'AND DO YOU ALSO PLAY THE VIOLIN?'
Carl F. Flesch

'AND DO YOU ALSO
PLAY THE VIOLIN?'

Carl F. Flesch

**With a Foreword by
SIR YEHUDI MENUHIN**

**TOCCATA
PRESS**

First published in English by Toccata Press, 1990
© Carl F. Flesch, 1990
Published in German under the title, '. . . *Und Spielst Du auch
Geige?*', by Atlantis Musikbuch Verlag, Zurich, 1990.

British Library Cataloguing in Publication Data

Flesch, Carl F.
    'And do you also play the violin?'
    1. Violin playing. Biographies
    I. Title   II. 'Und spielst du auch Geige?' *English*
    787.2092

    ISBN 0-907689-36-1
    ISBN 0-907689-37-X

Set in 11 on 12pt Imprint
by Alan Sutton Publishing, Stroud
Printed and bound by SRP Ltd., Exeter.

CONTENTS

5

Appendices

LIST OF ILLUSTRATIONS

8

FOREWORD
Sir Yehudi Menuhin

This book by the son of the great violin pedagogue, Carl Flesch, contains many gems which only filial insight and continuous interest in his father's work could provide. We meet the great of a very recent generation which has become curiously remote in my own life-time.

The metamorphosis of the world now and the world I knew has been so drastic and far-reaching that even a distinguished man speaking about his great father brings us back a measure of life which we might otherwise too easily forget.

I believe this book will be of interest not only to violinists, musicologists and contemporary historians, but also to what is known as the general public – a body of readers of growing importance who want and need that broader knowledge of human experience and aspirations which seems crowded out from the hectic lives of those who need it most.

Yehudi Menuhin

To my children
and grandchildren

INTRODUCTION

During my childhood, the question '. . . and do you also play the violin?' was practically inevitable within the first five minutes of meeting a stranger. This explains the title of this book, but not necessarily my qualifications as its author. For, although I am the son of a well-known violinist, the answer to that question had always to be 'No': I have hardly ever touched a fiddle – not, at any rate, with the intention of playing it.

On the other hand, I have in my time met a great many remarkable personalities, by no means all violinists; I have witnessed numerous interesting events; and I possess quite a large collection of intriguing and hitherto unpublished letters from many of my father's prominent contemporaries.

But was this sufficient for a book? I began to look at some of the existing literature – biographies and autobiographies; books on the history of music, of stringed instruments, orchestras, opera houses; collections of letters (with or without annotations); anecdotes; anthologies; and much else. Some proved very interesting or amusing, others rather less so. But, cither way, none was exactly like the book I had in mind.

Since it has never been my intention to become a professional musician, I tend to regard myself as a kind of part-outsider, or as someone with a ringside seat able to see some of the sights and hear a few of the grunts people sitting further back might miss. This enabled me at times to form independent opinions on some of the attitudes, habits and occasional sacred cows to which the artistic profession seems prone. They do not always conform to traditional views, but I make no apology for that.

And last but not least, I have experienced at first hand the

13

problems – and pleasures – of being the son of a famous father, a subject about which surprisingly little seems to have been written. I have tried, with hindsight, to make my modest contribution towards filling this gap.

All in all, I felt, there was sufficient material to comment on certain aspects of musical life as I knew it.

But I was still not quite satisfied and so did something against which I had been repeatedly warned: I asked the advice of a number of acquaintances with literary experience on how best to organise and present that material. The success exceeded my wildest expectations: the number of contradictory recommendations equalled that of the persons I had asked – surpassed it even, since I received in some instances alternative suggestions.

Serious; humorous; not too light; not too heavy; anecdotal; not too many funny stories; autobiographical; avoid writing in the first person; the book should consist solely of annotated letters; too much correspondence gets boring; don't express your own views – nobody is interested; some of your opinions seem original – why not include more; chronological; anything but; maximum 120 pages; minimum 350; restrict yourself to one or two subjects; the more variety the better; as many illustrations as possible; not too many; all chapters of the same length; all as different as possible; and so on – the list could easily be doubled.

When advice differs so widely, then – however grateful the recipient – there is only one thing he can do: proceed in the manner he himself thinks right. My book will therefore remain the mixture I had originally had in mind; 'serious; humorous; not too light; not too heavy. . .' – comparable, say, to an informal chat among people with shared interests.

I appreciate the risk: I was warned that people interested in a specific subject prefer to take their information 'neat'; that is, books intended for musical experts and serious students should be very learned, dealing with their subjects in depth, whereas those for music lovers in general should be anecdotal and light. But not both – the two don't mix.

It was with some diffidence that I decided to disregard this opinion, which is held by many people far more knowledgeable than I. But the simple fact is that my experience is quite different: I have met a large number of leading musicians and musicologists of every type who could – and did – discuss technical and professional subjects for hours or days on end. But this did not mean that they were unable to talk about other matters, both serious and light, exchange gossip, jokes, anecdotes or discuss questions of the most mundane nature. Indeed, if they didn't, they were regarded as bores.

Or take my father's *Memoirs*.[1] By general consent they are regarded as a very important contribution to the history of violin playing. Yet they contain numerous light-hearted anecdotes and remarks. And far from harming it, they make the book more readable. Then why should mine not relate an amusing story or two about Furtwängler, Casals or Kreisler, and, in addition, offer a good deal of material published here for the first time? Why not include a letter from Artur Schnabel containing what I regard as 'the Credo of the unrecognised contemporary composer'; another from the violinist Alma Moodie giving her opinion about the Stravinsky Violin Concerto; a *cri de cœur* from the composer Franz Schreker after his dismissal as director of the Berlin Hochschule? Modesty forbids me to add that even some of my own opinions may be worth reading – for instance, on the anxieties of public performers; Green Room visits, Furtwängler's personality; the 'show must go on' syndrome; and other subjects.

And so, to paraphrase the Duke of Wellington's well-worn saying, 'Mix it and be damned!'

Some readers may wonder why I have, in a number of cases, omitted to mention names – usually where the persons concerned are hardly known to the general public of today. The reason is that in these instances I have been interested mainly in describing events for their own sake whereas it was incidental whether they concerned Mr X or Miss Y. I have kept to this rule particularly where the story concerned anything unfavourable about the people involved. Of course, where the name of a person has added to the interest, I have mentioned it. In a very few instances, however, I have intentionally changed or omitted certain details – never the

[1] *The Memoirs of Carl Flesch*, Rockliff, London, 1957; reprinted by Da Capo Press, New York, 1979.

facts – in order to avoid giving a clue to the identity of the people involved.

This left me with one last problem; the role my father was to play in this book. Without him it could not have been written. He it was, after all, who made possible the experiences I wanted to describe, to whom the letters were addressed, and who was the focus for the musical scene around me.

On the other hand, was his personality still sufficiently interesting for the general public? Or, to put it another way, of more interest than 98 per cent of all those who have to be mentioned in a modern musical dictionary if it is to serve its purpose?

Well, he was indisputably a pioneer in the field of violin teaching, and almost half a century after his death his work has lost none of its importance. In addition, a set of historical recording of his playing, published in 1988,[2] makes it clear that he was an interpreter of the first order. He and his opinions should therefore still be of interest today.

But this is not the main point. The purpose of this book is not to write his biography – however often his name is mentioned – but to give a multi-coloured profile of musical and kindred happenings as I interpret them from the sources handed down to me, or as I saw them myself. Nothing systematic, then, but – since practically none of this material has been published before – rather the filling-in of an occasional gap or the independent confirmation of a fact already known. But not infrequently also something new or unexpected.

The reproduction of letters in facsimile has of necessity left some of them rather small. Since most are translated in the text, I hope this will not detract from their visual interest.

I am hoping that this book will interest and entertain music lovers: professionals because it has been written by the son of a colleague, non-professionals because it has been written by one of them. And both because it touches on subjects which never cease to fascinate us.

[2] CD 1032/3/4, Symposium, London.

ACKNOWLEDGEMENTS

I would like to express my gratitude to all those who have advised and encouraged me in the writing of this book; the many friends, acquaintances, curators of musical archives and in particular former Flesch pupils who so readily placed additional material at my disposal. My thanks are due also to Martin Anderson of Toccata Press for all his help; Mrs Joan Townsend and Mr Karsten Windt for looking through the manuscript and checking general details; and, of course, Sir Yehudi Menuhin for his generous introductory words. Thanks, too, to Guy Rickards for his help in reading the proofs and to Malcolm MacDonald for copying the music examples. Finally, my thanks go to those who have kindly permitted me to quote letters and other material which strictly speaking were still protected by copyright. In a number of cases I have been unable, in spite of all my efforts, to ascertain names and addresses of possible copyright holders, I hope that they will not hold my unintended omission against me – it has not been for want of trying.

I
CONCERTS

Question: who would chose an occupation which demands the
highest readiness and fitness at all times, requires literally
ceaseless training, involves a high risk of failure, is financially
extremely uncertain, means a lot of inconvenience and 'un-
social hours', and, last but not least, is likely at times to cause a
good deal of anxiety?

Answer: an artist performing in public, and in particular a
musician, who, apart, of course, from talent, perseverance and
courage, possesses strong extravert traits, preferably with an
admixture of conscious or sub-conscious exhibitionist tendencies. Otherwise he will probably be unhappy, and, more
likely than not, unsuccessful in his profession.

Admittedly, these characteristics are not always clearly
defined; many artists have an ambivalent attitude towards
'concertising', to use the current ugly expression. In a letter[1] to
my father, the cellist Hugo Becker[2] quotes a remark by Joseph
Joachim: 'It is a wretched trade, being a concert artist.
Preferably one ought to make music only for oneself and a few
friends'. Becker himself, incidentally, had retired from the
concert platform comparatively early and enjoyed the 'autumn

---

[1] Dated 30 December 1932.

[2] See note 2 on p. 287.

of his life not encumbered by public commitments', as he put it.

But this can obviously not be compared with the case of an artist who has an active dislike of appearing in public or suffers from severe inhibitions. The latter express themselves, of course, in the first place as stage fright, a state of nerves with which sooner or later every artist has to come to terms. My father – the subject nearest at hand in whom I could study this phenomenon – used to say that an artist *had* to be nervous in order to give of his best. But he meant this in the sense of being keyed-up, rather than suffering from 'nerves'.

Ida Haendel, one of his most renowned pupils, asserts in her autobiography[3] that 'Flesch was not keen on public performances owing to his suffering from "Lumpenfieber" (stage fright)'. Apart from an amusing misprint (the correct German expression is 'Lampenfieber', literally 'footlight fever'; 'Lumpenfieber' would mean 'rag and bone fever'), I am afraid she was wrong in the matter itself – an interesting illustration of the fact that on occasion even the most gifted pupils can misunderstand their teacher. Of course my father was nervous before a concert but, as far as I could ascertain, no more so than other artists; and, in particular, it did not affect his performance in any way.

In his younger years and middle age (before Ida came to know him) he concentrated on concerts rather more than teaching. And he enjoyed it, as a diary entry[4] shows: 'To make music oneself is incomparably more entertaining than listening – as every professional musician in a concert audience knows'. In his last letter to me[5] – which I received only after his death – he expressed his satisfaction at his undiminished powers, enabling him, despite his advancing years, to continue playing in public with outstanding success. He was very self-critical and would without a doubt have recognised 'the right moment to make room for the younger generation', to quote Hugo Becker once more.[6]

[3] *Woman with Violin*, Gollancz, London, 1970, p. 63.

[4] 12 September 1931.

[5] Dated 13 October 1944.

[6] In the letter quoted above, p. 19.

The art of mastering stage fright is, of course, part and parcel of the curriculum of every young artist intent on following the career of a soloist. In his writings my father detailed every potential impediment known to him and demonstrated technical and psychological ways of overcoming them. In his lessons, he used to say that an artist, before a concert, should aim at being 'prepared 200%' so as to offset a possible 'loss of 100%'.

All his pupils had the right, amounting almost to an unwritten law, to attend, whenever possible, co-students' lessons. Many have told me that playing in front of so expert an audience, with authoritative criticism following immediately afterwards, was a worse ordeal than – and thereby an excellent preparation for – real concert life.

He also encouraged pupils to attend his own concerts. I always found this rather puzzling: suppose he were to play, for once, badly? Would the loss of face with his students not be catastrophic? It never seemed to worry him, which lends added weight to the view that, as far as he was concerned, the condition of stage fright was well controlled.

One idiosyncrasy, however, he never lost. Unlike many other teachers he found it impossible to attend a pupil's important concert debut. On the other hand, he liked to listen to his present and former students over the radio, afterwards writing them a postcard, praising or constructively criticising.

I would not recommend to my non-professional readers that they bring up the subject of stage fright as a topic of conversation with professional musicians, who don't seem to like discussing it. This was brought home to me by an incident, small in itself, in my early childhood. At lunch on the day of a Berlin concert, my sister, who must have been nine or ten at the time, asked in all innocence: 'Daddy, are you nervous about tonight?' Unexpectedly, this question seemed to cause him considerable annoyance, and she received quite a severe ticking-off. It taught me early on that this topic was all but taboo. Ever since, I have shied away from talking to other artists about it. Experience shows that they prefer to keep it in the closet – something that may be significant in itself.

There are, of course, exceptions. Jascha Heifetz, for instance, renowned for his platform cool, used to amuse himself sometimes during orchestra rehearsals by pretending to suffer from a trembling bow. He seemed to enjoy the disconcerted embarrassment of conductor and orchestra and their obvious relief on realising that it had all been a joke. Similarly, he had a private party piece – a most amusing impression of a nervous beginner appearing in public for the first time. To me, this seemed so life-like that I began to suspect that a subconscious fear was being worked off in this way. I never found out whether I was right but, not so many years later, he unexpectedly cancelled two London appearances at very short notice and for reasons which at the time were not regarded as particularly convincing. Regrettably, they caused very serious difficulties to one of the promoters concerned.

One of the lucky people hardly ever plagued by nerves seems to have been the cellist Heinrich Grünfeld, famed perhaps more for his wit and charm than for his art.[7] An unusually wide circle of friends ensured excellent attendances at his concerts, making them more like social occasions.

A number of slightly malicious stories about him made the rounds, but there was a suggestion that some of them had been invented by Grünfeld himself; he was under no illusion about the fact that he was not the best cellist in the world and gave himself the nickname 'Professor humoris causa'.

There was, for instance, the story told by a colleague who visited him in the Green Room after one of his recitals to offer the customary congratulations. 'Get away', Grünfeld replied, 'I played rotten and I know it; but I was so nervous.'

'Nervous? You? Whatever for?'

'There was a man sitting in the first row whom I did *not* know.'

Or, again: he had a young pupil who, despite all efforts, showed no progress whatever. The lessons were paid for by the boy's grandfather whose fondest wish was that his grandson play something for him on his seventieth birthday. So as not to disappoint the old gentleman, it was decided to tell him

---

[7] When, at a ripe old age, he asked my father to appear with him at the fiftieth-anniversary celebration of his subscription-concert series, he did so with the words 'This is the last but one honour you can show me'.

that the boy was so nervous that he could play only in the adjoining room; there, Grünfeld was to do it in his place, so that the grandfather could enjoy the boy's apparent progress. On the great day, he listened to Grünfeld's performance next door, always in the belief that it was his grandson who was playing. But he became more and more agitated; clearly he was anything but happy with the result of the lessons. At the conclusion of the concert he summed up his feelings in one terse sentence: 'Grünfeld goes tomorrow'.

For some artists, 'nerves' are their severest difficulty. Their mental agony before and during a concert is matched only by that of their friends who feel honour-bound to turn up. For an excellent artist to know what he *can* do, only to find it impossible to achieve it when it matters, must in the long run be unbearable. Technical preparation, however thorough, is of no use. In some instances psychiatric treatment may help; but there are 'incurable' cases where the sufferer eventually has to accept his limitations and concentrate on teaching, frequently to the advantage of his pupils.

There are, of course, innumerable causes for a performance to go wrong, or for an artist to fear that it might. But first of all, let us exclude insufficient technique: if an artist has not mastered a work completely, or it is altogether beyond him, he should not attempt to perform it. But assuming adequate technical means, his path is still strewn with banana skins: an incompetent accompanist; misunderstandings with the conductor; something wrong with the instrument; a tummy upset; bad acoustics; a badly heated hall; a cold (or colds, in the audience) – the list is endless. And leaving all this aside, might there lurk somewhere, possibly in the subconscious, one fear, overshadowing all others?

I would like to put forward, in all modesty, a theory which I know will be regarded by many professional musicians as entirely misconceived, not to say ridiculous: could it possibly be that one of the most important reasons for stage fright is the fear of a memory lapse? Or, to put it another way, do audiences and professional musicians lay too much stress on works being played by heart?

Over the years I have heard diametrically opposed views from the experts.

'Playing from memory is essential, lest the printed page interferes with the contact between arm and brain, thereby destroying concentration.'

'Modern works should always be played from the score, because learning them by heart is probably not worth the effort considering how infrequently they are performed. If artists were to adopt this suggestion, it would be to the advantage of contemporary composers – their works would be heard more often.'

'If your memory temporarily fails, your fingers automatically take over'.

'The public don't mind whether or not a performer plays from the score.'

'Audiences expect us to know a work by heart, or else they will suspect that we haven't prepared ourselves properly.'

'Not having to worry about my memory means that I can concentrate more on artistic expression.'

'Playing from the score actually inhibits artistic expression.'

And so on, *ad infinitum*.

Everyone of these opinions is supported by reasoned argument. There can be no unanimity.

To look at the question in simple practical terms, performing solo works without the music seems (today) – with notable exceptions – to be the rule, even for those performers who would prefer the opposite.[8] Most artists conform to apparent audience preferences. But are these really so clear-cut? Admittedly, I once heard an old lady remark to her companion about a violinist who had just finished a more than pedestrian rendering of a Beethoven *Romance*: 'He is a great artist: he plays everything by heart'. But this, one may hope, is rare. What a musical audience wants to hear is the best possible performance of a work. Knowing it by heart is not an essential ingredient as it is in opera or the theatre where it is indispensible. And there, of course, performers can fall back on the equivalent of the score – the prompter.

Although in chamber music other factors play a part, it is

---

[8] The Flesch pupil Roman Totenberg considered the question sufficiently important to write to his teacher in 1935: 'I am playing the Brahms sonata from memory'.

nonetheless noteworthy that ensembles, even duos, almost invariably perform with the music before them. Those few who make a point of dispensing with it are to my knowledge not regarded as artistically superior. Indeed, I have heard it said that they are liable to suffer from a somewhat limited repertoire. Moreover, I should not be surprised if these feats were to absorb nervous energy that could be used to better advantage elsewhere.

I remember a charity concert I had arranged at which the Amadeus Quartet turned up without the cello part of the 'Hunt' Quartet.[9] The chances are that every member of the Amadeus could have performed this work in his sleep. But starting before the missing part had been procured? Out of the question!

I should add that since the players were quite upset by this unexpected mishap, I tried to cheer them up with the (true) story of my father arriving at the hall to play in a Furtwängler concert only to discover that he had left at home a removable bridge with which his dentist had recently supplied him and which he had not yet got used to. My mother had to make a mad dash through Berlin in a taxi, arriving back with it five minutes before he was due on the platform. My story fell flat. The Amadeus maintained that this was a purely cosmetic problem and that a violinist, in any case, had to keep his mouth clamped shut on the stage, except for smilingly acknowledging applause.

So why do so many people deny the single performer the fail-safe so readily granted to an ensemble? If only because 'it has always been done this way', one should remember that violin soloists invariably perform standing up – or did, until the emergence of Itzhak Perlman. His remark that many colleagues secretly envy him for being allowed to sit down, whilst jocular, probably contains more than a grain of truth.

The point is that sitting down, although unusual, does not seem to affect quality of performance and most certainly not

---

[9] The incident gave a popular daily, which would otherwise not have dreamt of reviewing the event, the inevitable opportunity for the headline 'Hunt for the Hunt Quartet'.

Carl Flesch by Mopp (see also p. 341)

public success. Granted all the differences, a parallel with the problem of playing by heart is not out of the way.

Of course, there are those fortunate enough genuinely not to mind the occasional memory lapse. Emanuel Feuermann and Lili Kraus seem to have been cases in point: if such a mishap forced them to stop, they just laughed and started again; they found it simply funny that something like that could happen to *them*. But this kind of self-confidence is granted only to the very few.

Except for modern works, my father played his solo repertoire by heart. But he invariably had by him at the concert hall the score of the works he was to play – presumably in order to resolve any possible doubts that might occur to him while warming up. The only time when I saw him being really nervous was when he (wrongly) suspected that he had left the music at home.

As far as I know, he played from the score during wireless performances. At any rate this is what he recommended to his pupils.[10] And I believe quite a few artists do it. It shows the importance accorded the problem by many soloists. A letter to my father from Bram Eldering, at the time professor at the Cologne Music Academy, may be of interest:[11]

With pupils possessing a good memory I don't discuss the matter except for showing them how to avoid some pitfalls. In the case of those, however, who, if they make a mistake, lose the thread, I advise [. . .] practising from the music a great deal, especially during the last few days prior to a concert, and during the performance itself to think only of the interpretation. A very talented female pupil who can't play by heart I make play from a lowered music stand.

The success rate of these methods seems a little doubtful. And

[10] In a letter, dated 24 November 1933, to Ricardo Odnoposoff, at that time already a very successful soloist, he wrote: 'I heard you over the wireless. On the whole you played excellently – a pity, of course, that you made such a bad error in the 1st movement of the Goldmark concerto. Am I right or not if I always try to drum into my pupils that when playing over the air, they should have the score before them?'

[11] Dated 24 January 1923.

the letter suggests the thought: 'Why make it simple if you can
make it complicated?'

It cannot be gainsaid that playing by heart represents, as it
were, the 'ideal'. Or, as Furtwängler puts it:[12]

> Conducting by heart has also a great advantage. It requires the
> interpreter to occupy himself with studying the work inten-
> sively and for a long period – always a necessary pre-condition.
> And that he does so again and again.

All this is correct, of course, but not the point I am really
trying to make: without a doubt, playing by heart confronts
many interpreters with a very substantial technical and psychological problem, or else it would not be dealt with in the
literature in so extensive and contradictory a manner. Is it
certain that this is worth the effort?

If a musician feels that he really does not need the score or
even that it would seriously impede him, fair enough: no one
wants to pressurise him into *not* playing by heart. What is
under discussion is whether playing without the score should
be 'compulsory'. Most high-wire acrobats perform with a safety
net, but they very rarely have to use it; its presence is simply
intended to remove an avoidable hazard. And even if there are
people for whom the thrill of an acrobatic performance lies in
the possibility of witnessing a catastrophic accident, this is not
usually the mood in which an audience settles down to listen to
a Beethoven or Brahms concerto. Admittedly, I have met
artists who were of a different opinion – but usually only when
they suspected the presence of a somewhat hostile colleague in
the audience.

My father used to tell that after performing the Beethoven
Concerto in a German town, as likely as not an elderly member
of the audience would visit him in the Green Room to tell him
that he had been present at a concert in which the aged Joachim
had suffered a memory lapse. (This incidentally raises an
interesting point: as we grow older, our memory becomes
progressively less reliable; one has only to recall Toscanini's
catastrophic last wireless concert – although Toscanini, of
course, was too short-sighted to read a score without glasses,

---

[12] *Vermächtis*, F. A. Brockhaus Verlag, Wiesbaden, 1975, p. 18.

and too vain to wear them. But should one expect an elderly artist to start playing from music, say, when he reaches 70, thereby advertising the fact that old age is beginning to catch up with him? Hair restorers and dyes, hearing aids and so on are based on the desire to correct conditions caused by advancing years in an unobtrusive manner. Why go to the other extreme on the concert platform?)

Gregor Piatigorsky confessed to me in a weak moment that he had a fear of memory lapses and always liked to start the season with a few unimportant concerts.[13] Joseph Szigeti seems to have been another sufferer. He told the charming story of once expressing his worry to my father shortly before a concert: there was a certain passage where his memory might fail him. My father was able to point to a solution, only to spoil it all by adding that there was another passage where *he*. . . – thereby causing poor Szigeti to jump from the frying pan into the fire. And my father's pupil Alma Moodie,[14] writing about the pianist and composer Eduard Erdmann: 'I am told he made a mistake during the concert. Bechstein had, without telling him, exchanged the grand piano, and he suddenly noticed, and pondered about, the fact that the black keys had sharp edges instead of round ones as during the rehearsal – and he had already lost his thread for a moment'.[15]

---

[13] He made this remark just before a Prom appearance, his first of the season. It throws a revealing light on the way the Proms have developed since. Gone are the days when it was the BBC Symphony Orchestra with Henry Wood (as he then was) conducting every night; I still recall Laurie Kennedy, the leader of the Orchestra's cello section, complaining bitterly about the resulting physical and mental strain with the inevitable lowering of artistic standards. Rehearsals – at least one I happened to attend – consisted of little more than playing a work through just once; there simply was no time for more. And Piatigorsky's remark shows that soloists performing in these concerts did not always have a high opinion of them; many made fun of the prevailing conditions. The violinist Henri Temianka used to say that he measured his success at a Prom appearance by the number of standing members of the audience who fainted – until a colleague voiced the opinion that this was only a ruse for some people to leave before the end of his performance without hurting his feelings.

[14] See chapter IX, pp. 171–86.

[15] In a letter dated 11 December 1931.

My father writes about 'one of our most famous violinists' who was playing the Bach Chaconne in a concert. On mounting the platform he noticed two music students sitting in the first row and following his playing from the score. This made him so nervous that 'after a short time his memory left him'.[16] I regard this story as particularly significant: if an experienced interpreter can lose his cool in a standard work such as the Chaconne for the sole reason that some listeners are following the performance with the score before them, and can therefore 'check' on him, is it really worth the trouble?

Many artists will answer yes: inspiration, 'losing onself', 'talking directly to the listener' – they are possible only when you play by heart. Does this mean then, that all this is missing from a chamber-music performance?

Others hold the opinion that, when it comes to the crunch, the score will be of no help: the interpreter cannot 'change gear' that quickly. Of course, I lack the personal experience, but I can refer to my father's *The Art of Violin Playing*,[17] where he distinguishes between acoustic, motoric and visual memory – the latter 'an unfortunately frequently under-rated expedient'. And there are well-documented cases of artists who always played from the score, such as, for instance, the pianist Raoul Pugno, *inter alia* Ysaÿe's long-standing sonata partner and no mean figure in musical history.[18]

In fairness let me add that in exceptional cases the presence of the score can *cause* the mishap instead of preventing it. Literally the only time I witnessed my father having to stop during a public performance was when he happened to play from the music. It was the first performance of a then contemporary violin concerto with the composer himself conducting.[19] The work started with a *Presto* and my father

[16] 'Aus dem Tagebuch eines Geigers', *Der fortschrittliche Geigenlehrer*, Nos. 7/8, June/September 1933.

[17] Carl Fischer, New York, 1924, rev. edn. 1929, p. 167.

[18] I have heard Sviatoslav Richter, too, perform, an entire London recital with the music before and a page-turner beside him; nobody appeared to mind in the slightest.

[19] I am afraid I cannot remember the name of the composer – a Freudian repression?

had the misfortune to turn two pages at once, landing him from page 1 directly on page 4. He hastily turned back and all would probably have been well, with the public little the wiser, but for the fact that the conductor had already stopped the orchestra and they had to start all over again. In order to compensate the composer for this annoying mishap, my father performed the work again at a subsequent festival of modern music – this time without trouble and, I should not wonder, without a fee either.[20]

Exceptions prove the rule for which one could cite many more examples. Not all, of course, end in disaster. Max Rostal tells of an occasion during his time as orchestral leader when a well-known violinist came entirely unstuck. Rostal took over from his desk until the soloist had sufficiently recovered to continue himself. He has so far steadfastly refused to disclose the name.

No doubt, a temporary loss of concentration is the most likely cause of this phenomenon. On the other hand, concentration can on occasions be too much of a good thing. There is a story concerning the Russian violinist Alexander Schmuller, about to play the Beethoven Concerto. He was so absorbedly thinking of his first entry that he entirely forgot the long orchestral introduction and started to play immediately. I understand conductor and orchestra rose to the occasion.

So much for playing by heart as one of the main causes of stage fright. The argument will go on, but I believe there is a lot to be said for the opinions I have expressed.

Concert fees are obviously of real importance. Before the advent of the recording industry, they constituted an interpreter's main income and even the most romantic figures had

---

[20] In the first round of the bi-annual Carl Flesch International Violin Competition every entrant has to play a contemporary work for solo violin specially composed for the occasion. Playing without the score is obligatory. It lasts only about ten minutes. Yet every time a somewhat disproportionately large number of candidates withdraws from the competition at the last moment. I have been wondering for some time whether the necessity for playing this short piece by heart has anything to do with it; and if so, whether this memory feat is really sufficiently important to prevent an otherwise excellent violinist from participating.

to give the commercial side of their profession a lot of thought. A page from Paganini's diary shows that the question of income and outgoings for each concert was foremost in his mind.[21]

The figures give an idea of the ravages of inflation over the centuries. But we don't have to go back that far. Fees customary at the turn of the century would nowadays hardly cover the railfare.

And how they fought for every hundred Deutschmarks (and, no doubt, pounds and dollars and francs)! It is amusing to read letters from concert societies of that period; sometimes they tried to get away with reduced fees at the same time creating the impression that they were particularly generous. Pfitzner to my father from Strasbourg in 1918,[22] after having agreed to a fee of 1,000 Deutschmarks: 'We never pay more than 800 Deutschmarks. You will oblige me if you will treat this exceptional amount as confidential'.

A letter in 1910 about a Bach Festival in Heidelberg: 'Heidelberg is, as you know, a small hole and I could not exceed 450 Deutschmarks. But I am hoping that the "Mammon" will not be an obstacle for you either'. This was for two concerts! I like the 'either'.

Reger, from Meiningen on 24 April 1912: 'May I express the hope that you will play the Beethoven Concerto for us at a fee of 500 Deutschmarks? I can't offer you *more* with the *best* will in the world, since we don't have the means! Even so I must ask you to regard this offer as provisional, as I still have to ask his Highness the Duke of Meiningen for his approval'. Reger's next letter[23] shows that he thought of every eventuality.

Max von Schillings from Stuttgart in 1912: 'Please regard 20 February 1913 with a fee of 800 Deutschmark as firm. Concerning the latter, I would ask you to consider whether in view of the charitable purpose for the widows and orphans of our Court orchestra and as a favour to its members and

[21] See p. 34.

[22] 14 June 1918; see p. 37.

[23] Reproduced on p. 38.

myself, you would agree to a reduction'. I don't know my father's reply, but I do know that he interpreted the term 'charity concert' literally, as an event at which the artist played without, or at least for a much reduced fee.

And finally a letter dated 31 December 1904 from Bram Eldering, who was at the time orchestra leader and professor at the Music Academy in Cologne. My father had asked for a fee of 900 Deutschmarks, which the City of Cologne claimed to be more than it could afford. His friend Eldering, whom he had apparently consulted, replied – no doubt without the knowledge of his superiors – 'Frankly, I feel it would be infra dig for you to play for such a fee' (referring to the lesser amount being offered). As the correspondence shows, this advice was not always followed.[24]

Free tickets are another somewhat controversial question. As far as I know, my father was generous in this matter where pupils or good friends were concerned. Artur Schnabel, on the other hand, apparently gave free tickets very rarely indeed, even to his pupils. I remember a sonata evening when a Schnabel pupil, Leonard Shure, who could not afford the price of a ticket, asked me whether I could get him in for free. When I complied he said: 'As a token of my gratitude, you can attend all of my concerts free for as long as I live'. He had the nerve to emigrate to the USA one year later so that I could never make use of his generous offer.

I have to thank Hans Keller's widow, Milein Cosman, for the story about his mother who as a young girl attended every concert conducted by Gustav Mahler but could afford only the very cheapest seats. One day she managed to penetrate into the presence of the great man himself and, summoning all her youthful charm, asked him for a better seat at least for one concert 'so that she might be able to appreciate his great art even better'. Mahler showed considerable dexterity in extricating himself: 'But my dear young lady, the acoustics in the Gods are far superior!'

---

[24] Not all that much changed during the inter-war years: I possess a letter written in the 1930s by Sir Robert Mayer, in which he offered Ida Haendel a fee of £12 for an appearance in one of his Children's Concerts: he justified this as being 'on the reduced educational scale'.

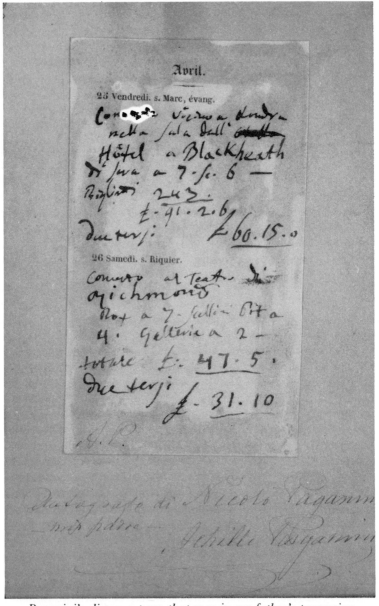

*Paganini's diary: a page that was in my father's possession.
It is authenticated by Paganini's son Achille.*

In the privately published collection of letters to Bronislaw Huberman[25] there is an example dating from 1931 which says it all. From a young female admirer:

> [. . .] If Beethoven himself had been in the audience, he would have realised that his concerto had never been performed with the perfection with which you played it that evening. After the concert [. . .] someone alleged that even you don't make music for its own sake but for purely financial reasons. I was furious [. . .] and [. . .] said that if I were to ask you for a free ticket for your concert on 20 February you would grant me this request. Please give me the opportunity to disprove the offensive opinions of these people.

To which Huberman replied:

> If your friends need the supply of a free ticket as proof for a musician's artistic convictions, if they cannot read sufficient into the artistic accomplishment to rid themselves of such childish ideas, then I am not in the least interested in convincing them of the contrary. [. . .] Apart from this only a dreamer would deny for one moment that even the most precious artistic matters have an economic ingredient, namely at the point in time at which they are being sold. [. . .] the essential requirement is that an artistic product must be free from such considerations at the moment of its creation.

What is there to add, except that the collection contains a letter in which Huberman placed a free ticket at the disposal of an impecunious fan – unasked.

I have little first-hand experience of an artist's preparations on the day of a concert, except my father's when he happened to appear in a place where we were living at the time. He would give no lessons on the day, take a nap in the early afternoon and practise in a mild way; he combined this with what today I suppose we would call 'meditation' but what at the time was the Coué method of auto-suggestion, which worked well for him.

He had a very light meal including, invariably, some chocolate. Alcohol was out, as officially laid down in his book

[25] *The Listener Speaks*, compiled after his death by his former secretary Ida Ibbekken.

The Art of Violin Playing.[26] But as one amused conductor told me, it did not prevent him from occasionally breaking this rule himself at a post-rehearsal luncheon.

There was no question of disturbing him with any but the most urgent matters. I vividly recall his being summoned to the telephone on the day of a Berlin concert, the caller stating that the matter was of considerable urgency. It turned out to be a call from his tailor reminding him that it was time for him to order new tails – indeed quite important for a soloist, but a case of unfortunate timing if ever there was one. I have rarely seen him more annoyed, and I believe the firm lost him as a customer. My first lesson in the pitfalls of high-pressure salesmanship and a permanent blight on my performance in my own profession – insurance.

At the hall itself, there was equally no possibility of seeing him before, or in the interval during, the concert. I can't remember whether my mother was the exception, but I believe she was frequently posted in front of the artist's room in order to stop unwanted – and that meant all – visitors. I remember a story she told with wry humour, of her encounter in this capacity, in Budapest of all places, with a girlfriend from my father's long-distant past (whether before or after his marriage I was too tactful to ask). The lady felt that the rule did not apply to her. My mother won. Pity – I am still wondering what the effect of this romantic meeting would have been on my father's playing.

I don't know how much has been written outside films and fiction – where the artist has taken to drink or is otherwise on his way down – about the strain on an artist's family before and during a concert. The stress can be considerable. I remember, for instance, meeting the wife of Adolf Busch leaving the hall the moment her husband appeared on the platform as soloist in a symphony concert (I believe she did not need to do so during the Busch Quartet's chamber-music concerts). Seeing me, she murmured somewhat shame-facedly: 'Here goes Mrs Busch' – quite unnecessarily, because I knew how worrying these occasions could be for wives,

---

[26] Vol. II, Carl Fischer, New York, 1930, p. 90.

*Hans Pfitzner's letter in which he asks my father not to
disclose the fee involved in a Strasbourg concert*

Max Reger writes to Carl Flesch about rehearsal arrangements, and expresses his hope that the Duke of Meiningen – then 86 – will survive until the date of the concert. The letter also reveals Carl Flesch's rather disrespectful habit of punching holes in the correspondence he received.

especially before passages they had heard their husband practise over and over again.

Of course, at a very young age, when you still regard your parents as infallible, the idea of anything going wrong for my father did not enter my head, unless some inept conductor – say, Nikisch, Mengelberg or Furtwängler – were to make a mistake (at that age even the greatest could not compare with my father). I therefore tended to regard cadenzas as the safest and easiest part of a performance – an opinion, I soon learned, not necessarily shared by the profession. At a later age you do begin to worry, but since I can truthfully say that I never attended an unsuccessful Flesch performance and, moreover, he never showed the slightest outward trace of nervousness on stage, the problem simply did not become acute for me.

Like probably every musician's family ours had some peculiarities. It was, for instance, an absolute rule that no member of the family was to sit in one of the front rows. My father firmly believed that the sight of wife or child would adversely affect his concentration – a somewhat unrealistic fear since he was short-sighted in the extreme and performed without glasses, unless, of course, he played from the score.

It was not the done thing in our family to applaud at any of my father's concerts. At the time, I accepted this as a matter of course – it did not even occur to me to enquire which of my parents had decreed this. It was only when I noticed, somewhat to my surprise, that this rule did not apply to other artists' families that I began to ponder the reason. The simplest explanation is probably that it would have looked bad if the family had been seen trying to augment the applause. Possibly it may also have been some kind of snobbishness, perhaps a tacit expression of opinion that my father's playing well was such a matter of course that there was really no particular reason to applaud him for it.

Of course, as a small child, before I had been conditioned accordingly, I used to clap enthusiastically. Indeed, I used, towards the end of an item, to hold my hands in front of me in order not to lose a single precious moment. This caused one of our friends to remark to my mother, with tears in her eyes: 'Look at the boy, how he adores his father. He even worships before him'. Thus are legends born.

When we were a little older, we were able to move around more freely. On one occasion my brother, on seeing an acquaintance leave the hall after the second encore, rushed up to him with the words: 'Don't go yet, my daddy has prepared three encores!'

The Green Room was for us youngsters the place to be asked the question which forms the title of this book. It became so irksome that Stefan Schnabel and I at one time contemplated appearing at one of our fathers' joint sonata recitals with placards round our necks proclaiming 'No, I don't play the violin/piano'. This idea was firmly scotched by our parents.

As small children we used after a concert to plant a congratulatory kiss on our father's cheek. It made me realise at an early age the immense physical and mental effort of a public performance. But then, my father always maintained that he could gauge precisely how well he had been playing, by the need or otherwise of having to change his shirt afterwards. The more soaked the shirt, the better the performance.

This particular topic seems to have some fascination for musicians generally and, of course, it *is* important especially for violinists. I have heard female members in the audience tut-tutting disapprovingly on seeing a lady violinist – who obviously has more important matters to think about at that moment – carelessly wiping her hands on her expensive frock. As it happens, this subject is unfortunately my only memory of Arthur Nikisch, who mentioned to my father after one of their concerts that he had been perspiring more than usual.

For friends and acquaintances, after-concert visits to the Green Room can sometimes be a doubtful pleasure. Not surprisingly, many artists experience a 'high' at that time and cannot be judged by normal standards. They are understandably anxious to receive all the praise going – possibly more so if they feel that they have not been playing all that well. I have sometimes gained the impression that it is the quantity rather than the quality of visitors that matters most to them. On the other hand, if, after queuing for some time in a long line of well-wishers, you are eventually nearing the front, you will sometimes see the artist's glance already resting on you while he is still talking to someone else. Do not be misled into

49, HALLAM STREET,

LONDON, W. 1.

LANGHAM 3693.

17.November 1937.

Hochverehrter Herr Professor!

Lassen Sie mich ein aufrichtiges Wort sagen. Wie furchtbar gerne
wäre ich gekommen! Aber gerade einem
so verehrten Manne wie Ihnen gegenüber
soll man keine Unwahrheit sagen. Ich
muss nachmittags einem alten Versprechen gemäss zu Babin und Vronsky ins
Konzert gehen - nun mein Geständnis -
ich kann nicht zweimal im Tag Musik
hören oder ich wäre beim zweitenmal
ein schlechter Zuhörer eines solchen
Meisters, wie Sie es sind. Solch ein
Sakrileg muss ich mir verbieten, aber
ich hoffe Sie in allernächster Zeit
sehen zu dürfen, bis ich meine Arbeit
fertig habe. Erlauben Sie mir nur,
dass ich Ihnen als Zeichen meiner
herzlichen Gesinnung ein neues Buch
für Ihre schöne Bibliothek überreiche.

Ihr getreu ergebener

Stefan Zweig

*Stefan Zweig to Carl Flesch: 'Let me be honest with you. I
would so much have liked to come! But I just don't want
to tell an untruth to a man I esteem as highly as you. I
promised long ago to go to a matinee concert given by
Babin and Vronsky. And now for my confession: I can't
listen to music twice in one day or I would be, the second
time round, a bad listener for a master such as you. Such a
sacrilege I cannot permit myself, but I hope you'll allow
me to see you soon – when I have finished my present
task. Permit me, only as a token of my sincere regard, to
send you a new book for your fine library'.*

imagining that he is particularly pleased to see *you*! When you are eventually face to face with him, you will notice that he is, in turn, already looking beyond you – presumably in the hope that the next person will prove to be more interesting. It can make you wonder why you are there at all.

Personally, I like to duck some of these visits unless the artist is a friend or close acquaintance, or I have a social obligation – and always provided I can feel certain that my absence will not be noticed. Curiously enough, however, performers seem to remember those who are not there more than those who are. 'Why weren't you at my concert the other day?' 'But of course I was there. You played marvellously well.' 'Then why didn't you come to the Green Room?'

Incidentally, it is a fairly safe bet that if there is a crowd, the artist does not remember the names or recognise the faces of half the people who have come to greet him. But he will rarely admit it and instead simply smile and say something like 'Thank you, thank you very much. So pleased you could come!' Szymon Goldberg likes to tell the story of Bruno Walter – under whom he had frequently played in his capacity as leader – who did precisely that, when after one of his concerts a long line of admirers was wending its way past him. When it came to Goldberg's turn, Walter murmured the same phrase, but then, looking up, recognised him and exclaimed joyfully: 'Ach, it's *only* der Goldberg!'

Green Room visitors on their part can vary considerably in their behaviour. Some are shy and get out as quickly as they can. Others, often strangers, can be very pushing and try to spin out a chat – even if no more than the simple request for an autograph – for as long as possible, much to the irritation of the others waiting in the queue, their congratulatory smiles slowly freezing on their lips. It is not always easy for the artist to deal with this situation in a tactful manner. Sometimes the people behind can help; a good technique is an 'accidental' push followed by lengthy gushing apologies, giving the host the opportunity to turn to someone else.

At the other end of the scale are some very unassuming people. One of them is the broadcaster Richard Baker. I was being introduced to him by an artist whom we had both come to visit after her concert. At that time he had just been promoted from his job as regular reader of the BBC '9 O'Clock News', but his face was still familiar to every adult in the country from his nightly visits to their drawing rooms. Yet he found it necessary to introduce himself to me by name – a trait of such genuine modesty that it left me temporarily speechless.

It is not always easy for the visitor to find the right words. Basically, you have come to say something pleasant; this is what is expected of you, especially if the performance has not been quite as successful as it might have been. If you are not a professional (for that matter, even if you are), the first rule is to avoid 'expert' opinions. Artur Schnabel – who could afford to – used to reply to remarks like 'I thought the instrument sounded a little hard' with 'No, that was me'.

If you were not over-impressed, but don't want to lie, it is best to remain non-committal. A number of bon mots have been developed for this purpose such as 'If Beethoven could have heard you. . .', or '*Good* is not the word!' Or you avoid mentioning the playing altogether and pay an indirect compliment, such as 'I hope you'll be playing here again soon!'

But always remember that the artist's sense of humour after a concert is likely to have sunk to zero. Hence, under no circumstances any funny jokes such as the tired 'There was only one voice of praise. I talked to the gentleman myself'.

One of the most pleasurable things to watch (for outsiders, that is) are visits by a rival. The praise is always extravagant, both parties knowing full well that none of it is meant. It is not so much what but how it is being said.

The best Green Room story is attributed to Louise Wolff, the doyenne of Berlin pre-war concert agents. She was an impressive personality – an ex-actress – and an important figure in Berlin concert life. Her daughter has written an interesting book about the artists and musical scene during that period.[27] Quite a number of malicious sayings existed about her, such as the answer to the question as to her postal address during a holiday in Venice: 'But Grande Canaille, of course'. Or the words sung to the well-known theme in

---

[27] Edith Stargardt-Wolff, *Wegbereiter grosser Musiker*, Bote & Bock, Berlin, 1954.

Tchaikovsky's *Pathétique*, 'What have you ever done for art, Louise?'

But her own Green Room performance cannot be bettered. It is an untranslatable play on words, though non-German-speakers can still appreciate the joke after an explanation. It was one of her duties to be present at her artists' concerts. But she often played truant, managing, with an impeccable sense of timing, to turn up at the precise moment the concert ended. Entering the Green Room, she would approach the artist with outstretched arms and exclaim enthusiastically, and perfectly truthfully: 'Noch nicht dagewesen wie Sie gespielt haben!' This sentence can have two meanings: 'I have never heard anybody play as well as you' or 'I hadn't yet arrived when you were playing'.[28]

Not surprisingly, most musicians regard their concerts as something so important as to put everything else in the shade. For this reason it is not always easy to find a plausible excuse if one does not want to accept an invitation to come along. I have a number of letters to my father, *inter alia* from Joseph Joachim[29] and Stefan Zweig, in which they, especially the latter, solve the problem in a charming manner. Perhaps that from Zweig may be of use to the one or other of my readers should the occasion arise.[30]

One thing is certain: what goes on behind the scenes is at least as intriguing as the concert itself.

---

[28] I had always assumed this story to be too good to be true until I recently read it – in a slightly different version – in Wolfgang Stresemann's memoirs *. . . und abends in die Philharmonie*, Albert Langen und Georg Müller Verlag, Munich, 1981; he claimed to have been present on such an occasion. (On Stresemann, see p. 166n.)

[29] See p. 162.

[30] See p. 41.

II

'THE SHOW MUST GO ON'

'Why must the Show go on?'
NOEL COWARD

'The Show Must Go on' – the Eleventh Commandment for actors, musicians, indeed, for all those who are in some way concerned with public performances. Everybody will do his or her utmost to avoid calling off a concert or show, even in the face of seemingly unsurmountable obstacles – an admirable principle. In taking a closer look at it, I mean no disrespect. I would just like to give some thought to two questions. Might there be more to it than meets the eye? And has there been, during the past few decades, a trend towards watering down this attitude – 'dogma', rather – in some respects?

Let me say right away that this problem hardly ever arose in my own experience as far as it concerned my father. He was spared serious illness until shortly before his death. He sometimes suffered from bouts of sciatica and, on one such occasion in the United States, performed the Brahms Violin Concerto sitting down, at that time apparently an unusual feat which earned him, as he describes in his *Memoirs*,[1] a hero's acclamation. What he does not mention in his book is another occasion when he came very near to cancelling a performance. I well remember the exact date – 8 October 1923 – because his fiftieth birthday fell on the following day – hardly a propitious time for a catastrophic public appearance.

He had arranged an orchestral concert jointly with a young conductor (his name does not matter) who was anxious to make his Berlin debut and was prepared to bear part of

---

[1] Pp. 349ff.

45

the expenses; considering the ruinous economic conditions following World War I, this suited my father very well. It seems that for this reason he had – untypically for him – not enquired very closely into the young artist's qualifications. No doubt he felt that anybody prepared to lay out a substantial amount for an orchestra concert would possess the appropriate technical and artistic equipment.

The programme contained two solo items, the Brahms Violin Concerto and the *Fantasie* by Josef Suk, a work my father liked enormously and played superbly well; on the occasion of one of its early performances he played in the presence of the composer.[2]

But the young man was anything but a good accompanist. This would not have mattered with the Brahms, where the Berlin Philharmonic could, if necessary, have followed my father without a conductor, especially since they had played it with him dozens of times in the past. But the Suk was different, because it was – and still is – performed only very rarely and the orchestral part is complicated.[3] The conductor simply could not master it.

My father became so worried that he seriously considered calling the concert off. This was not one of those situations, such as with illness, in which cancellation had become unavoidable, but one in which he had to decide whether to take the risk of damaging his professional reputation through no fault of his own. In the end the 'Show-Must-Go-On' axiom prevailed. The concert performance of the Suk showed in places distinct 'Flesch improvisations' and cuts so as to avoid, as far as possible, parting with the orchestra. As he said afterwards, it had been one of the most nerve-wracking experiences of his concert career, earning him, incidentally, the undying admiration of the leader of the Berlin Philharmonic, Maurits van den Berg. Apart from my father, he

[2] A letter from Suk is reproduced on p. 48.

[3] As Suk himself acknowledges in a letter dated 19 May 1911: 'The Fantasie is not one of those solo works where one rehearsal is sufficient for conductor and orchestra, and the conductor has to be fully familiar with the score; but, of course, in this regard one can rely on Nikisch absolutely – others would have to be told beforehand'. See also pp. 153.

had probably been the only person in the hall who really knew what was going on; and this includes the conductor.

The reviews were favourable. One of them mentioned that the soloist had initially been playing in a somewhat 'carefully probing' manner. 'The man doesn't know how right he is', was my father's laconic comment.

The 'Show-Must-Go-On' phenomenon has two aspects, one factual, one psychological. My knowledge of the first stems mainly from a very inartistic source – my professional activities as an insurance broker. In the course of my career I became, not surprisingly, something of a specialist in 'Non-appearance Insurance', as it is called in insurance jargon. To avoid any misunderstandings, let me say right away that this is not a commercial. My work in the insurance field is now purely consultative, and arranging policies as such no longer forms any part of my activities. But the subject is both of interest and relevant in this context. I am restricting myself, incidentally, to 'serious' music, not pop, jazz and the like, where conditions are somewhat different.

Understandably, the musical profession and the insurance industry view the subject from two diametrically opposed angles: musicians claim that cancellations practically never happen; insurers take a more jaundiced view. To some extent both sides are right, because individual attitudes adopted by artists or promoters can be substantially different.

Most artists are extremely reliable and some promoters most helpful and inventive in order to avoid cancellations. It would be wrong to single out any one individual, but I cannot forbear from mentioning two names. The first is Daniel Barenboim who once, at a moment's notice, agreed to deputise for a colleague at an Edinburgh Festival concert, cut his finger while shaving and yet went on. Ever since I tried to negotiate reduced rates for him whenever I was asked to insure him (he does not know this; most insurances of this kind are taken out by promoters, not the artists themselves).

The second is the impresario Victor Hochhauser, who is uncannily successful in surmounting a crisis and keeping a show going. He certainly had to employ all his diplomatic skills when, many years ago, he managed to avoid the Bolshoi Ballet calling off a London appearance in the face of strong

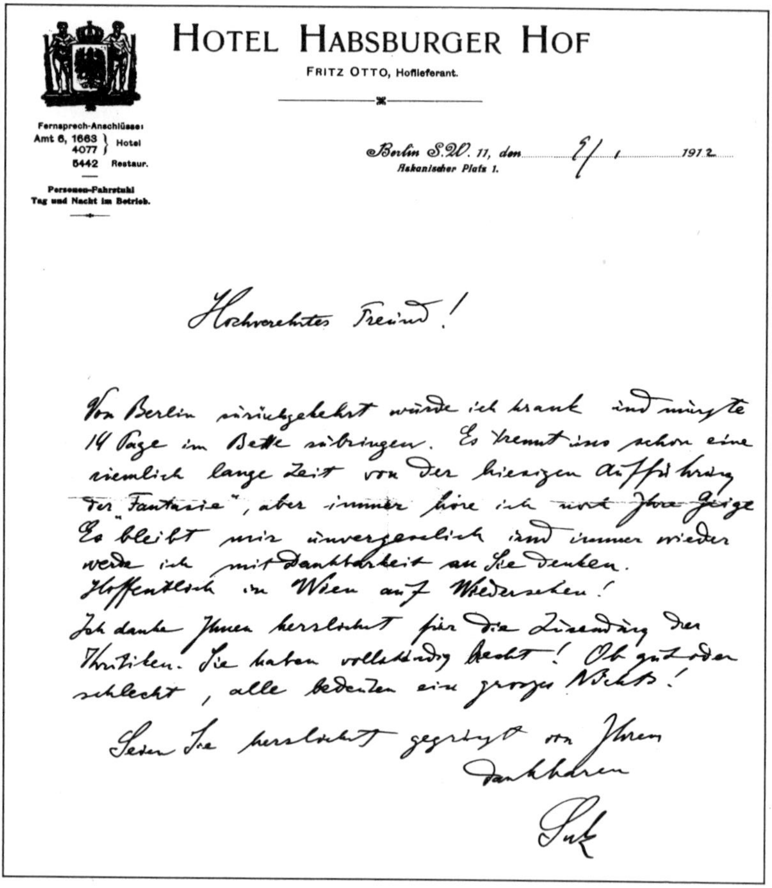

HOTEL HABSBURGER HOF

FRITZ OTTO, Hoflieferant.

Fernsprech-Anschlüsse:
Amt 8, 1663 } Hotel
4077 }
6442 Restaur.

Personen-Fahrstuhl
Tag und Nacht im Betrieb.

Berlin S.W. 11, den 8/1 1912.
Askanischer Platz 1.

Hochverehrter Freund!

[handwritten letter in German]

Josef Suk to Carl Flesch: 'On my return from Berlin I fell
ill and had to spend a fortnight in bed. Quite some time has
passed since the time of the performance of the "Fantasie"
here but I can still hear your violin. It remains
unforgettable for me and I will think of you with gratitude
again and again.
Au revoir in Vienna, I hope.
Many thanks for sending me the press reviews. You are
absolutely right! Whether good or bad, they all mean a big
Nothing!
Kind regards from your grateful
Suk'.

political agitation, culminating in throwing drawing pins and releasing mice onto the stage. Another achievement was his obtaining permission to go ahead with a public performance (almost certainly the only one) on a day of national mourning after the death of King George VI. Hochhauser had arranged a concert by the Vienna Boys' Choir and managed to put it on by the simple expedient of changing the programme to exclusively religious works. I hope the rumour that the audience demanded *The Blue Danube* as an encore is unfounded.

At the other end of the scale are artists known to be so unreliable that insurance for them is obtainable only at near-prohibitive premiums, if at all. A marked proportion of these consists of singers of either sex whose vocal powers are on the wane. Obviously, I am not going to name names, except – and this for a special reason – that of Richard Tauber. In his case, non-appearance insurance was practically impossible, because he had once called off a sold-out Albert Hall matinee shortly before it was due to start: he had felt that he would not be able to 'give of his best'. In order to make a successful insurance claim, the policy-holder has to prove that cancellation has been due to force majeure (including illness). Tauber's non-appearance was thus outside the scope of the policy, since the abandonment of the concert was entirely his own decision, based on artistic considerations. Luckily, all this happened well before my time so that I was not professionally involved.

To hear the understandable emotion with which the late Harold Holt, the promoter of that concert – or rather non-concert – recounted the story was an experience in itself. And no wonder: having to send an audience home before the start of a sold-out concert must be, for any organiser, one of the most traumatic experiences of his professional career.[4]

But what was apparently held against Tauber was the fact that he was seen visiting a cinema the self-same evening.

---

[4] Incidentally, Holt and members of his team could on occasion be quite witty. I remember the charming biblical adaptation with which a director of the firm turned down one of my insurance propositions: 'Flesch is willing, but we are not'.

There is, of course, no reason that someone with a sore throat should not attend a film show; and television, at that time, was still a thing of the future. But one has to admit that the moment was not particularly well chosen.

Yet I remain convinced that his motivation was perfectly honest and genuine. He was the last person to let anyone down, be it public or promoter. Indeed, this was probably the key to his decision – he regarded a bad performance as one way of 'letting the audience down'. That he was a real trooper became clear to me during a matinee performance when I witnessed a basically unimportant yet quite significant example of the way in which he comported himself.

The concert took place at Queen's Hall in London – alas destroyed in the early days of the Blitz. I was listening from a small ante-room immediately behind the stage; all artists had to pass through it on their way to and from the platform. Those old enough to have been present at one of Tauber's performances will recall his exaggerated arm movements, a habit which I always found rather irritating – until the day of that concert.

At the end of his first number, Tauber walked off, as usual, in full flight, arms flailing. There were three steps leading down from the stage to the ante-room and when he reached them he *jumped* them. It was only then that I realised that he had one rather stiff leg and that all his movements, and of course the jump, were designed to divert attention from this disability.

Many people considered him conceited. Though he had every reason to be – some of his Mozart recordings are pretty well unsurpassed even today – he was not. He was easy-going and approachable if perhaps somewhat naively egocentric – a character trait he shared with many another artist. He once asked me to insure him against the risk of losing any piece of paper on which he might have sketched a tune that had just occurred to him. It is improbable that a Schubert or Mozart would have felt a similar necessity of protecting themselves against the loss of their inspirations, no doubt musically more valuable. The funny thing was that I did succeed in finding a Lloyd's Underwriter prepared to accept this proposal. At that time I was still very young and inexperienced; today I can only shudder at the thought of how I would have arrived at a satisfactory claims settlement if a loss had occurred; luckily it never did.

I cannot remember from my own experience any performance Tauber ever cancelled, although he made his last opera appearance – on the occasion of a visit to this country by the Vienna State Opera – when he was already terminally ill.

I value the memory of a great artist and a charming personality.

Now for the 'psychological aspects': for what reasons would a show normally *not* go on? Apart from genuine force majeure such as an earthquake or a fire destroying the concert hall, it would in the first place be illness or accident suffered by an indispensable member of the cast; or a performer's severe emotional upset caused, for instance, by the death of a close relative. In these cases, no one would normally expect a business or professional man to come to work. Either a colleague will substitute for him, or it just has to wait; it must be something of quite outstanding importance for this rule to be broken.

Not so in the artistic profession. According to the 'Show-Must-Go-On' axiom, *any* public performance is of over-riding importance. The underlying idea is that the artist must not let down his colleagues, the promoter and, above all, the public.

This deserves closer examination. Unless there are special circumstances – for instance, the artist being one of those rare people who, due to some flaw in their mental make-up, are known to cancel appearances without good reason – experience shows that colleagues will accept the situation with good grace. After all, it might be their turn next. In some cases, a substitute can be found. If the artist is irreplaceable, there may well be insurance. At any rate, the occasional non-appearance is a fact of life normally appreciated by the artistic fraternity.

Naturally, promoters take a somewhat less relaxed view. The theory mooted occasionally by actors that the whole 'Show-Must-Go-On' syndrome is nothing but an invention by agents and theatre managements is intriguing but hardly realistic. But these professions, too, recognise that the occasional cancellation is an inevitable 'law of nature'; indeed, I happen to know that most of them budget for an annual percentage of such cases. Of course, if they are let down too often by one particular artist, they will sooner or later write him off as unreliable.

Interestingly, a few promoters, when insuring against cancellation, sometimes stipulate that the artist in question must not be told of the policy's existence lest it would weaken his resolve to appear in the face of adverse circumstances. While there is something in this, I believe that it overrates the importance of insurance cover in the performer's mind: conscious and sub-conscious motivations are usually stronger than merely practical or financial considerations.

And the public? Of course it is annoying to arrive at a theatre or concert hall only to find that the performance is off or that the star one had come to hear has been replaced by an unknown. But is it really more serious than, say, a train cancellation due to a wildcat strike or because a guard or driver has simply not turned up? This happens most days of the week – we have only to listen to early-morning radio or TV. It can cause inconvenience, hardship and even financial loss to more people and to a larger extent than the occasional cancellation of a public performance. But how do we react? We grumble, but by and large take it in our stride.

So the argument that the show *must* go on looks perhaps a little more threadbare than appeared at first glance.[5] In cases where one casts doubt on a long-standing well-established tradition it is often rewarding to try and trace its origin. This may not necessarily be as extreme as in the well-known story of the bench in a military barracks guarded, since time immemorial, by a sentry 24 hours a day; until someone had the sense to enquire after the reason. It turned out that, 100 years before, the bench had been freshly painted and a sentry had been posted in order to stop anyone using it before the paint had dried (obviously the military commander of the day

---

[5] Incidentally, I am by no means alone in this opinion. Many years ago Noel Coward composed a chanson with the title quoted at the beginning of this chapter, in which he made disrespectful fun of the matter (recorded on *Noel Coward in New York*, Columbia ML 5163).

had no great confidence in the literacy of his men). The
subsequent cancellation of the order for a guard had been
overlooked. A similar explanation seems unlikely in our case.
But could it possibly lie in the performer himself?

There are facts supporting this view. The missing train
guard, for instance, is anonymous, the missing performer
well-known; hence there is no public acknowledgement for the
former, but keen appreciation for the latter who is working
although he does not feel up to it. Then there is the artist's job
satisfaction, the heady sensation of success without which
most performers would probably not be able to function
adequately – something entirely outside the train driver's
experience. Third, there is the publicity, the glamour inherent
in keeping his trust with the public – something again which is
not granted to a train guard. And finally, there is the artist's
egocentric make-up (an expression not used here in any
derogatory sense), which may lead him to believe that his
absence will be more deeply felt by his public than may be the
case.

However valid these reasons, none of them seems to me to
be strong enough to explain the lengths to which an artist may
go in order to put in an appearance in the face of almost
overwhelming odds and genuine hardship. I believe that there
must be an additional far less obvious ingredient. But before I
risk putting every artist friend's back up, let me reiterate that I
am in no way wishing to disparage the tradition and
motivation. All I am trying to do is to look at the phenomenon
objectively. People often act in an admirable way for reasons
which are not fully apparent to the outside world or even
themselves.

It is my belief that in quite a number of cases – not, of
course, in all – the subconscious motivation is a flight from
reality. This enables the victim of a calamity to push it into the
background, even if only for a short time, and instead to allow
him to immerse himself in a somewhat unreal activity, which
will demand his single-minded concentration and make him
forget his immediate problems. It permits him to postpone
action which, realistically, he ought to be taking right away.
And last but not least, all this will earn him sincere praise for
his dedication, having been able to convince the public and

himself that what he is actually doing is more important than the realistic steps he ought to be taking.

Ridiculous? Fanciful? Far-fetched? Well, I at least don't know of any case when an artist has ever been blamed for behaving in this manner. In one significant example, a famous artist, about to start a series of performances at an important festival, heard on the day preceding the premiere that his wife had been involved in a serious accident and that her life was in danger. Clearly, his place was at her side. But he chose to leave the show only after the first night – at the end of which he received an ovation for his dedication and heroism. But there can really be no doubt about the objectively relative importance of the two events.

And now imagine an ordinary business or professional man going to the office immediately following the death of a close relative. Would he not be condemned as unfeeling and heartless? And, for that matter, if he were to go on working while ill, would he not be accused of acting irresponsibly towards his colleagues, himself and his family? Yet there can surely be no doubt that the work of a solicitor or archi- tect – looked at purely in terms of its necessity and urgency – is in most cases considerably more important than that of a performer. This has nothing to do with a comparison between the value of an artistic and any other profession, but solely with the question how realistically we react to a temporary interruption of one person's activities compared with another's.

Of course, one has to beware of over-simplification; there are a number of complicating factors. In the case of medical men, for instance, and especially surgeons, the overriding importance of an urgent life-saving operation is beyond question. A surgeon continuing his vital work in the face of an event which is for him personally catastophic will earn high praise. But he might insist on cancellation for a different reason, fearing that the risk of his troubled state of mind might affect his concentration. Here, at least, realism wins the upper hand: the doctor's responsibility to his patient is recognised as more important than that of the artist to his public.

On the other hand, consider the case of a leading statesman faced with the problem of whether or not to cancel an important conference on account of a personal tragedy. Experience shows that normally he won't – although one might argue that if he were to commit a technical or political error he would be responsible to a far larger number of people than the surgeon to his solitary patient. On the other hand, the cancellation of the conference might affect the plans of many other persons, more important than the man in the street. And finally, a politician usually has the back-up of many experienced specialists, so that his own role may be less important than it often appears. In brief, there are many possible variations, so that most cases are not strictly comparable.

Altogether it seems extraordinarily difficult to bring all these contradictory features to a common denominator – which only shows that the problem is far more complicated than meets the eye. I should not be surprised if, as so often, the key is the public position of the person concerned. The mystique, the aura of unreality surrounding people in public life, seems to have been probed surprisingly little.

As a further point, the therapeutic effect of 'The Show Must Go On' should not be underrated – and not only for the artistic profession. I myself experienced this when, during the Second World War, I heard of my father's sudden death in Switzerland by reading, completely unprepared, in a London morning paper a brief paragraph headed 'CARL FLESCH DEAD'.[6] The report had been picked up from a Swiss broadcast the night before; a personal telegram reached me only two days later. I telephoned a client to cancel an important appointment for that morning. This caused such consternation and violent protests, with a complete disregard for my personal situation, that I eventually decided to keep the appointment; there was no possible communication with Switzerland, and absolutely nothing I could do. As I found out, the necessity of concentrating on an entirely different problem was probably the best method I could have devised to absorb the initial shock.

So why do I think that present trends point to a weakening of the 'Show-Must-Go-On' principle? To start with, there is an interesting antithesis, 'The show must *not* go on' as it

[6] See p. 56.

Carl Flesch dead

Carl Flesch died in Lucerne yesterday at the age of 71, the Swiss radio announced last night. Flesch was accepted as one of the world's finest violinists.

The announcement, in the News Chronicle *of 16 November 1944, of the death of my father*

were – the strike. Here everything possible is being done to prevent a 'show' (in the widest sense of the word) from taking place. Of course, the political and the artistic situations are completely different and it would be foolish to attempt a direct comparison between the two. And yet, some remarkable parallels are discernible: for instance, the firm conviction of the persons involved in the moral justification of their action (or rather, inaction); their efforts to underpin it with realistic and idealistic reasoning; the not infrequently over-rated idea of the effect on the public.

To be sure, a striker usually makes a financial sacrifice, whereas an artist who keeps an engagement does the exact opposite – he saves his fee. But political considerations apart, I doubt that the financial question represents the main psychological motivation. For the artist, it is the job satisfaction; the effect on his public; and the flight from reality. As against that, a striker often finds his normal job anything but satisfying and welcomes a good reason for interrupting it; he receives no publicity for his work – except when he stops doing it; and he has the chance of temporarily neglecting the realities of everyday life, namely, the necessity of earning a living. It would be going too far to follow up the similarities and contradictions any further. But perhaps one day a sociologist will consider them sufficiently interesting to make them the subject of his thesis.

The artistic profession itself, of course, is not free from cases in which the principle is completely disregarded. Strikes by members of orchestra and chorus are today no longer as unusual as in former times, especially in the United States, where they are often an inevitable side effect of negotiations about the renewal of salary-scale agreements. This can pose severe problems, in particular for opera house managements, since internationally famous singers have to be engaged several years ahead of the performance date and usually demand a clause in their contract to the effect that they will receive their fee even if the date of their engagement coincides with a strike.

But even individual artists do not always give the fullest consideration to the principle. As an example I can quote a somewhat startling entry in my father's diary:[7]

> The conductor Ansermet: 'No, I no longer believe in Casals'. I: 'Why?' Ansermet: 'I had a concert with him, in Montreux. He was to play the Haydn Cello Concerto in the first, and the Don Quijotte [*sic*] solo in the second part of the concert. During the interval he says to me: 'Where is my fee? I always have to have it in the interval, otherwise I don't continue'.
>
> Ansermet makes an urgent call for the cashier – he is not to be found. Casals: 'Well, then I won't play'. Another search. The audience is becoming impatient; catcalls and stamping of feet. Casals waits – at long last the cashier appears, hands Casals a bundle of notes. Casals, with the cello under one arm, counts the money – carefully, from time to time wetting his thumb with his tongue – the amount is right. 'Et maintenant nous pouvons continuer' – mounts the platform and starts the solo with his enraptured Casals expression, 'Depuis ce jour-là, je ne lui crois plus', Ansermet concludes.[8]

'Must the show go on?' the objective answer lies probably somewhere between the two extremes. But as a member of the public – and, to be frank, as a former insurance broker – my firm answer is: 'Yes, please, if at all possible!'

---

[7] Dated 19 September 1931.

[8] Well, nobody is perfect. Casals' towering artistic importance is not diminished by an episode of this kind. Alma Moodie pertinently expressed it in a letter she wrote to my father on 11 December 1931, acknowledging the receipt of a treatise dealing with the 'Problems of Sound on the Violin': 'You can't put all of it into words – I realised this again last week in a Casals concert in which he played like a God in a half-empty hall. In the last resort it is not possible entirely to explain the effect of his playing; and that is something which, these days, I for one particularly welcome'.

III

THE ARTIST AND HIS PUBLIC

'The toughest thing about
success is that you've got to
keep on being a success.'
IRVING BERLIN

All of us who have to work for our living measure our success
in different ways: if we are employed, normally by the
appreciation shown by our employers and the amount of our
salaries; if self-employed, usually by the number of customers
or clients and the size of our free-lance incomes. But frequently – for instance, in arts, science, sports and politics – there is
an additional factor: prestige and recognition, irrespective of
material rewards. And in occupations involving public performances we have yet another significant ingredient: the
spontaneous and directly expressed appreciation by spectators
or listeners – public applause.

What do you suppose would be the reaction of your dentist
if, after a painless tooth extraction, you were to jump up from
his chair and treat him to a prolonged demonstration of
hand-clapping? He would conclude either that you were
temporarily deranged or that you wanted to pull his leg.
Admittedly, since you are at that moment presumably the only
member of the audience, you could render your thanks to him
simply in a few well-chosen words. But usually you don't do
even that; you accept the quality of his work as a matter of
course, and he on his part does not count on any spontaneous
expression of opinion.

The performing artist feels quite differently. Not only does
he, after a concert or play, expect enthusiastic applause, but
he would regard its absence, or too little of it, as a definite sign

of failure. In other words, the immediate reaction by the audience as a whole is, for an artist, of decisive importance.

But here we encounter a curious paradox, at least if my personal observations are anything to go by: although public performers consider success with the audience – as a body – outstandingly important, they accord surprisingly little value to appreciation by individual members of the public. Indeed, it is not unknown for continually expressed admiration from individuals to be regarded as a nuisance, an intrusion. But even in less pronounced cases professional musicians show a condescension bordering on snobbishness.[1]

Of course, the professional musician knows incomparably more about music than the average concert-goer. Vincent d'Indy, for instance, estimated the percentage of genuine cognoscenti at a concert as no more than 5% of those present.[2] But a similar comparative discrepancy in expertise applies also to other walks of life: on the one hand, to professionals whose main activities consist of giving advice to laymen, although they have usually no such dismissive attitude towards those who cannot compare with them in professional competence; and on the other, to certain academics such as archaeologists, lecturers in philosophy, mediaeval history and similar subjects, who not infrequently develop a state of mind leading them to regard everything and everybody non-academic as inferior – but with the difference that they do not seek, nor need, any publicly expressed appreciation of their work by more than a few persons of a standing equalling their own.

---

[1] At the same time it is worth mentioning that some artists have a confidant who, intellectually and technically, is anything but their equal but to whom they accord preferential treatment – sometimes to the annoyance of their immediate families. This is by no means confined to musicians. Thomas Mann, for instance, had a purely literary relationship with an elderly lady whose intelligence and cultural standard did not, as far as I could judge, go beyond a good average. She told me that she possessed numerous letters from him containing important and profound observations and reflections. On meeting one of Mann's sons I asked him whether he knew this to be true. His somewhat unflattering reply: 'Yes, she was the wall on which my father wrote his graffiti'.

[2] Quoted by Carl Flesch in a paper, 'Individual or Classroom Teaching?'

The ambivalence I have described appears to be a trait peculiar to musicians.

A typical entry in Carl Flesch's diary:[3]

> The other day [Piatigorsky and I] discussed in detail the present-day material conditions of the concert artist's profession. The conclusions were shattering [there follows a list of expenses, discomforts, and so on, ending with] and finally having to listen, in the artist's room, to the remarks of 'musical' people [. . .].

And this although many artists consider a well attended Green Room to be of enormous importance.[4]

Of course, there are music lovers and amateurs whose musical education and knowledge are in no way inferior to – and sometimes better than – those of professional musicians. On the other hand, there are probably few subjects about which more nonsense is talked than music. No wonder, then, that professional musicians usually have a fund of anecdotes and stories in their repertoire illustrating this state of affairs.

One glorious instance can be found in the (authentic) remark by Queen Wilhelmina I of the Netherlands who, eighty years ago, during a charity concert in which my father was participating, looked down from her Royal Box on to the orchestra, conductor and soloist who were playing their hearts out and then turned to her lady-in-waiting with the question: 'Tell me, what do these people do during the day?'

This episode is not quite as out-of-the-way as one might think, for a similar case once happened to me. I kept a business appointment with the director of an important firm of Lloyd's brokers. On the previous night the finals of the Carl Flesch International Violin Competition had been transmitted live on TV. The conductor on that occasion was Sir Charles Groves. Since we are both portly and sport a short white beard, we are to some extent look-alikes (a fact, incidentally, which did not seem to please Sir Charles very much when I once happened to mention it to him). The secretary of the man I was to meet received me with fulsome compliments on

[3] Probably for 7 September 1931.

[4] See pp. 40–44.

my conducting the night before. She was obviously under the impression that conducting an orchestra was a part-time occupation that could easily be managed alongside the full-time profession of insurance broking.

Or take our encounter on holiday with a man who was highly pleased to make my father's acquaintance: 'Greatly honoured to meet so famous an artist', rather spoiling the effect by adding 'Who wouldn't know Flesch', at the same time moving his hands as if playing the piano. This became part of the Flesch family folklore.

Into this category falls a question someone asked my father after he had played in a private concert in the house of a friend: 'Tell me, in which café do you usually play?' So, too, does the remark made to my mother by a friend after a concert: 'Carl played wonderfully well today, especially on the G string'.

Then there is, of course, the old chestnut of the two friends at the opera. 'Beautiful, Lohengrin's voice today!' says the one. 'But they are not performing *Lohengrin*; this is *Freischütz*', replies his friend. '*Freischütz*? I know every note. Let's go!'

And finally a letter from a member of the audience at a charity concert I had arranged in which Karl Ulrich Schnabel had given an admirable performance of Schumann's *Kinderszenen*. The writer advised us that, in his youth, he had 'learnt' the *Kinderszenen* himself and therefore knew how easy the work was to play. Considering the price of the ticket, he had been expecting something more difficult. The member of the charity committee who handed me this letter with an accusing glance was somewhat taken aback when I suggested sending it to a music magazine as 'Joke of the Week'.[5]

---

[5] This reminds me of a *bon mot* by Artur Schnabel: 'Mozart is too easy for children, too difficult for adults' – a very clever observation, possibly losing a little of its force if one takes it to its logical conclusion, since the two lines are bound to cross at some point when Mozart's work is neither too easy nor too difficult for the player. In my opinion this moment should be scientifically ascertainable in the same way as, say, a solar eclipse. I think I've managed to do it: after lengthy calculations I have come to the conclusion that the exact age at which this phenomenon occurs is fifteen years, four months, two weeks and three days.

But all this does not offer a full explanation of the slightly schizophrenic attitude of musicians. The general public is, after all, nothing but a conglomerate of individuals; one should think, therefore, that what applies to the former, should apply to the latter with at least equal force. Is it possible to draw from this rarely noted ambivalence any conclusions regarding musicians' general motivation and attitude of mind?

I cannot claim to have found a satisfactory answer, but I have tried to collect some material towards it. Where, for instance, is the borderline between 'individual' and 'general public'? Mere figures cannot be the sole criterion. I don't know of any artist with a sense of responsibility who would consciously take less trouble when appearing in a small town before a half-empty hall than when playing in an important or sold-out concert in a big city. He may be kicking himself for having played much worse in London than the evening before in Little Ambridge, but this does not mean that he treated the concert in the Styx less seriously.

Similarly, it is no criterion whether or not the audience has paid for its tickets. The concerts of many unknown artists on the threshold of their career are padded with as many freebooters as can be induced to attend. Some of the London concert halls, as well as the National Theatre, regularly arrange lobby concerts of about one hour's duration by professional musicians before the advertised events; doubtless, their success is measured by the performers – as in any other concert – according to the amount of public applause they receive.

Perhaps one gets a little nearer to a solution by defining 'the public' as an audience with most of whose members the artist has no personal relationship, so that their reaction is solely governed by the quality of his performance. This, after all, is what he has spent years of preparation to accomplish. Looked at from this angle, the whole audience means more to him than simply the sum total of single persons.

But I am sure this is not the full answer. For it does not take into account the lack of musical understanding on the part of individuals in the audience. If d'Indy's remark about a mere 5% being knowledgeable is correct, the next question, logically, is why an artist should take all this enormous trouble for so small a part of his public, seeing that a far lesser effort would be sufficient for 95% of it. What is it that motivates him?

Perhaps another of my father's diary entries might throw a flickering light on one aspect of the question:[6]

> For the artist as well as art itself, creative striving is of far greater significance than the achievement, development more important than ability.[7]

So does this mean that there always exists continuous striving towards further perfection? In some cases, no doubt, yes, but not always; for the diary entry continues:

> For this reason a phenomenal executant such as Heifetz is, in the last resort, less interesting than his compatriot Elman, because the former has stood still whereas the latter continually, albeit with problematical results, works at his art, endeavours to progress.

One has to remember, of course, that this is an opinion expressed from the expert's, not the concert-goer's, point of view. But if the assessment of Heifetz has validity – something which many will not regard as proven – then, clearly, the striving after improvement is not always the motivating force nor the prerequisite for maximum achievement. And although for a man like Heifetz his overwhelming success was such a matter of course that it cannot have affected him much, he would no doubt have been anything but indifferent to a sign of diminishing public approbation.

But whatever the artist's state of mind when performing a work, the amount of effort invested into studying it, whether old or new, is immense. Every single nuance is considered, experimented with, discussed, frequently

---

[6] Entry for 21 September 1931.

[7] This is a somewhat clumsy translation of the more simply expressed German original: 'Für den Künstler und für die Kunst ist das Werden von weit grösserer Bedeutung als das Sein, die Entwicklung wichtiger als das Können'.

changed. In Appendices III and IV I quote extracts from letters which give convincing proof of this.[8]

What else can motivate an artist to his untiring efforts? Is he thinking, in the first place, of his professional colleagues – like some ladies who, when buying new clothes, allegedly (indeed, even by their own admission) do so with an eye on the probable judgement by other women, rather than the men whose approval they are supposedly seeking? Partly this is no doubt true, for we all find satisfaction in approval by our professional equals; it is even possible to adduce a logical reason for this, since those who have to decide on artists' engagements frequently – though not always – are musical experts.

Does the artist have the critics in mind? Surely he must have, whatever his attitude towards that particular profession. D'Indy's 5%? No doubt, that too. But if you add up all these factors and personalities, they represent only a fraction of the general public.

What remains? The artist himself! His own satisfaction at playing a work to the best of his or her ability. Additionally, proof of his ability to influence circles outside his immediate personal sphere. And last but not least the public approbation which, whether he knows it or not, becomes a necessity to him.

We ought not to lose sight of the ritual form and character of public applause: in the first place, not so much the conduct of the audience as that of the artist himself – most markedly, incidentally, in opera and ballet. No artist would ever dream of behaving in real life as he does on these occasions on stage or platform: the exaggerated hand movements, the 'surprised-grateful' mien[9] or even the complete immovability on first appearing, allowing the applause to envelop him or her like a delicious shower (for me the most typical example of the latter is Jessye Norman). The crowd is treated on these occasions in a manner entirely different from that used with acquaintances or individual fans. But the audience is only too willing to play

---

[8] See pp. 355–61.

[9] My father, who looked very serious on the platform, maintained that a smile usually guaranteed an additional call.

its part. It is almost as if they and the artist are giving a joint performance. The rules of normal behaviour are being temporarily suspended.

Much as all this means to an artist, it has been known for disenchantment to occur in some instances. My father's diary again: on his fifty-eighth birthday he had decided to retire from concert life at the age of 60, although 'I have only now attained my artistic zenith. However, with advancing age I am realising more and more the innate spuriousness of the concert artist's profession, and no longer possess the ability to believe in the illusion about the interpreter's importance'.[10] Thus, at that time he no longer needed outward confirmation – he found his main satisfaction in teaching. And yet when emigration compelled him to resume public appearances, he used to report the number of his engagements and his successes with obvious satisfaction. But in his case it was probably the confirmation of his continued technical mastery that gave him the deepest pleasure.

And the relationship to the critic? We all know how much has been said and written about this subject. My personal experience is limited in that bad reviews about my father were practically non-existent.

By and large, artists have a negative attitude towards critics – behind their backs, that is; personal relations are mostly by no means bad. If there is sometimes a degree of truth in the cliché that 'He who can't, criticises' (or, in a different version, 'teaches'), in the majority of cases it is quite unjustified. Too many people overlook the difficulties of the critic's controversial and, to some extent, self-contradictory task. He writes in the first place for the reader interested in what is happening in musical life; for the concert-goer who likes to be confirmed in his own opinion, though sometimes he needs to know whether or not he, in fact, liked a particular concert he attended! The least important of his tasks is writing for the artist himself, although a beginner may need favourable reviews. (On the other hand, there is no point in over-rating these if only because in most case even the worst review can be processed

[10] Entry probably for 5 September 1931.

for publicity purposes in such a way that it says something good.)

His main problems are lack of time; that he is expected to know about every aspect of music – instruments, compositions and much more; and that he is supposed to write in an interesting manner. All this means that, however broad his all-round knowledge, it will be inferior to the specialised expertise of many of those about whom he writes, and yet at the same time he has to keep his articles variegated and different. Considering how frequently he has to listen to the same works and artists, one can appreciate the critic's difficulties. There is an additional obstacle: frequently his copy will be changed or cut as remorselessly as inexpertly by sub-editors whose main objective is to fill a given space, with the result that his intended meaning can be severely distorted in print.

Obviously an artist wants to read as much – and as favourably – as possible about himself; and who can blame him? He will be offended if the reviewer concentrates on the programme, and deals with his performance in only a few words, especially if these are not particularly enthusiastic or even tend to be critical. But how many ways are there of saying that Mr or Miss So-and-So gave an excellent perform-ance? And for that matter, who, except the performer himself, is all that interested, unless it concerns a newcomer or a very special event? Should the critic make comparisons? Surely, this would only aggravate his problems.

And who can take it amiss if, without adopting an unnecess-arily malicious tone, he mentions something he did not approve of? On the other hand, a critical remark can give the unintentional impression of coldness or unfriendliness, especi-ally if the success of the concert with the audience had been outstanding.

Writing about the programme itself doesn't help him much, either. If it contained the first performance of a new work, he is accused of being a charlatan – how could he possibly judge a work at first hearing? Very true in most cases (although he may have been able to look at the score beforehand), but what is he to do instead? Write, however truthfully, that he did not understand the work and therefore cannot express a valid opinion? That would cost him his job.

On the other hand if he writes, say, after a chamber-music concert, about the history of a Beethoven quartet that had been performed, it will be said that he has copied it all from books which anybody could have read. But where else should he have got it from? And if professional musicians already do know it all – as, indeed, they should – 99% of his readers do not. But probably some of those will say that they, too, would have preferred reading something about the performance rather than the programme.

In brief – the poor chap just can't win. Nobody, of course, likes to read an unfavourable notice about himself, but as long as it is pertinent and objective he has little grounds for complaint. In artistic questions, subjective opinions, sympathies and antipathies are unavoidable. A reviewer can't be the exception, but he will recognise his subjective tendencies and be doubly circumspect – provided he knows his job.

This, unfortunately, is not always the case. Everybody knows stories of reviewers who became objects of ridicule in one way or the other, as in the age-old – but to my knowledge true – tale of the critic with an Austrian provincial rag who concluded an enthusiastic review of the newly founded Rosé Quartet with the words: 'It is to be hoped that the young artists will soon be in a position to augment their small orchestra'; or the cases (not all that rare) in which a critic did not notice an alteration in the programme with the result that he reviewed a piece at length which had not been performed at all; not to mention those who write about a concert which they had not taken the trouble to attend so that they had no knowledge of the fact that it had been cancelled at the last moment.

Of course, criticisms can sometimes be extremely cutting or hurtful – unfortunately, from a purely journalistic point of view, they are usually the most interesting. But unless they deal with an important question of principle, there is no call for them to be written in this way. It is always possible to express an unfavourable opinion tactfully without blunting its force. Bad notices for purely personal reasons are, of course, unforgivable, but newspapers dealing with music in a serious way usually do what they can to take avoiding action. I remember meeting Peter Stadlen, for many years chief critic at *The Daily Telegraph*, queuing for a ticket before a concert. 'Are you here professionally or privately?' I asked. 'Privately. Otherwise I wouldn't buy a ticket. There is a firm rule on our paper to review only those concerts for which we get free tickets.' Noticing my surprise, he added: 'So as to avoid any suspicion that we may have written a bad review because we had been refused free entry'.

A similar attitude, albeit from a somewhat different angle, was expressed by the violinist Robert Perutz in the 1930s:

> I was recently asked by a very important Polish paper to become their permanent musical correspondent in the USA. I declined [. . .] *inter alia* because I am convinced that an artist, however unimportant, who plays in public himself, ought not to criticise others in print.[11]

The artist's motivations as well as his relationship with the public at large, individual fans and critics are somewhat more complicated than meets the eye. The problems inherent in this subject have so far by no means been exhaustively treated, let alone fully explained.

---

[11] Letter to Carl Flesch; Perutz never dated his letters properly.

IV

TEACHER AND PUPIL

'As a teacher you live on in
your pupils like a father in his
children.'
CARL FLESCH

Wilhelm Busch, a German poet of the late nineteenth century, comparable, perhaps, to Edward Lear, wrote a poem whose beginning is still popular in Germany today:

Vater werden ist nicht schwer,
Vater sein dagegen sehr.

which in translation gives us:

Becoming a father is easy enough,
But being a father is really quite tough.

Replace the word 'father' by 'teacher' and you have something just as valid.

Carl Flesch would no doubt have confirmed it: as he confesses in his *Memoirs*,[1] he started his teaching career at the age of twelve. But his pupil, a boy of about his own age, profited little from these lessons, since it was mostly not he but my father who did the playing, using the opportunity to practise his own repertoire. In this way he earned his fee – a bowl of stewed fruit per lesson – in an easy and (for him) doubly convenient way. By the time, twenty years on, he had matured into one of the foremost violin pedagogues of his time, he had realised that there was rather more to it than he had imagined in his youth.

[1] Pp. 55ff.

Over the years every prominent teacher is bound to train several first-class artists. Leopold Auer's school, for example, probably produced the largest number of world-famous violinists of that generation. My father was, in this respect, not all that far behind, but held the view that in the case of an outstanding natural talent a teacher's main task should be to develop what already existed in such abundance and to give students of this type a last polish, being careful at the same time to avoid undoing anything. In his view, the real test for a teacher was his ability to guide normal talents to the highest peak of their potential. This did not necessarily mean a concert career: pupils who subsequently applied, and possibly improved on, their teacher's methods, were equally important, even if they were not above average as soloists.

Of the professionals playing a particular musical instrument, about 1% are famous and 99% relatively unknown. In the last resort it is the ability of the latter that matters: without them, musical life could not continue to exist. A first-class orchestra, for instance, does not need members of Heifetz or Rostropovich calibre. Indeed, I suspect that their presence would actually be counter-productive, because even the greatest conductor would probably find it next to impossible to weld a team of this kind into a homogeneous whole. It is also true that some talents are more suitable for collaboration than for soloistic activity – and vice versa. In this respect, a diary entry by my father about a world-famous violinist (whose name I am not prepared to divulge!) is relevatory:

> Heard [. . .] yesterday for the first time. Excellent standard, outstanding violinistic talent, a lack of musical upbringing [Kinderstube] notwithstanding. Like so many others, finished his apprenticeship too early. Large tone albeit at the expense of all too frequent changes of bow. Noble, chaste tone quality. Many unnecessary portamenti, capricious alterations to the score. But all in all, a pleasing figure among the youngsters because basically natural and uspoilt.
>
> Next day, played quartet with him – clue-less angel – agonising both for players and listeners.

How important is 'star quality'? Most public concerts – as, indeed, opera and theatre performances – take place without the participation of a world-famous artist and are no less successful and culturally valuable for all that.

This became clear to me on a very special occasion – a concert organised by the European String Teachers Association (ESTA) in 1973 to celebrate the centenary of my father's birth. It was a unique event: a chamber orchestra conducted by Yehudi Menuhin with members of the Amadeus Quartet as section leaders. The Flesch pupils Bronislaw Gimpel, Ida Haendel, Max Rostal and Henryk Szeryng (who insisted on participating at least during the first half of the concert; he was scheduled to fly to the United States that self-same afternoon, and his place in the second part was taken by Yfrah Neaman) were soloists in the Vivaldi Concerto for Four Violins and Orchestra and a similar piece specially commissioned by me.[2]

It was fantastic! And in the middle of it all – without in the least wishing to appear ungrateful – the heretical thought occurred to me: would it sound any worse if the solo parts were played by four competent orchestral leaders accompanied by a normal orchestra? The ESTA audience was, of course, highly professional, but would more than a small percentage of an ordinary audience have noticed the difference? I rather doubt it. 'Horses for courses': works like these do not necessarily gain by being performed by such outstanding soloists. Of course, to hear them accompanied by that orchestra under that conductor was a musical sensation *per se* which remains unforgettable. But this has nothing to do with the original question – not to mention that if artists and orchestra had been asking for their normal fees (they all gave their services for nothing) nobody could have afforded them.

Contemporary music, too, would develop far more slowly if its performance were to be the preserve of only the most prominent.

In brief, although, of course, no teacher would ever dream of refusing to accept a particularly gifted pupil, it is the student of average talent who represents the more attractive and rewarding task. A letter from such a pupil who writes 'People who hear me now don't recognise my playing

[2] See pp. 159–60.

*A rehearsal for the Carl Flesch Centenary Concert in 1973.
The conductor is Yehudi Menuhin and the soloists, from left
to right, are Ida Haendel, Henryk Szeryng, Bronislav
Gimpel and Max Rostal. The orchestra includes, from left
to right, Alan Loveday, Norbert Brainin, Yfrah Neaman,
Siegmund Nissel, Suzanne Rosza-Lovett, Robert Masters,
Peter Schidlof, Nannie Jamieson, Joan Dickson and Martin
Lovett. (Courtesy of Suzanne Rosza-Lovett.)*

compared with what it was two years ago' will satisfy a teacher
no less, and in many cases more, than the triumphant report
from a genius who basically was already first-class before he
ever came for lessons.

Of particular interest are the problems, difficulties and
fiascos of young and promising students, the growing pains of
young artists just out of school, and the teacher/pupil relationship as such. If young musicians do not succeed in rising
above and overcoming their weaknesses, one will rarely read
anything about it; should they ever get around to writing their
autobiography they will usually touch only very lightly, if at
all, on their disappointments; and a teacher will obviously
prefer to mention his successful pupils rather than those who
did not make the grade.

Those with little or no talent will be referred to at best in private, as, for instance, in the case of a young (and later very successful) ex-student whom my father endeavoured to help by recommending suitable pupils from time to time:

> Miss [. . .] has contacted me and now takes regular lessons. [. . .] suffice it to say that she is neither gifted nor young, but takes her studies very seriously and is in better financial circumstances than talented pupils can ever be. This latter point is of importance to me during this time of the year – outside the concert season.

As I have said, reports about failures are usually far more instructive. They show that from a certain point onwards even the best teacher becomes powerless. Sooner or later the pupil has to stand on his own feet. And sometimes circumstances intervene which are outside the player's control.

In his *Memoirs*, for instance, Carl Flesch mentions Frank Gittelson, a pupil whom, as he writes, both Nikisch and Godowsky regarded as a possible successor to Ysaÿe. However, he was forced by the conductor Walter Damrosch to make his Carnegie Hall debut with the Bach E major Concerto – a work entirely unsuitable for a first appearance in New York. His inevitable failure so affected him that he subsequently never achieved the position to which his talent should have entitled him. On such uncertain feet sometimes stands the career of a budding young artist if he does not have it in him to overcome occasional set-backs. At the same time it shows how much damage a self-opinionated conductor can do when he is not prepared to listen to justified and reasoned arguments and will not tolerate contradiction. Gittelson's letter[3] says it all:

> I did not want to answer your very welcome letter until I had finished my recent tour. Now I am able to tell you that with the exception of New York I have had splendid success everywhere. [. . .] As to New York it was a choice between the Nardini and the Bach E major.
> While I thought that both would scarcely appeal to the public, still I concluded that the Bach is a really great work, and

[3] Dated 10 February 1915.

I had had a big success with it wherever I had played it. My father and I made a special trip to N.Y. to see Damrosch and to protest against the Nardini, which he had selected, but he insisted on having a short classical piece and had already refused the Lalo, Brahms, Bruch, etc. [. . .] We did not want the Bach either, but it was all that was left. I see now that I could possibly have suggested a Mozart, but I had not played them in years, and it would have been risky.

The accompaniment was very bad, too. [. . .] and we were hardly ever together.

There is no use crying over spilt milk, and I am trying to forget the *damned* concert as quickly as possible. I am more than tempted to become a professional chess player, street cleaner or vermin exterminator. [. . .]

I can follow the reasoning as far as the last two are concerned. But if newspaper reports are anything to go by, the profession of a chess player seems to be almost more stressful than that of a musician and would have meant a jump from the frying pan into the fire. Anyway, the young man stuck to the violin, but the brilliant career of which he had originally been considered capable eluded him.

Or take the case of one of my father's best former students, anonymous in this story (for he is still with us) but world-famous except in Great Britain where, surprisingly, he simply could not manage to secure a foothold. When during a renewed attempt the question of a London BBC engagement became acute, he was asked – an artist with numerous well-known gramophone recordings to his credit – to undergo an audition before anything else. Had he been able to ask my father's advice – at that time no longer alive – I am sure he would have declined this precondition. As it was, he agreed. Result: he was considered not good enough! Well, we all make fools of ourselves at one time or another – why should the BBC be an exception?

Another to some extent tragi-comic case is that of a young fiddler who had made an excellent London debut, but could not maintain this success elsewhere. In a letter to my father (written in 1913) he complains not only about his agent who apparently served him very badly, but also about British audiences:

I have now been on tour in England for 6 weeks, and have rarely had to suffer as much as now when I have to play in front of the most unmusical people in Europe – the English; I except, of course, London, Manchester, Birmingham and Liverpool, but otherwise the British people are disgracefully unmusical. Sometimes the accompanist has to play 'God Save the King' in order to make people realise that the concert is finished.

This hilarious misconception about the reason for playing the National Anthem – the almost invariable custom after a public performance at that time – makes one wonder how justified was the wide-spread opinion at the beginning of the century about the British lack of musical culture.

'Heart-rending' is an apt description of the plight of a highly gifted young girl who originally had been regarded as a prodigy, only to experience psychological difficulties which turned many of her public appearances into nightmares. She had originally studied with a teacher well-known for his success in producing 'Wunderkinder', but who could not do anything with her once her defects had become apparent. My father managed to achieve considerable technical progress, but he could not cure her inhibitions. What surprises me in her letters to him is the gratitude and absolute confidence in him one can read in every line in spite of the fact that he had, after all, not helped her either. It is an interesting question whether with today's better-developed psychological insights and therapeutic methods a more positive result could have been achieved.

I don't know what is the matter with me – I have no vitality whatsoever, and I wish I were dead. The Goldmark seems to be getting worse and worse the more I play it [. . .]. I'd like to give the whole darn thing up, smash my violin and drown myself. Please tell me what is the matter with me. The notices were very good [. . .] but that doesn't mean a thing. [. . .] I don't think I'll ever be anything – all this time and money has been wasted – because all people think of is the glory of fame – and I am finding out it is a dog's life. [. . .] this whole tour is a terrible nightmare to me, and I wish morning would come quickly. I wish you could come and wake me up. Please help me! Tell me what I can do.

And on another occasion:

I must be one of those people who play well in a room and at
rehearsals and can't play in public. At the rehearsal I played –
well, my best, conductor and orchestra and the few listeners
went mad! [. . .] And then I got up to play last night and it was
all gone, all inspiration, all pep – it was as though someone else
played for me [. . .].

In this vein it went on. The young girl took more lessons,
played better and better – and failed every time when it really
mattered. She tried many things on her own – a different way
of bowing and several other technical amendments. Unfortunately my father did not approve of any of them. There
followed a tearful goodbye. As far as I know, she subsequently
gave up playing in public. A great pity, for she had an
exceptionally beautiful and beguiling tone. All this proves that
once a pupil has completed his (or her) studies he has to rely
on himself; it is perhaps also proof of the importance of not
'leaving school' too early.

Another – as it were, reverse – problem can be that of a
talented pupil meeting opposition on account of his or her
choice of teacher. This seems to have been the case with no
less a person than Ginette Neveu. In 1937 she was already
following a very successful concert career but was still an
occasional Flesch student. She had not been in touch with him
for some time and he did not conceal his resentment. Her
reply:

[. . .] Please believe me, Dear Maestro, that nothing is further
from my thoughts than any hint of ingratitude. [. . .] Do rest
assured that in spite of all that people say to me and the
difficulties I am encountering in France on account of being
your pupil[4] my feelings for, and my confidence in, you have not
changed. Unfortunately I know from experience how malicious
certain people can be towards me merely because I am successful [. . .]. I am even asking myself whether there may not be
some persons in London who would be only too pleased if I
were to be discredited in your eyes [. . .].[5]

---

[4] Curiously enough, my father was not particularly well liked in France
although he had spent most of his student years in Paris.

[5] Letter dated 14 May 1937.

*Ginette Neveu announces
her success in the 1935
Wieniawski Competition*

With other pupils the problem can be – and often is – financial. As already mentioned elsewhere, in these cases my father – like no doubt many other teachers – did not hesitate to give lessons to really gifted students at a reduced fee or none at all. However, he took care not to overdo it, frequently citing Busoni as a cautionary example; according to him, Busoni had been opposed on principle to accepting money for his lessons with the inevitable result that on his death he had left his family in dire financial straits. Some letters from Frau Busoni's friend, the sculptress Annette Kolb,[6] show that she had to eke out an existence by letting rooms. I know that my father tried to help her through the charity he had founded for just these cases.[7]

[6] See pp. 80 and 82.

[7] On the Hilfsbund für deutsche Musikpflege, see pp. 190–91.

Ginette Neveu   le 14 Mai 1937.

Cher Maître,

Ginette Neveu protests her gratitude to Carl Flesch and mentions the hostility she has encountered in France as a result of her decision to study with him.

Once a student has completed his training, there are still ways in which he can be assisted further, in particular through recommendations. Well-known teachers are frequently asked to suggest a suitable candidate for an orchestral job or the position of second violin in a string quartet. For young artists, however high their ambitions, such a post can be excellent practice, not to mention the financial security it offers during their first difficult years.

Sometimes there is more at stake, namely the position as leader of a prestigious orchestra; in these cases the teacher's function can go beyond the merely artistic. This can lead to intriguing situations. The conductor George Szell, for instance, wrote to my father[8] about his ex-pupil Henri Temianka with whom Szell had been negotiating about the post of leader in the BBC Scottish Orchestra, of which he had just been appointed conductor:

> [. . .] I ascertained by telephone last night that it might not be impossible to obtain for Temianka the remuneration which you suggested yesterday as the correct and necessary one (£300 including 2 solo engagements). May I ask you when discussing the proposition with him to deal also with the financial aspect and to convince him that this amount would be the right one for him? Please do not mention this letter to him, nor that this salary is very likely achievable, but try to steer the conversation in such a way that Temianka writes to me and asks for this salary. If this is agreed, with the additional remark that such a high fee has never been paid before (which is the truth), this will please him far more than if we were to offer this amount from the outset.
>
> I am relying on your friendship and help [. . .].

This looks to me as if the figure suggested by my father – I hope agreed with Temianka beforehand – had been on the low side. I don't know how precisely my father carried out Szell's request, but in any case, Temianka accepted the position. The letter is instructive in that it not only provides an insight into pre-war salaries but also the somewhat devious ways in which even the greatest musicians managed to combine art and

---

[8] Letter dated 19 January 1937.

Annette Kolb to Carl Flesch about Gerda Busoni: 'Years ago you were kind enough to mention to me, à propos Frau Busoni, a fund for acute cases of hardship. Fortunately help would be necessary for only a short time. However, as her tenants have moved out, she will (until her own removal in April) be in a catastrophic position for three months since she has to meet the expenses for her large flat entirely on her own. What is your present address, dear Professor? I am not sure that this letter will reach you. Is it true that you have a villa in Baden-Baden; could I visit you there some time? Frau Busoni does not know that I am taking steps on her behalf. Please regard the matter as confidential'.

cultural high-mindedness with sound business sense, then as now.

Pupils usually fully appreciate the interest their former teachers take in their careers; this was certainly the case with many of my father's students. A pleasing example is a letter[9] from Ricardo Odnoposoff on his appointment as leader of the Vienna Opera Orchestra (clearly his teacher's advocacy had played a part in this case):

[9] Dated 30 December 1933.

Busoni by Mopp

[. . .] For quite some time I have been longing for the moment when I could write you this letter. I am happy to be able to tell you now at last that your [*sic*!] long-standing wish has been granted. [. . .] After I had signed the contract, my first thought was to go to the Post Office in order to send you a cable. Today I would like to report to you in greater detail [. . .].

Not that the position of leader always turned out to be the ideal start to a career, as is shown, for instance, in the letter from a very promising ex-pupil who was not at all happy in that position. He had the feeling that a colleague (as it happened, a former co-student) was scheming against him and was being given preferential treatment; as a result he did not find the work satisfactory, not even the solo performances that formed part of his contract:

Dear Professor, I should be very grateful if you would write to me. My future, which seems to be entirely devoid of prospects,

Annette Kolb
by Emil Orlik

looks very bleak to me and you are the only person who can help
me [. . .].

He must have received a satisfactory reply, for two months
later he writes

[. . .] Thank you again for your letter. The knowledge that you
will always be prepared to help me with advice means very
much to me.[10]

Finally, a letter[11] from Josef Wolfsthal, who was occupying
the position of orchestra leader in Oslo:

[10] Letters dated 26 April and 9 June 1927.

[11] Dated 17 January 1927.

I can answer your question whether I am making savings out of my salary, with a resounding 'Yes'. I am confident that you will be satisfied with the result at the end of the season.

'*Your* long-standing wish'; '*You* are the only person who can help me'; '*You* will be satisfied': there can hardly be better proof of these young people regarding it as a matter of course that their teacher remained closely involved with them and their progress; and that is as it should be.

Sometimes, of course, matters went a little too far, as, for instance, when a Dutch impresario suggested that my father should change his programme (Brahms) for a forthcoming appearance with the Amsterdam Concertgebouw Orchestra because Ginette Neveu had expressed the wish to play the Concerto in Holland the following week herself. I should imagine that this suggestion was not received with much enthusiasm. At any rate, a few days later Ginette's agent wrote a letter of apology assuring him that the suggestion had been made without his, or her, knowledge.

Since my father liked to listen to his pupils' wireless performances whenever possible, some of them made a point of bringing these appearances specifically to his attention. Ricardo Odnoposoff again:[12]

I am happy to tell you that I shall be playing the Goldmark and the Prokoffieff with orchestra on the 22nd. It would please me very much to know that you will be listening [. . .].[13]

Similarly, his pupil Roman Totenberg:[14]

The last concert of my tour will be broadcast from Stockholm, I am playing the Beethoven Concerto, perhaps you will be able to hear me, it would please me so very much.

If they did hold him in awe during their student days, this certainly seems to have disappeared at that stage; or was it

[12] Letter dated 18 October 1933.

[13] The postcard quoted on p. 27n very probably refers to that concert. The Prokofiev work must be the First Violin Concerto of 1916–17; the Second was not composed until 1935.

[14] Letter dated 20 August 1935.

perhaps the hope for some free advice in that way? Perish the thought!

The custom, incidentally, was not confined to pupils but occasionally extended to colleagues, as, for instance, to Georg Kulenkampff (1898–1948), among the foremost German violinists of the time. According to Boris Schwarz,[15] one of the highlights of his career was the performance in 1937 of the rediscovered Schumann Violin Concerto:[16] 'I was greatly touched by your cordial and complimentary message about my Hilversum broadcast [. . .]'.[17]

My father was always happy for ex-students to play for him when the occasion arose. A letter from one of them, who had already made an excellent career, is typical. He wrote cancelling a proposed visit for private reasons and then continued:[18]

> In any event I would not have been able to play for you at this time. The reason is that I am utilising the present vacation to change my bowing! You have long advised me to do so, but I never had the courage. So far I do not feel entirely comfortable with the new method. But I won't drop it again, because I can see already now that it has its advantages. [. . .] I shall be very interested in your views when I see you next April.

All this shows that, very often, the relationship between teacher and pupil never really comes to an end.

But the situation during the learning period itself is rather less clear-cut. And here, although the name of Carl Flesch may seem to crop up rather often, because I am relying entirely on his correspondence and diary entries, I believe that much of the material has general validity.

One can, I think, characterise the teacher/pupil relationship with one word – 'ambivalence' – for it does not differ all that much from that between parents and children. At any rate this was how Carl Flesch saw it; several diary entries point in this

---

[15] *Great Masters of the Violin*, Simon & Schuster, New York, 1983, p. 328.

[16] See Appendix II, pp. 353–54.

[17] Letter to Carl Flesch dated 15 March 1938.

[18] Letter dated 9 February 1937.

direction. For instance, as my father wrote on a brief concert tour in Holland:[19]

> I feel as if I were on holiday, due to the prospect of not having to give lessons for 5 days. Of course, I love teaching, but it wears me out through my intense involvement.

And here he goes a little more into detail:

> For me, every pupil represents a technical, a spiritual and a development problem. The first can be easily solved. The second requires a personal human approach, something that can be risky especially with young girls. Finally, the development potential is shrouded in darkness, being very little susceptible to educational influences.

As to the technical problems, I obviously have nothing to add. The other two overlap in regard to eroticism and sexuality – subjects on which he comments in his diary several times. But disregarding this aspect for the moment, he was certainly conscious of the dangers of too close an involvement, even of a non-sexual nature:

> It is the bane of powerful personalities that, as teachers, they are bound to destroy the individuality of their pupils – not, of course, knowingly, but pupils are so fascinated by them that they voluntarily surrender their own personalities with the subconscious intention of exchanging them for that of the Master. However, it is a regrettable fact that in most cases the first thing one acquires are the faults and fads of the idol; its good points are rooted too deeply to be readily accessible. Vide Joachim, Busoni, Ysaÿe, perhaps also Schnabel. The one exception was Liszt.[20]

I don't believe, though, that he regarded himself as one of these personalities. To my knowledge, those he named did not consider it as one of their prime tasks to deal with purely technical matters in their lessons; they took these more or less for granted and concentrated on questions of interpretation instead. This inevitably placed more emphasis on their own personalities. Carl Flesch, on the other hand, did give tech-

---

[19] Diary entry, probably for 9 November 1933.

[20] *Ibid.*

nique, too, his full attention. With his partly less spiritual
approach the risk he mentions was therefore smaller in his
case. But in any event, having recognised it he would do his
best to try to avoid it. Opinions differ on how well or how
badly he succeeded and on the impact his methods had on his
students generally.

Some who knew him well – Max Rostal, for instance – saw
in him a hard, almost unbending task master who regarded it
as his first priority to make the pupil malleable – 'wax in his
hands', as the German expression has it.[21] Only then could he
mould him according to his wishes. Others – as, for instance,
Henryk Szeryng, in one of the last interviews he gave before
his untimely death[22] – asserted that they had no difficulty in
expressing opinions differing from his, to argue, to insist on
their own views and interpretations. They found that he gave
them the widest possible freedom and thereby the chance to
develop their own personalities and ideas.

There is no gainsaying that he possessed considerable
natural authority and it is possible that this much impressed
the weaker personalities among his students. Hence I believe
that the many divergent opinions about him have a good deal
to do with the individual attitudes of the various pupils
themselves, his substitute 'sons' and 'daughters'. But however
intimate and friendly the relationship, there was usually some
barrier that even former students were unable to cross.

This could show itself in unexpectedly small details, such as
the question of names. Alma Moodie, for example, had, after
many years of friendship, got on to the equivalent of first-
name terms with my parents – 'equivalent' because she could
never bring herself to calling my father by his actual first
name. Instead she addressed him in her letters as 'Dear
Dolcissimo' or even 'Dear Papi'. And another pupil of about
my own age, with whom I for my part am on first-name terms,
until recently used to avoid using my real forename – Carl,

---

[21] In a speech given at the Carl Flesch centenary concert organised by the
European String Teachers' Association (ESTA) in London, 29 October
1973; see also p. 71.

[22] *The Strad*, Vol. 99, No. 1181, September 1988, and in conversation.

The young Henryk Szeryng with Carl Flesch,
around 1931

like my father; he addressed me as 'Carlos'. The third commandment?

This letter from a girl pupil far from her home shows yet another angle:

> For me your father was more than merely a great teacher. He was equally friend and adviser and he and your mother looked after me like second parents.

Finally, an observation from someone who was not directly involved, Professor Max Dessoir:[23]

[23] *Buch der Erinnerung*, Friedrich Enke Verlag, Stuttgart, 1947, p. 259. See also pp. 335–37.

It was moving and refreshing to see how much his pupils, old or young, male or female, were attached to him, always returned to him, the teacher, physician, friend.

Parents of pupils, too, saw in him someone whose authority was capable of exerting a stronger influence on their children than they were. A letter in 1939 from the father of a Dutch boy is characteristic:

> I am still very worried about [. . .]. The crisis in his life, which we discussed the other day, is by no means over [. . .]. He has not given me the opportunity to discuss this with him in any detail [. . .]. I have to remain in the background and can merely try to do something for him behind the scenes. Very probably your influence is stronger [. . .]. I have the greatest confidence in you, not only with regard to his musical education but also to your psychological insight.

Here, then, are many different views of the same man. They seem to offer ample proof that the assessment of a teacher's personality is highly subjective and depends more on how his pupils see him than on himself. I am certain that this applies to many teachers generally.

It is noteworthy, incidentally, that I have not come across a single document or entry referring to drugs. At that time the problem was apparently of very minor importance. The same cannot be said about sex. Although, self-evidently, sexual problems existed half a century ago as they do now, their nature has fundamentally changed. Sex is no longer 'verboten'. (Whether this is one of the reasons for the drug problem to have emerged so prominently – having in a way to replace one forbidden activity (and the need for its transgression) by another – is an intriguing question.)

The problem of pupils' sexuality can be divided into two categories: the erotic relationship between pupils themselves, and that between teacher and pupil. The two, I think, sometimes overlap.

Again the Flesch diary:[24]

> The erotic disposition of pupils is a secret which they anxiously strive to protect. The teacher can only sense it but he must not –

[24] Probably for 9 November 1931.

at least openly – take it into account. Otherwise he would have to advise many a male pupil to 'go to a woman'.[25] Or if he masturbates, not to burden himself with unnecessary twinges of conscience. Whereas in the case of young girls similar remarks would soon create a state of familiarity which, assuming the appropriate inclination on both sides, would inevitably lead to an affair.

My father was, I believe, by no means averse to the occasional extra-marital adventure, but, as he writes, 'what was missing was the irrestible urge of the born Don Juan (see Thibaud) to take advantage of every favourable opportunity presenting itself'.[26] Sentiments such as this are why I don't believe that – at least in his later years – he ever had sexual relations with female pupils. A further diary entry seems to me to bear this out:[27]

When I observe the various slightly erotic relationships that develop in course of time between pupils of different sex, I get sad and envious. The story of Adam and Eve repeats itself in every human being. The Garden of Eden from which he or she[28] is banished for ever is his or her first love.

The story of Adam and Eve may not necessarily have been the only reason for his feeling 'sad and envious'. How many parents have not on occasion, whether or not we are prepared to admit it, envied their children their young and attractive boy- or girl-friends? But my father's views show that it was not his intention to allow relations with his female pupils to go beyond the platonic stage.

Incidentally, I have the distinct feeling that friendships between pupils were not always quite as innocent as he suggests in that particular passage. Indeed, the diary refers elsewhere[29] to a very different situation:

---

[25] In the German original 'zum Weibe zu gehen'; note the paraphrasing which people found it necessary at the time to employ even in their most private thoughts.

[26] Probably for 23 September 1931.

[27] Entry for 18 March 1931.

[28] The German 'Mensch' can refer to either sex.

[29] Entry for 19 March 1931.

Jacques Thibaud in 1903. The postcard demonstrates that he and Flesch were friends from an early age, as he proudly reports his 'succès énorme' in New York.

One of my pupils had an affair with a female colleague – he a baptised Jew, she an 'Aryan' of purest stock.[30] After some time she refuses herself to him. At first she declines to give a reason but then she confesses: she does not want sexual intercourse with him although she loves him; her antisemitic friends have told her that intercourse with a Jew, even if not leading to pregnancy, would affect subsequent Aryan issue with the result that they would turn out to be 'Jewish types'.

I remember the case well. Until I heard of it I had always considered this nonsense to be a badly invented fairy tale. But obviously some people did believe in it; others disseminated it possibly with the idea of improving their own chances.

If my father had inclined towards erotic relations with

---

[30] And exceedingly pretty, as I can confirm from my own observations.

female pupils, his diary would presumably not have contained this entry:[31]

> When I listen to the Grieg Piano Concerto I automatically remember Pugno, Ysaÿe's fat bearded partner [. . .] who through the interpretation of that concerto in 1893, at the age of 41, became famous overnight. He died on a concert tour through Russia in the arms of his beautiful 20-year-old pupil Nadia Boulanger who was travelling with him. For him, the concepts of 'pupil' and 'lover' were synonymous [. . . .] he was an outstanding artist in particular as a chamber musician. I once played with him, Marsick and Hollmann the 2nd violin part in the Schumann Piano Quintet in a public concert in Paris.

On the other hand, his principles did not make him blind to the charms of beautiful girl pupils, and while I do not think that they influenced his assessment of their talent,[32] I suspect that he was a little more forbearing towards them than towards male or less good-looking female pupils of similar standing. I believe the case of the violinist Lisa Minghetti is an apt illustration.

In 1930 he received a very urgent letter[33] from an acquaintance with a deep interest in music, the painter Paul von Schlippenbach:

> I am writing to you under the very strong impression of a young violinist in whose destiny I have, on the spur of the moment, taken an active interest [. . .]. Wherever she showed herself, all heads turned on account of her charming face and extra-ordinarily striking red hair [. . .]. We arranged that she should play for me [. . .]. Already the first few notes showed me that here was an extraordinary talent [. . .]. Of course she has no money whatever. On what conditions could she come to you? [. . .] She bears the impossible name Liesl Pollak, but this will be changed, of course.

I remember the afternoon she appeared at our flat for an audition. Intrigued by the glowing description of an un-

---

[31] Entry for 22 September 1931.

[32] Otherwise, the case of Marlene Dietrich (see pp. 305–6) would hardly have been possible.

[33] Dated 19 July.

doubted connoisseur, one of my friends and I decided that we could not possibly miss the chance of submitting the young lady to an unobtrusive inspection; we came to the conclusion that von Schlippenbach had not been exaggerating. My father accepted her as a pupil. He recorded his opinion of her in his diary:[34]

> During the summer I had 5 pupils who interested me [. . .] and finally Liesl Pollak alias Minghetti, a red-haired Viennese girl with a delightful harmony of colours[35] without being convent- ionally beautiful – with an enormous desire to express herself as well as great ambition as driving force – technically still in the development stage.

Everything undoubtedly correct, but without wishing to do her an injustice, I can't quite get rid of the feeling that her appearance played a somewhat disproportionate part. And in spite of the opinion which Henri Temianka expressed in a letter two years later – 'Minghetti now stays most of the time in London and has, I believe, an excellent future here'[36] – I think it somewhat improbable that her talent would have been sufficient to gain her admission to the select circle of world renowned violinists. But where, after all, is it laid down that an artist's beauty or elegance should not add to the enjoyment of his or her performance? Tragically, she died very young, so that no one can say for certain what final success she might not have achieved. At any rate, it was always a pleasure to hear – and see – her play.

Nobody is perfect, and even the most prominent teacher cannot be an exception from this rule. Carl Flesch certainly wasn't – he had his fair share of faults and idiosyncrasies. I don't believe that they caused him to be unfair to pupils, except on one occasion which I happened to witness. This was during one of his courses in Baden-Baden which were open to violinists regardless of whether or not they were his students. One of the participants had been a pupil of Otakar Ševčik (1852–1934) whom my father had originally much admired. I

[34] Entry for 22 September 1931.

[35] The photograph reproduced opposite unfortunately does not do justice to this, her most striking feature.

[36] Dated 15 June 1933.

Lisa Minghetti in 1934

clearly remember his pride in the 1920s on receiving a letter from Ševčik enthusiastically praising the first volume of his *Art of Violin Playing*. Later, my father's assessment of him changed and he did not hesitate to express his adverse opinion quite openly. Although his sentiments are well known, I think it may be instructive to quote a diary entry,[37] for it shows clearly the reason for his violent criticism – the damage he felt Ševčik had caused to a large number of young violinists.

> Today I accepted – I admit, reluctantly, but I have to earn a living[38] – a former pupil of Ševčik. This man, by now 80 years old, is one of the most striking examples of artistic decadence. He started as a relatively young man in the 1880s to create a new

---

[37] For 16 October 1931.

[38] An inelegant translation from the German 'Der Not gehorchend, nicht dem eigenen Trieb' – a quotation from Friedrich von Schiller's play *Die Braut von Messina*.

basis for the study of violin technique, to 'rationalise' it – i.e.,
save time and energy – and this with indubitable sucess.

During the past 20 years, however, he began to adopt
methods that were increasingly stupid. He made pupils play
passages backwards, omitted slow movements of concertos as
technically uninteresting, and dissected compositions into
minute parts of 2–4 notes at a time, which he made his pupils
repeat again and again as finger exercises – all this a sympton of
senile dementia.

Nevertheless, pupils came to him in droves and delighted in
letting him ruin them for life. Clearly these unfortunate young
people were bound, sooner rather than later, to lose all contact
with living art and to be degraded into soulless machines –
which function badly, to boot. It is infinitely difficult to get
these shipwrecked people back onto dry land. The harm caused
by this man to those who entrusted themselves to his guidance
cries out to heaven. As a theorist, on the other hand, he has
created exercises of lasting value.

I am certain that Flesch's exceptionally harsh judgement was
not motivated by personal envy – of, for instance, his very
large number of students[39] – for he himself recommended
Ševčik's exercises in suitable cases. This is confirmed by a
letter from one of his favourite pupils, Alma Moodie: 'I
practise a great deal and notice that my bowing is improving thanks to Ševčik [. . .]'.[40]

The young man in the Baden-Baden episode was a
typical product of his teacher and his playing demonstrated
everything my father condemned in Ševčík's method. During
the performance my father became more and more irritated
and in the end criticised the poor fellow more harshly than I
had ever heard him do before or since. He seemed to have
completely forgotten that he did not have Ševčík but an
innocent victim of his method before him. I am certain that
this unthinking criticism, however honestly felt, did the young
man a real disservice.

Another point that could be held against him was the fact

[39] Gracian Černušak and Boris Schwarz (in *The New Grove Dictionary of
Music and Musicians*, Vol. 17, Macmillan, London, 1980, p. 200) put the
number at an astonishing 5,000.

[40] Dated 30 July 1921.

that he sometimes misunderstood his pupils' attitudes and actions and read into them motives which had not – or not always – been intended. He had a very low opinion of the gratitude shown by pupils towards their teachers as a body:

> Why is it that pupils generally are so ungrateful? The teacher, provided he is conscientious, gives them his heart's blood, and they give him nothing [. . .]. I have had amazing experiences in this respect [. . .].[41]

Numerous letters from pupils, which he kept, show the exact opposite and I believe that he sometimes over-reacted.[42] What hurt him were unduly long silences from successful pupils and ex-pupils for whom he had, during their studies, taken particular trouble. A disproportionately large number of letters from pupils start with apologies for their long silence and the promise – rarely kept – to do better in future.

Pupils who were child prodigies were at times, predictably enough, exploited or over-exposed by their parents or third parties – often more from snobbishness than financial motives. He was rightly of the opinion that public appearances that were too early or too frequent, or an unsuitable choice of programmes, could disproportionately damage these young people and he insisted that all such matters be submitted to him for his consent. One of the most virulent disputes on this theme took place with a wealthy industrialist who was the patron of the boy genius Josef Hassid and in this capacity interfered in questions which in my father's view were outside his province.[43]

Something else that could annoy him was the failure to mention his activities as teacher in interviews, newspaper articles and brochures by or about successful students – not that he set much store by public acknowledgement but he took it apparently as proof of ingratitude. In 1936, for instance, he had a dispute with Harold Holt, Ida Haendel's agent, because of a lengthy newspaper story about her in which his name did

[41] Diary entry dated 14 October 1931.

[42] For the case of Josef Wolfsthal, see pp. 307–12.

[43] See Artur Weschler-Vered, *Songs Ephemeral*, John Murray, London, forthcoming.

not appear at all. Although Holt, as well as Ida's father (her manager and constant companion), repeatedly assured him that this had not been their fault – whether correctly or not is a matter for dispute – it was initially not possible to mollify him. I suspect, though, that in this particular case there was a contributing factor – a rumour that Haendel senior had been forming the intention of letting Ida take lessons with Enescu – something which, to judge by her somewhat ambivalent stance in her autobigraphy[44] could well have been possible. He declared that in the circumstances he was not prepared to continue with Ida's lessons. At the same time it seems that he accused her father of having acted behind his back. Mr Haendel replied in a letter which for diplomacy left nothing to be desired. He remarked mildly that if my father were to persist in his refusal to continue Ida's lessons, he was, after all, left with no alternative but to look for a different teacher.[45]

In the end, the matter was smoothed over. Ida remained with my father until he left England in 1939. In a personal remark to me Harold Holt said that he would have been much happier for Ida to have been able to stay with him for one more year so as to receive the ultimate artistic and stylistic polish. But I don't think that this premature end of her studies affected her subsequent career in any way: for me she remains one of the best women violinists of her time – if not the best.[46]

In course of time the number of Flesch pupils still active on the concert platform has naturally been reduced more and more. But that many of them have, for their part, trained

[44] *Woman with Violin, op. cit.*

[45] She was less than fourteen years old. It appears from a letter written by a Dutch concert agent at about that time that the authorities made her cancel a few concerts in Holland because of her age.

[46] An unfortunate remark as it turned out, when I was rash enough to make it to Ida herself. After asking me 'Have you heard all the others?', she pointed out that she saw no reason for discriminating between male and female musical performers – a good point, underlined by Henry Wood who is reputed to have said that, since Ysaÿe's day, he had heard no one else play as well as she did.

prominent violinists and that the importance of his work for the profession remains undiminished are the aspects of his life's work that would undoubtedly have pleased him most – for to live on in future generations must be the highest aim of any teacher.

V
CHILD PRODIGIES

'It is easier to make a talented
pupil into a "Wunderkind"
than into a "Wundermann".'
CARL FLESCH

It is a well-known fact that parents of violin-playing prodigies can sometimes pose bigger problems than the offspring. Where several such children are pupils of the same teacher simultaneously, rivalry between parents – rarely the children themselves – is usually fierce and unremitting. They will monitor the respective numbers of lessons and the comparative treatment of their young; they will watch the other children like hawks. Considering the subsequent successful careers of many artists who were regarded, in their childhood, less than benevolently by competing mothers, I can only conclude that the alleged efficacy of the evil eye is exaggerated.

But, as so often, there is rather more to it than that; and it is about time someone put the case for the defence. For one thing, one must acknowledge that the care, dedication and sacrifices of many parents both in time and money, which can be immense, are admirable and sometimes very touching. For another, most of them are inexperienced in the field of classical music and are out of their depth. Their position is entirely different from that, for instance, of parents of fledgling film actors, particularly in the world of commercials. As long as they have a son or daughter with good looks, charm and an extrovert personality, they may expect immediate financial returns quite out of proportion to the duration and thoroughness of the child's training. Against this, the talent of a youngster seriously studying music may take years to reach

98

full maturity; the outcome is always uncertain; initially there is no money in it; and last but not least, control over development, speed of progress, and so on, is largely out of their hands.

They have to rely on the judgment of a teacher who may be so opinionated as to regard the parents' natural concern as interference – and make them feel it at every opportunity. At the same time they will very likely be ceaselessly bombarded with contradictory advice from family and well-meaning friends, not to mention those whose motives may not always be entirely disinterested or who for purely personal reasons begrudge a teacher a talented pupil.[1]

All these difficulties can cause alarm and despondency; and it must be said that it is not necessarily unjustified. Prodigy parents as a class probably receive less sympathy and understanding than they deserve. Yet, taking all mitigating circumstances into account, the fact remains that they often can, at least, have a nuisance value and at worst a very damaging influence on their children's development.

This does not always specifically involve music. If, for instance, the teacher does not happen to live in the pupil's home town, it will obviously be the mother who accompanies and supervises the child while away from his or her usual environment; the father remains in the background. For boys, this is not always the right thing. In the case of a Flesch pupil aged about fourteen the problem was recognised by an

---

[1] For instance, Artur Schnabel in a letter to my father (22 July 1920):

> Miss [. . .] has now after all become my pupil. It was by no means her alleged illness that held her up before she found her way to me, but objections on the part of certain friends and patrons. [. . .] It was only my complete indifference towards disclosures of this kind that made her mother save for a future opportunity the name – already on the tip of her tongue – of the person so hostile to me. However, I don't think it needs a great deal of intelligence to guess his identity: Adolf W.

I assume this refers to the prominent Berlin critic Adolf Weissmann who was not every artist's favourite reviewer. A letter from Alma Moodie (dated 21 December 1927), for instance, tells of a performance of the Mozart Violin Concerto in A major:

> At the matinee Weissmann attended and his review was mean and insolent in the way so typical of him. All others were excellent.

educational charity supporting him; a letter from its honorary secretary shows an insight as refreshing as it was unusual at the time (1937):

> So far his mother has been here with him and devotes her life to providing for and looking after him. It is thought in some quarters that the time has now arrived when the boy should not be continually under his mother's wing and that different arrangements should be made for him.

My father was asked for his opinion and I assume, agreed. I don't know about the mother's reaction to this proposal – correct in principle but no doubt hurtful to her.

At the opposite end of the scale are the (happily very rare) cases in which children from poor families are supported by cultural organisations or wealthy patrons and where it turns out that the monies received are being used for the support of the whole family instead of the pupil for whom they are intended. In these cases the primary consideration must be to avoid any damage to the child itself, but at the same time to acquaint the parents with the facts of life very firmly. Usually the threat of all support ceasing immediately if not used for its original purpose will be all that is necessary to remedy the position.

For my father these cases were particularly annoying when it had been he who had induced a well-to-do acquaintance to place the necessary means at the pupil's disposal. In the course of a heated talk during which the father of the child in question replied that the money was necessary for the support of the whole family because he could not find any work, my father gave a reply which became a household word in the Flesch family on occasions when it was felt that a piece of advice was not altogether practicable: 'In that case you will have to become a packer at Wertheim' (Berlin's best-known department store at that time) – not very realistic if one considers the fact that such a job, if available at all, required accomplishments which I don't think my father possessed himself; except on the violin he was comparatively ham-handed, and I doubt that he ever made up a parcel himself.

Parents sometimes have the most peculiar ideas on how to motivate their children. Scarcely credible (but told me by a

Carl Flesch at the age of six. He was not a child prodigy, although the photograph is undoubtedly intended to make him look like one.

'usually reliable source') is the story of the father of one Flesch pupil who, no doubt with the best of intentions, addressed his son one hour before his public debut, thus: 'My boy, you will now have to prove that your years of study and all the immense sacrifices your mother and I made for you have not been in vain. Your own future and the honour of your family depend on your performance tonight', concluding with the classic line: 'And now go out there and do as you like!' Not surprisingly, the boy played nothing near his best, and but for his immense talent, which in time took him to the greatest heights, his career might have foundered there and then.

At the other end of the scale, Heifetz's father is said to have told his son before his Carnegie Hall debut: 'Remember, you can spit on them all'.[2] And Mischa Elman's father, the butt of many prodigy jokes, is reputed to have replied, when asked whether his son Mischa would tour Europe that year: 'No point. Who is there for him to play against?'

There are many ways in which parents can do potential damage to their children. I still treasure a letter from the father of a talented American girl. He had obviously requested that his daughter be made 'concert-ready', but my father felt that the time was not yet ripe; she would have to develop further before making public appearances of any importance. His reply was apt but flowery, if I may mix a metaphor: 'An artist must have time to mature, like a fruit which, even when of the finest kind, does not taste perfect when taken from the tree, still unripe'. To which the parent replied: 'I contend that a young artist may be "far from ready" for an international concert tour and yet be able to give an extraordinarily fine performance of *2 or 3 numbers*' (my italics). The unbridgeable gulf between these two viewpoints requires no further comment. Since the correspondence was interrupted by World War II, I don't know the outcome. I hope that the young lady's career suffered no lasting emotional or artistic harm.

Then there are the parents who will reluctantly agree to their son or daughter taking up the study of their chosen instrument professionally – 'but first you must learn something respectable/acceptable/solid'. This failsafe is by no means unreasonable, but what these parents are overlooking is the fact that an instrumental career demands full-time training from the earliest possible age onwards. Otherwise it may be too late for the artist to achieve his full potential. All too often such delay will lead to disappointment, frustration and even tragedy.

But a teacher, too, can have a very adverse effect on his pupil. This is particularly true of those who 'specialise' in child prodigies. If they lose interest or even fail – perhaps because progress has been less rapid than originally expected –

[2] André Benoist, *Memoirs*, Paganiniana Publications, New Jersey, 1978, p. 275.

they simply will not or cannot adapt their methods. It is very difficult for a subsequent teacher to retrieve this situation.

My father was more interested in helping as many talents as possible to the highest standards they could achieve than in cultivating 'Wunderkinder'. He regarded this as a bigger challenge and a more worthwhile task. But of course, he accepted prodigies with alacrity when they were offered to him.[3] In this context, though, I remember his only chance encounter, during a stroll in Baden-Baden, with the young Yehudi Menuhin, already world-famous but still in the studying stage. Although Yehudi does not know this, my father remarked afterwards:

> I can only hope that I shall not be asked to take him on as a pupil. If I were, I could not possibly bring myself to refuse. But I know precisely what would happen: if he lives up to his promise, it will be all Menuhin; if he falters, it will be all Flesch.

In the event, of course, he was never asked, since Menuhin, after finishing his studies with Louis Persinger, was already fully committed to his teachers Busch and Enescu.[4] And my

---

[3] On the other hand, he was a complete failure teaching less gifted children. A few lessons he gave my sister during the school holidays at a summer resort ended in tears (on her part!). He had originally entrusted his pupil Josef Wolfsthal with the task of teaching her, which he did usually seated on a rocking horse in our nursery. Subsequently my sister expressed the wish to change over to the piano, but then changed her mind again and decided to try lessons with Wolfsthal once more. He was at the time recovering from 'flu; my father, on learning of my sister's decision, remarked dryly: 'When Wolfsthal hears of this, he'll suffer a relapse'.

[4] Indeed, the story is even more complicated than this. My father's correspondence contains two letters from Louis Persinger – undated but almost certainly written in the early 1920s. In the first he writes:

> May I hope that you will accept me as a pupil? [. . .] I spent last summer with Thibaud and prior to that was, for two years, a non-paying pupil of Ysaÿe. [. . .] Perhaps you would permit me to play for you; if you plan to go on holiday only later in the year, I should be very pleased if I could start working with you before.

My father apparently agreed, but the plan could not be realised, for a few weeks later Persinger wrote again, this time in French, stating that he was having trouble with his left arm and that the doctor had ordered complete

father was wrong: Yehudi never ceased to pay the highest tribute to his teachers.

Incidentally, since my father had rarely heard Menuhin play, except a few times over the wireless, he did not refer to him in his *Memoirs*, which are mainly concerned with the often very frank technical appraisal of those of his contemporaries whose playing he did know well. When, many years ago, I mentioned this omission, somewhat apologetically, to Yehudi, he retorted drily: 'Thank Heaven for that! I shudder to think what he would have written about me' – the true modesty of a great artist.

One of the most awkward problems that can confront a pupil or his parents is a change of teacher at the parents' request. This can be because of incompatibility, because the pupil is not making the expected progress, or because the teacher simply cannot cope with the standard to which the pupil has advanced. It is to the credit of many teachers that when they realise that a pupil has outgrown them, they are sufficiently fair-minded to suggest an upgrading themselves. My father had many pupils referred to him in this way both by former students and others. But not all teachers are that unselfish; they can sometimes prove very difficult. Whatever their attitude, the personal element can create uncomfortable situations, especially if the pupil has much to thank the master for and would hate to hurt him unnecessarily.

---

rest for some time. He never reverted to the matter, but a letter of 1 June 1938, in which he introduced one of his pupils to my father, showed that he had a high opinion of the Flesch method.

These letters were a find so unexpected that I took the precaution of asking Yehudi Menuhin to verify the signature. His reply (13 October 1988):

> I cannot but think that the letters to your father from Louis Persinger must be [from] my teacher. It is indeed his signature which I remember perfectly well. [. . .] What wonderful French he wrote! He was most cultured, and his German is equally beautiful. [. . .] the letters] bring back a man to whom I shall always remain profoundly grateful and whom I have always loved.

It is intriguing to speculate whether Persinger, if he had carried out his intention of studying with my father, would have suggested that the young Yehudi complete his studies with him.

The young Carl Flesch

My father was in this position with his Viennese teacher, Jakob Grün. A letter of his had obviously been returned after Grün's death. Even discounting the writer's youthful age – he was not yet seventeen – it is a model of tact. To understand it, one has to know that both Grün and he were suffering from severe antisemitic hatred and persecution by Josef Hellmesberger, the director of the Vienna Music Academy at the time.

12. 5. 1890

Revered Maestro,
Already before my departure from Vienna my father had asked your advice and agreement regarding my projected move to Paris. I explained to you at the time the reasons which had persuaded me to take this decision: the utterly unjustified hatred with which 'His Majesty' (Franz) Josef Hellmesberger deigns to honour me has convinced me that I shall never be successful in making a career in Vienna. I hardly think that I would even obtain a post with the Orchestra, of the Court Opera because His above-mentioned 'Majesty' would always be

able to prevent this with the help of his yes-men on the board of the Opera.

But enough of these unsavoury matters. [. . .] I decided to explore the possibility of going to Paris. However, my parents and I wanted to proceed with this plan only if you had no objection. Since you have been kind enough to give your consent to this important step, Maurus Deutsch [a Paris friend of my father's] wrote a few days ago that it would be very helpful indeed, if you, honoured Maestro, were to provide me with a letter of recommendation to Massenet, Delibes, Massart or another leading musician. To ask you for this favour is the reason for my writing to you today.

At the examen d'admission I shall play the Vieuxtemps E major Concerto, at the Concours d'admission the Paganini Concerto in D. [. . .]

May I assure you, dear Maestro, that to be a credit to his teacher will always be regarded as the prime duty of your grateful pupil.

Karl Flesch.[5]

My father maintained contact with Grün and kept him informed of his progress. Grün, who must have been a particularly nice and modest man, wrote on 22 May 1903 in reply to my father's letter advising him of attaining a teaching position at the Amsterdam Music Academy: 'It gives me great pleasure to know that you have not entirely forgotten your old teacher; thank you for this sign of remembering me'. This exchange is a good example of how the teacher/pupil relationship should continue even where there has been a parting of the ways.

An interesting case is that of a highly gifted fourteen-year-old, whose parents had decided to entrust his future musical education to my father, a step which so annoyed his teacher – a lady with whom my father was on friendly professional terms – that she repeatedly asked him not to accept the youngster. This is one of the rare cases where my father kept a copy of his reply;[6] he apparently felt that the question was of general interest:

[5] At that point he still spelled his name 'Karl' and only later (by 1905) changed it to 'Carl'. But as a point of fact, being Hungarian by birth his first name was 'Károly'; some might have regarded this as God's gift to an artist, but flamboyance was not in his nature.

[6] Dated 7 April 1918.

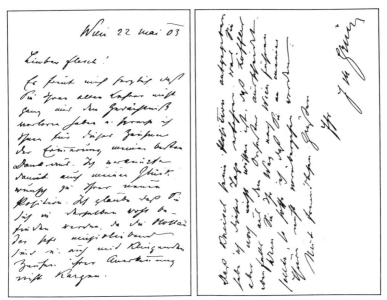

Jakob Grün expresses his pleasure that Carl Flesch stays in touch

Permit me to confess that I cannot understand your insistent demands not to accept the boy. There is no teacher who has not, at one time or other in his career, had the experience of a pupil wishing to leave him. As far as I am concerned, I always readily agree, with my best wishes [. . .]. Under no circumstances would I try to obstruct his future career.

I fully appreciate, of course, your great annoyance with his parents, for doubtless you have done a great deal for the boy and have received nothing but ingratitude for your pains. On the other hand, I have to concede to every pupil the right to part with his teacher if he believes that there is someone else from whom he can learn more or something different. Haven't we all done exactly the same? As far as I am concerned, I did not hesitate to leave my teacher Grün at the Vienna Conservatorium for Prof. Sauzay at the Paris Conservatoire, and when I came to the reluctant conclusion that this 82-year-old was no longer able to teach me anything worthwhile, to become a pupil of Marsick. There are certain selfish actions which in the interest of artistic development are not only justified but in fact imperative. In the present case, of course, the way in which it was done was objectionable. The parents ought to have come to you first and then have arrived at an agreed decision.

You are asking me not to accept the boy. In other words, a punishment. If this were to affect only the parents, you might have an arguable case. But the main sufferer would be the boy himself. Do you really feel so little for him that it would give you satisfaction to see him start his career with no or, worse, wrong guidance? I know that you and your late husband have ordered your lives according to rules of conduct far too ethical to wish to repay the injustice you have suffered by inflicting untold damage to the future career of this entirely innocent child. [. . .]

I am quite prepared to obtain for you from his parents any reasonable satisfaction as long as this does not entail any damage to the future of the most important person in this case. [. . .]

Predictably, this letter had the desired result. The previous teacher was mollified, the boy could effect the change-over without more ado and developed into one of my father's best students. I feel fairly certain, incidentally, that in the last resort my father would have taken him on even against the wishes of the previous teacher if he had been unable to convince her.

The sentiments expressed in his letter are without doubt wholly sincere. But I feel bound to add that there could be a difference between theory and practice. On at least one occasion I can recall my father having been quite upset when he was at the wrong end of such a change.[7] In that particular case, however, the negotiations had been conducted behind his back – something he specifically condemned in his letter. I cannot be certain what his reaction would have been otherwise, because the situation arose very rarely indeed. But in any event it would never have entered his mind to try doing anything to spoil the ex-pupil's career.

Not all prodigies, of course, fulfil their early promise. To my knowledge there are no statistics – how could it be otherwise? – but I feel certain that failures outstrip successes by a very considerable margin. It can have many reasons: talent can simply dry up and wither, for instance; a child may suddenly realise that what it had been doing instinctively and

[7] See pp. 95–96.

Charles-Eugène Sauzay (1809–1901), Carl Flesch's teacher at the Paris Conservatoire

without fear hitherto, is in fact extremely difficult; or the existence of an inborn natural talent may lead to the neglect of purely technical training.

Other artists die tragically young as, for instance, Ginette Neveu who perished in a plane accident in 1949, at the age of 30, and Josef Hassid, a uniquely talented boy who in 1945 succumbed to schizophrenia at a mere 21 years of age.[8] And sometimes an artist simply loses the urge, the motivation, and decides to change to a less arduous profession. Such a case was the young Iso Briselli, a highly talented child.[9] His talent was

[8] Although there are many recordings by Ginette Neveu, Hassid recorded only a few genre pieces; these have been issued by HMV under the title *The Complete Hassid* (EH 29 12301). Bryan Crimp, the author of the sleeve note, quotes Kreisler's well-known remark that 'A fiddler such as Heifetz is born every 100 years, one like Hassid ever 200 years'. But Mr Crimp's otherwise excellent note is wrong in naming Heifetz: I have it from a witness present on that occasion that Kreisler's remark referred to another equally famous artist (who, I hope, will be with us for many years to come). It is a minor error, yet a typical instance of the fact that not everything in print is necessarily correct.

[9] A programme of his Berlin debut, illustrated by Emil Orlik, has been preserved: see p. 110.

Emil Orlik's programme for a recital by Iso Briselli

very impressive indeed and a brilliant future was predicted for him. It is amusing to read a letter from Alma Moodie, his co-pupil, very much older than he:[10]

'How is Isaac doing?[11] The other night I dreamt of him playing

[10] Dated 14 June 1924.

[11] Isaac was Briselli's original first name – at that time already absolutely impossible for a career in Germany.

such unbelievable octave scales that I woke up in a furious temper and practised them myself.

In the early 1920s my father took him to the Curtis Institute in Philadelphia (which, incidentally, earned my parents and the boy at night's stay on Ellis Island[12] on arrival). In the United States a wealthy industrialist offered to provide the means for his subsistence and training, with the unexpected result that he adopted him a few years later, whereupon Briselli gave up playing the violin professionally – a pity considering the time and trouble expended on his training. But my father did not complain. He knew only too well the difficulties and disappointments besetting the artistic profession.

Moreover, one may assume that Iso, in his newly won financial independence, became a patron of the arts and continued to make music in a non-professional capacity. I don't know who it was who first said that 'the good amateur plays for his *pleasure*, the bad one for *his* pleasure', but Briselli undoubtedly belonged to the former – and thereby was able to achieve a Happy Ending not granted to all child prodigies.

[12] Ellis Island was 'the purgatory for undesirable aliens ' (*Memoirs*, p. 349).

VI
COMPETITIONS

> 'There is something that is
> much more scarce, something
> rarer than ability. It is the
> ability to recognise ability.'
> ROBERT HALE

Competitions are a controversial subject. They are certainly not a modern invention – singing and minstrelsy contests took place in the Middle Ages, after all. Obviously, with the advent of newspapers, radio and TV, their character and importance have changed enormously, but the basic idea can't have been all that different. And the public probably got as agitated about wrong decisions then as it does now.

My own experience is, naturally enough, based in the main on the Carl Flesch International Violin Competition which is held biennially in the City of London. I can lay claim to having been if not the co-founder, then 'one of the fathers' of this particular event. When, one day during the Second World War, I saw a brief notice in the now defunct *News Chronicle* of the death of my father in Switzerland[1] – Zurich Radio had obviously included it in its news bulletin the previous evening – the first of my friends whom I contacted was Max Rostal, one of the oldest Flesch pupils and at that time professor at the Guildhall School of Music.

In the event of a family bereavement, the first shock is often cushioned by immediate vigorous activity concerning the inevitable routine formalities as well as the wish to honour the departed by as dignified a funeral or memorial service as

[1] See pp. 55–56.

possible. Since during the War the impossibility of any contact with Switzerland, let alone being present at the funeral, precluded this outlet, I expressed my need 'to do something' by suggesting to Max Rostal that we should try and devise some kind of memorial perpetuating my father's name. Rostal immediately concurred and was able, within a few days, to secure the co-operation of the Guildhall School's director Edric Cundel, who agreed to organise a 'Carl Flesch Competition' to take place annually or biennially.

I undertook to look after the creation of a medal to be awarded to the winners and commissioned the well-known German sculptor Benno Elkan who was living in London as a refugee from Nazi Germany. His best-known work, the German 'Freedom Memorial' ('Befreiungsdenkmal') had immediately been removed after Hitler had come to power. After the War he concentrated on sculptures depicting themes from the Old Testament: two candelabra by him have found a permanent place in Westminster Abbey and an over-life-sized 'Menorah' is positioned in front of the Knesset, the Israeli Parliament, and is one of Jerusalem's tourist attractions.

Elkan suggested a profile in traditional style. Since he had never met my father, he needed a good picture. It turned out that, try as we might, we could not unearth a single one showing Carl Flesch in profile; all we could do was to provide half-a-dozen photos showing his head from diverse angles *en face*. I shall never forget my astonishment on being shown Elkan's completed design: the way in which he had 'reconstructed' the profile, was quite extraordinary, as can be seen from a comparison between his work and a drawing by Emil Orlik I rediscovered after the War.[2]

I have never aspired to official participation in the conduct of the competition. In my opinion, these events have to stand on their own feet, as it were; any formal involvement by the family tends to diminish the value of the honour intended for the man after whom they are named. But I did take part in preliminary discussions, and well remember how impressed I was by the Guildhall School's young secretary whose effortless

[2] See p. 114–15. Orlik's drawing has been reproduced from the collection *Neue 95 Köpfe von Orlik*, Bruno Cassirer Verlag, Berlin, 1926.

*Benno Elkan's medal
for the Carl Flesch
International Violin
Competition*

authority and gift for organisation ensured that everything
went like clockwork. Unfortunately the competition could not
benefit from his talents for long. He soon moved on and after a
comparatively short time became General Manager of the
Royal Opera House, Covent Garden – Sir John Tooley.

Since initially the competition had to be organised on a
shoe-string, it was kept to very modest limits: one day in the
Great Hall of the Guildhall School; there were no money
prizes, just the medal itself and a few concert engagements for
the winner. Gradually, however, additional finance became
available and the Competition's importance grew until the
City of London became interested and made it an integral part
of its official Festival. Today, the 'Carl Flesch' is regarded as
one of the most important contests of its kind.

Outsiders usually do not appreciate the amount of time and
routine preparation required to organise an event such as this.
Take the jury, for instance. In accordance with regulations
laid down by the World Federation of International Music
Competitions it has to consist of at least nine members. For an
international competition of this importance you need prominent personalities, leaders in their professions; their diaries
are filled months, sometimes years ahead. Jury members have

Carl Flesch
by Emil Orlik

therefore to be engaged long in advance. In this respect conditions appear to be somewhat different from those in former times. Among my father's papers I have found an invitation from the Conservatoire de Musique in Paris to be a jury member at a 'concours de violon' on 12 July 1909. The date of the invitation was 1 July 1909.[3] Obviously the composition of the jury was regarded as rather less of a problem 80 years ago.

The invitation contains another interesting detail: jury members were not permitted to vote when it came to their own pupils. This rule is still being observed today in most competitions, but not, as it happens, in the 'Flesch'. In the opinion of the non-voting chairman of its jury, Albert Frost – a former director of several leading industrial concerns and now, apart from being an enthusiastic amateur violinist, on the board of various cultural organisations – the importance of this rule is much overrated.

[3] See p. 118.

The comparatively large number of jury members ensures that an unjustly favourable assessment by one particular judge does not affect the overall result decisively. Moreover, it would not be difficult to circumvent the rule anyway: the teacher of a candidate for whom he is not allowed to vote could simply reduce his points for that pupil's nearest rivals – always assuming that anybody deliberately tries to falsify the result. In practice, of course, it can safely be assumed that persons occupying the positions and enjoying the prestige that make them eligible for jury service on important international competitions will not resort to manœuvres of this kind. Similarly, any possible nationalistic influences are obviated by the fact that jury members are usually deliberately selected from many different countries with none predominating. In any event, the 'Frost Method', which incidentally entails the use of a computer, appears to have worked well in practice so far.[4]

But even the most ideal voting method does not preclude the possibility of some – and not infrequently many – of the participants and audience disagreeing with the jury's verdict. I confess that I myself was quite frequently among the dissenters. After a few years therefore I suggested the creation of a 'prize for the competitor who really ought to have won'. The idea appealed to the committee, chaired at that time by Yehudi Menuhin, except that it was felt that the name was possibly not entirely what they had in mind. The award was named 'Audience Prize'. Those members of the public who have attended all of the Finals (usually spread over two consecutive evenings) are entitled to vote in their turn for the contestant whom they regard as the winner. When all official awards have been announced, a sealed envelope is handed to the chairman of the jury and solemnly opened onstage. The delight if the Audience Prize differs from the official one – which happens in about 40% of the cases – is considerable. One can occasionally even learn something about 'mass psychology': I remember a competition in which the official result was so unexpected, indeed inexplicable, that it was

[4] For further details see Albert Frost, 'Voting Procedures in Music Competitions', Programme for the Flesch Competition 1988, City Arts Trust, London, pp. 12ff.

The Guildhall School of Music & Drama

(Founded in 1880 by the Corporation of London)

Principal - - EDRIC CUNDELL, Hon. R.A.M., F.G.S.M.

CARL FLESCH, MEDAL

PATRONS

SIR ADRIAN BOULT	DAME MYRA HESS	FRITZ KREISLER	YEHUDI MENUHIN
MAX ROSTAL	ALBERT SAMMONS	DR. MALCOLM SARGENT	ARTUR SCHNABEL

TO PERPETUATE THE MEMORY OF CARL FLESCH, and as a tribute to him for his discoveries in the scientific application of violin playing, a Medal is to be awarded annually by THE GUILDHALL SCHOOL OF MUSIC AND DRAMA. The recipient will be selected as a result of an annual competition which will be held at the School in October of each year, and approximately on the birthday of Carl Flesch, October 9th.

The competition will be open to all violinists, regardless of their nationality, but they must be under the age of 30 on October 1st of the year they compete.

A very high standard of violin playing will be expected, and the adjudicators have the right of withholding the award, should this standard not be attained by any of the competitors.

A performance of a standard violin concerto, and of one of the solo-sonatas of Bach, both works chosen by the competitor, will be required. Whilst it is expected that competitors resident in this country should provide their own accompanist, the special provision of an official accompanist will be made if desired for those travelling from abroad.

THE LONDON PHILHARMONIC ORCHESTRA, as a gesture of their appreciation of the founding of this award, have agreed to offer the winner an opportunity of appearing as Soloist with them at one of their concerts during the year.

An entry form is attached, and should be forwarded with the entrance fee of five guineas, before September 1st, to

The Secretary,
Guildhall School of Music & Drama,
John Carpenter Street,
Victoria Embankment,
London, E.C. 4,
ENGLAND.

The first announcement of the Carl Flesch competition show-
ing how it was started on a shoe-string – no orchestra, no cash
prizes, duration only one day (see p. 114).

received by the audience with some unrest and even catcalls. When it turned out that the Audience Prize represented the majority opinion in the hall, the atmosphere miraculously changed and all was well, an object lesson on how easy it is to mollify the masses with a graceful admission of a possible error that costs the authorities nothing!

Conservatoire National
de Musique
et
de Déclamation.

Prière de répondre d'urgence

Paris, le 1ᵉʳ Juillet 1909

Monsieur,

J'ai l'honneur de vous inviter à faire partie du Jury pour le concours de Violon qui aura lieu au Théâtre de l'Opéra Comique, le lundi 12 Juillet à midi précis

Si, comme je l'espère, il vous est possible d'accepter cette mission je vous serai reconnaissant de vouloir bien m'en donner l'assurance.

En raison des mesures de Police imposées pour les concours publics, je vous prie instamment d'avoir l'obligeance de présenter cette lettre à la porte d'entrée, le jour du concours.

Agréez, Monsieur, l'expression de mes sentiments très distingués

Le Directeur du Conservatoire,
Membre de l'Institut,

Gabriel Fauré

Les Membres du Jury doivent se récuser dans les concours où figurent des Élèves auxquels ils ont donné des leçons dans l'année. (Art. 84 du Réglement)

Monsieur Karl Flesch

The invitation, stamped with Fauré's signature, to join the jury of a 'concours de violon' at the Conservatoire National – dated a week and a half before the competition

At one time it was decided to permit the accompanying orchestra to vote for the Audience Prize as well. This seems to be a good idea in principle – after all, professional musicians who have heard all the finalists both at rehearsal and in the concert, thus for far longer than judges and public, are ideally placed to give a competent assessment. On the other hand, it contradicts the idea of the Audience Prize: an orchestra is not the 'public', which, however non-professional, is the final arbiter, determining the financial success of a concert. The combination of two elements, both important but diametrically opposed in knowledge and experience, is bound to obscure the picture.

Consequently the decision to include the orchestra in the voting was reversed. It is to be hoped that someone will come forward with the offer of an additional 'Orchestra Prize', if only because it must be highly instructive to get the undiluted and independent opinion of a second body of experts.

Incidentally, I find it somewhat surprising that the idea of involving the public in decisions seems to have been copied only rarely by other important competitions. Could it be that their organisers are taking themselves a little too seriously?

Originally I had donated this prize myself, but after a few years passed it to an insurance company which specialises in the insurance of valuable musical instruments. I carried out a different idea: in the first round of the Flesch Competition there is a mandatory modern piece for solo violin, of about ten minutes' duration, specially composed for the occasion; its purpose is to test the young artist's ability to cope with a contemporary work, which incidentally they have to learn by heart. I suggested a competition for young British composers; apart from a small money prize, the winner would have the guarantee of the piece being published and performed 30 to 40 times straight off.

The Society for the Promotion of New Music took this up and organised the contest in an exemplary fashion. But after two years I asked to be relieved of this particular award: I found the compositions, even after having listened to them a number of times, just as unintelligible and – I must confess – unattractive as on first hearing. I have not doubt that my decision was regarded as a sign of old age – probably rightly

so. After all, these compositions were the prize-winning ones
after a stiff competition – but I simply found no pleasure in
this particular prize. Happily, the organisers were able to
replace me as a sponsor quite easily.

Before I had discarded this particular award, I had tried
another tack. Through the introduction by a friend I had
made the acquaintance of Mrs Rosemary Brown, a lady who
claimed to be regularly receiving dictation of new compositions from composers long gone – from Beethoven
downwards. I had heard some of these items on tape and in a
concert and I am bound to say that I had not been impressed:
if I had been one of the composers in question, I would have
made strenuous efforts to prevent a public performance. On
the other hand, I had no doubt that Mrs Brown, who has
written an interesting book about her experiences,[5] had a
wholly genuine belief in her gifts. I must also add that a man
far more qualified than I, the late violinist Bronislaw Gimpel,
regarded the pieces with rather more favour.

Some months after meeting Mrs Brown the idea ocurred to
me to give her the opportunity of proving her abilities in the
Flesch Competition. In its second round the performance of
two Paganini *Caprices* is mandatory; Mrs Brown had
mentioned to me that she had 'met' Paganini several times, if
only as 'middle man'. I wrote to her publishers with the
suggestion that she should ask Paganini to write one or two
Caprices especially for the competition. Apart from the stir
this would have created, I reckoned that it would solve almost
beyond any reasonable doubt the question whether or not she
was a genuine medium. For a Paganini *Caprice* is not only
recognisable by its style – whose imitation might not be too
hard – but far more by the fact that it is extremely difficult
technically, yet still just playable, even if not necessarily by all
the competitors.[6] Imitating the technical features would

---

[5] *Unfinished Symphonies*, Bachman and Turner, London, 1971; see also
Immortals at my Elbow, Bachman and Turner, London, 1974.

[6] This reminds me of an occasion when Ruggiero Ricci was in the jury. The
Wieniawski *Faust* and Sarasate *Carmen Fantasies* were in the list of
virtuoso works the competitors had to play. The executions I heard left
much to be desired. In any event, I am not too keen on this type of music.

*Henri Temianka (right)
with me at the 1980 Carl
Flesch International
Violin Competition*

undoubtedly have been beyond the ken of the ordinary forger. Unfortunately there was no reaction to my suggestion – a disappointment also inasmuch as I had been hoping by this device to get rid of the modern composition prize without having to draw attention to my deplorable lack of culture as far as modern music is concerned.

I have since introduced a prize for the candidate 'whom the jury most regretted not to have been able to select for the Finals' and whom they regard as the most promising non-winner; it has aptly been baptised 'Special Merit Prize'. In addition, I have endowed the 'Ruth Flesch Memorial Prize', in memory of my late wife, for the best performance of a Mozart concerto, an obligatory part of the final round.

It is frequently maintained that competitions as such are

During a coffee interval I happened to stand next to Ricci and knowing his fondness for this type of genre, in which he specialises, I obviously had to be careful not to show my dislike. So I said the first thing that came into my head: 'I don't think I had ever heard the *Carmen Fantasie* until today'. 'You haven't heard it yet' was his laconic reply.

undesirable, even potentially damaging; and moreover that no reliable judgement is possible. Here are some of the principal objections.

First, it is said that in a sporting event the winner is clearly ascertainable – the athlete throwing the javelin over the longest distance, jumping highest, running fastest. But in an artistic performance? There are no 'best' pianists, singers, conductors, violinists – should one listen to the last movement of the Tchaikovsky or Mendelssohn Concertos with a stop watch so as to find out which player breaks the tape first?

It is, of course, true that the criteria for an artistic performance are relative and often subjective. But the same can be said about ice-skating, high diving, dressage, gymnastics and other sports. The Olympics could be considerably shortened if these disciplines were to be omitted.

Second, what criteria is one to apply? How, for instance, does one compare a fifteen-year old girl of whom it is obvious after five minutes that she will scale the highest peaks, but is as yet not quite 'ready', with a young man aged 22, of not quite the same calibre but possessing a perfect technique and a fully matured musical understanding?

One can judge only on what one hears at the time, not on how it is likely to develop in the future. Moreover, experience shows that artists who originally achieve only a minor award, or none at all, may return after a few years and, if they have continued to develop as anticipated, walk away with the top prize the second time round (not forgetting that – in the 'Carl Flesch' anyway – the above-mentioned young lady might well have received the Special Merit Prize).

Third, how can you compare competitors who may be playing partly different works?

Apart from the fact that it would be almost unbearable for jury and audience having to listen to the same piece 30 to 40 times (at least in the first round), there are certain absolute criteria that can be applied to any interpretation. A free choice of items within reasonable limits is therefore preferable.

On the other hand, I believe it to be wrong to allow players of different instruments to compete against one another. On two occasions, the Carl Flesch Competition was open to both

My late wife,
Ruth Flesch

violin and viola players. But the decisions gave a distorted picture and the practice was discontinued.[7]

Fourth, the result of a competition for the individual contestants depends not only on their own performance but to some extent also on the quality of the opposition.

Opposition is one of many incalculable factors. A manufacturer can suffer a catastrophic loss if someone else offers similar goods at a vastly lower price because he is able to produce them with the help of new modern machinery. The textile industry depends to a very large extent on the weather – as do summer and winter sports resorts. By the same token, an excellent musician may play before an almost empty hall, because a world-famous artist happens to be giving a concert on the same evening next door. This kind of thing is neither predictable nor avoidable. It is simply that life can often be unfair, not only in the case of violin competitions.

---

[7] Similarly, the necessity of having to compare players of entirely different instruments is to my mind the flaw in the BBC's annual 'Young Musician of the Year' Competition.

Fifth, it is claimed that failure in a competition can have catastrophic consequences for the individual even if it was due only to an off-night.

This is not correct – or ought not to be. On the one hand, one should not over-rate the influence of a favourable or unfavourable result on a young player's future. The first prize is no guarantee of an outstanding career: it represents no more than a springboard; what use the artist makes of it is his own affair. On the other hand, an unsuccessful result does not have to mean much if only because a failure usually does not become generally known. Moreover, the profession of a concert artist entails so many and varied risks that any musician is likely to be unsuitable for it if a solitary mishap is sufficient to take him out of his stride.

Sixth, decisions are frequently – whether intentionally or otherwise – wrong.

Intentional misjudgements are wholly objectionable and beyond the pale, whatever the circumstances. No doubt such cases do occur, but I am glad to say they are entirely outside my own experience.

Unintentionally incorrect? This is undoubtedly possible. After all, an assessment cannot help being to some extent subjective; but it can usually be underpinned by reasoned argument even if others are unable to go along with it. There is, of course, the considerable and understandable temptation for unsuccessful participants to lay the blame for a bad result on factors other than those within themselves.

A good example of probably one of the most notorious disputed decisions occurred in the Concours Ysaÿe in Brussels in 1937. It was widely predicted that the first prize would go to the Flesch pupil Ricardo Odnoposoff. In the event the winner was David Oistrakh. My father, a member of the jury was convinced that this was the wrong verdict.[8] But who can say today with absolute certainty which would have been the

---

[8] In an article he wrote for *The Strad* (May 1937, pp. 113–116) he stressed that the competition management had done everything possible to make sure of all decisions being absolutely fair, yet had omitted giving jury members guide lines on which to base their assessments; this had made matters somewhat confusing from the outset.

correct one? Both artists had excellent careers in which the question who was first and who was second prize winner probably played a very minor part.

The last objection one commonly meets is that a competition of this kind is, for the participants, 'cruelty to animals'. Moreover, for many competitors it is the first time that they perform with orchestral accompaniment.

An animal is trained, broken in and made to appear whether it wants to or not. A human being makes a free decision on whether or not he or she wishes to undergo this particular ordeal by fire. In any case, it is an excellent preparation for a concert career and undoubtedly provides the successful candidate with a unique chance.

As to the lack of orchestral experience, this is, after all, a matter of individual preparation. Moreover, from what I have seen, one of the most important factors is the accompanying conductor. I have particularly pleasant memories of Sir Charles Groves, who steered his soloists past reefs and sand-banks with a fatherly care and consideration almost touching to behold.

But just as decisions can be subjective, so can be the views regarding the value of competitions as such. Striking proof of this is offered by my own father, who was by no means an unconditional supporter of events of that kind. Yet this did not prevent him writing to his friend Georg Schünemann:[9] 'I don't know whether you have heard of the great satisfaction I had a few weeks ago? Among the 9 prize winners of the Warsaw International Competition for violinists were 4 of my pupils the first, third, seventh and ninth'.[10] As Mephisto says in Goethe's *Faust*, 'Grau, teurer Freund, ist alle Theorie'. The grey theory of my father's misgivings about competitions had been forgotten.

[9] Letter dated 8 April 1935.

[10] First prize went to Ginette Neveu – see p. 77. The second prize, incidentally, went to David Oistrakh.

VII

THE CARL FLESCH *MEMOIRS,*
HUBERMAN AND HANS KELLER

'The power of accurate
observation is commonly called
cynicism by those who have not
got it.'
GEORGE BERNARD SHAW

Although the title of this chapter may sound somewhat
contrived, the topics are in fact closely connected.

Before he reached the age of 50, my father had decided to
write a book which, although in the form of an autobiography,
would concentrate on the description of artists whom he had
met or at least heard. His accounts were not only to be entirely
objective but in a form which would pass on to posterity a
really expert and authentic picture of the persons portrayed.
The book's provisional and rather clumsy title was 'Material
for a Contribution to the History of Violin Playing, 1885 – ?';
The question mark was to be replaced by the appropriate year
once the total period covered had become apparent. He
intended to up-date the manuscript continuously. In order to
avoid being influenced by considerations of tact or friendship,
he stipulated that the book should be published only after his
and my mother's death.

To anticipate, the autobiography which first appeared in
English under the title *The Memoirs of Carl Flesch* and, later
on, in an abbreviated form in German,[1] was an outstanding

---

[1] And unbeknown to me, also in Russian. The German version is at present
out of print; the English edition was reprinted by Da Capo Press, New
York, in 1979.

success – a source work for historians and students of musical personalities and events during the half-century from 1885–1935. It is probable that since its appearance no musical dictionary, no book about violin playing of that period, has been published that does not draw some of its material from his work – sometimes dealing more or less critically with the assessments and opinions expressed.

My father had been lucky enough to find an expert and dedicated adviser in his friend Professor Georg Schünemann, a well-known musicologist and former director of the Berlin Hochschule für Musik – not that he required his assistance in dealing with the subject matter as such; but since he was, except for works of a purely technical nature, without literary experience, he welcomed hints concerning style as well as presentation of his material in a well-ordered way.

Some of the correspondence has been preserved, although it is not particularly interesting because it consists for the most part of progress reports by Flesch and complimentary remarks by Schünemann. Concrete suggestions were apparently inserted into the drafts themselves. One piece of advice (which I remember because my father happened to remark on it) was to delete as far as possible purely personal details, including his relations with the female sex; Schünemann felt that such topics would not fit into a serious book. This opinion corresponded probably to some extent with Schünemann's character, which came over to me always as somewhat dry and civil-servant-like. It may or may not have been the right advice in this case, but it did result in a rather scanty picture of the author's personality.

My father died unexpectedly in 1944, my mother surviving him by 27 years. The manuscript was in my keeping. In the early 1950s it occurred to me that it would be of no advantage to defer publication any longer: the material was sufficiently important to merit being made known to the musical world now instead of being delayed for a further considerable period. My mother agreed and I began to look for a publisher. At that time – shortly after the Second World War – a German edition was out of the question. This meant that the book had to be translated into English.

To my considerable astonishment I received nothing but

refusals from the publishing houses I approached. Part of the reason was, no doubt, the fact that there was only a German version in existence, which moreover contained quite a number of frankly critical remarks that might require a certain amount of editorial attention. Nevertheless, in my inexperience, I could not really understand the negative attitude of the publishing world, which appeared to me to be very short-sighted. There existed, after all, many technical works by Carl Flesch, still sufficiently up-to-date to be in constant and undiminished demand with the young generation of violinists. However, I came to the eventual conclusion that there was little point in banging my head against a brick wall, and since my time was fully taken up with my own profession, I began to regard the difficulties as virtually insuperable and to abandon the hope of seeing the book published in the foreseeable future.

Some months later we happened to be on holiday on the Isle of Wight. The weather was atrocious and I was so bored that I took refuge in the local library. It was there that I happened to come across a book of short biographies entitled *Violinists of Today*.[2] Not exactly un-put-downable – until it began to dawn on me that seven out of these 'famous violinists' had been my father's pupils. I wrote to the publishers to the effect that, since that book had been considered worth publishing (I took care to avoid expressing my own opinion) an autobiography by the teacher of a large number of their book's subjects was bound to be of even deeper interest. The publishers took my point and offered to read the manuscript with a view to examining its suitability for publication.

After a – with hindsight, surprisingly – few weeks, a director of the publishing firm took me to lunch and explained to me that, although the book could not possibly be a financial success, they were prepared to take it on for reasons of prestige, provided I agreed to forgo the customary advance on royalties. I accepted.

At that precise moment my host was called to the telephone and left his papers on the table opposite me. Without thinking of anything in particular, I cast a glance at the open file. One

[2] Donald Brook, Rockliff, London, 1948.

of the first skills you have to acquire if you wish to follow any profession in which negotiating plays a major part is reading anything written or printed quickly and fluently upside down. To do this when the occasion presents itself is almost a conditioned reflex, if only in order to keep in practice. The passage on which my eye alighted was the concluding sentence of the reader's report: 'Any publisher fortunate enough to secure this work for publication can count himself very lucky'.

There is an old story about an orthodox Jew who, on the Day of Atonement, the highest Jewish holiday, succumbs to the temptation of playing a lonely round of golf – lonely, because all his friends are at the synagogue where, on that day of all days, he ought to be as well. The Archangel Gabriel, who notices his transgression, asks God how he proposes to punish the sinner. 'Very simple,' says God, 'we'll let him do a hole-in-one.' 'But surely, that's anything but a punishment?' 'On the contrary – he won't be able to tell anybody.' I was in a rather similar position. I could never have admitted to having read anything in the file, however inadvertently and without leaving my seat. Gnashing my teeth, I had to stick to the conditions originally agreed.

The writer of the report had been Hans Keller, at that time a young, practically unknown musician and writer who later achieved a leading position in the classical-music department of the BBC's Third Programme, was invited by many universities as a guest lecturer, conducted highly acclaimed chamber-music courses, and whose name lives on as the author of several books and an enormous number of articles. He declared himself willing to undertake the translation and editing of the book – on one condition: the chapter about Bronislaw Huberman was to be 'cleaned up', as he put it. It was well-known that my father had a strong dislike of Huberman which might – however unintentionally – have affected his judgement. I agreed to Keller's request subject to one condition on my part: the basic assessment was not to be altered, and in particular not a single word was to be changed or added. The cleaning-up process was to be entirely confined to deletions.

During the ensuing two years Hans Keller and I worked closely together. He translated the original text and added numerous footnotes. I looked through his work, and we had arguments, frequently until late into the night, regarding style, his choice of words, number, length and tenor of his appendices, and much else. Looking back, I realise with some contrition how much irritation and annoyance I, a layman, must have caused him. He was generally regarded as difficult – and he was, on questions of principle. But he was invariably prepared to weigh up my arguments objectively, if not always politely. In nine out of ten instances he prevailed and whenever I happen to glance at the book I realise how valuable and profound his work has been and how much it contributed to the success of the book.

We had really only two serious disagreements, one because, like most writers, he would not keep to deadlines agreed for the delivery of finished instalments of his work. In the long run I felt highly irritated by these constant delays, especially since it was very difficult to contact him by telephone. Eventually I lost patience and when, on entering a restaurant one evening I saw him sitting at a table in deep conversation with his companion, I stopped and delivered myself of a few well-chosen remarks concerning his tardiness. Today I can't even begin to understand what came over me to make me act in this inexcusable manner. Keller waved me away and phoned me next day complaining in strong terms about my unheard-of behaviour, adding that I had interrupted and important discussion with a high-up in the BBC about a job there; the timing of my intervention had therefore been particularly ill-chosen. I could only apologise and offer to speak to the BBC official in person in order to clear up this unfortunate matter. Happily this proved unnecessary: Keller got the job and never referred to my *faux pas* again. If matters had not ended on such a favourable note, I might have inflicted, within the space of half a minute, untold damage on Hans Keller's career, not to mention British music.

Our second disagreement was more important, and concerned Bronislaw Huberman. Keller was of the firm opinion that my father's assessment in his case was factually wrong.[3]

_____

[3] In this (though neither of us knew it at the time) he differed from Professor Schünemann who, on receiving the relevant chapter from my father, had written (his letter is dated only '15.IV'): 'One can only

For this reason he had prepared a footnote of inordinate length in which he contradicted just about everything my father had written. I pointed out that, although for my part I could not judge which opinion was the correct one, this book was supposed to be my father's autobiography. Footnotes were OK as long as they did not threaten to develop into fully-fledged polemics. If he felt so strongly, he ought to go and write his own book. His note was, in this form, unacceptable to me.

This argument developed into a real crisis: Keller threatened to abandon the (almost completed) work and to issue a statement to the press explaining his reasons. I told him to go ahead – I could not, in my wildest dreams, have thought up a better publicity ploy. Eventually, and after long and heated arguments, we arrived at a compromise: Keller was to give his views in an appendix immediately followed by a reply from me. And that is what we did. In this way the book represents something of a literary curiosity. But what really crowned it all was the fact that Keller, after reading my reply in draft, considered it not sufficiently effective. So he helped me to improve it and state a better case – Hans Keller in a nutshell.

I had always been a little puzzled by the passion with which he was standing up for Huberman. The explanation came to me only many years later. I myself had been on friendly terms with Huberman. He had a secretary and masseuse – in the best meaning of the word! – in Miss Ida Ibbekken who accompanied him on all his travels. After his death she published privately a collection of Huberman fan letters. Personally, I am no great believer in anthologies of this kind – in particular with a man of Huberman's stature, who certainly did not need the confirmation provided by however many hymns of praise – but it did contain a few very interesting letters[4] and in particular one that was an eye opener: it was from the sixteen-year-old Hans Keller on the evening after he had attended one of Huberman's London concerts. It is charmingly and breathlessly innocent and shows an unexpectedly different side of the usually abrasive

---

congratulate you and the world of music on your characterisation, Kubelik – Huberman represents an excellent follow-up to your earlier portraits of Joachim, Marteau, and others'.

[4] See also p. 35.

Keller (although he could not entirely suppress his critical
faculties even at that tender age):

The evening of your London Concert   12. 12. 1936.

I have just arrived home after your concert and I have to write
to you. I am only 16 years old. I am writing this only so that you
don't regard this letter as too important; but I expect you won't
do that anyway. I just want to tell you how greatly I revere you
and admire your musical powers. You probably receive many
letters such as this, perhaps this one will never get into your
hands, but no matter – I shall feel much easier in my mind once
I have written this letter. I have been in London for only a short
time, completely starved of music, and today I was at your
concert. I am sure you were not in the same frame of mind as in
the Vienna Musikvereinssaal (I believe it is a frightful presump-
tion on my part to say this), but you were 'The Huberman' and
this is something so enormous that somehow one can't really
express it in words. One is conscious of the whole of your soul
being put into your playing – your antagonists don't hear this.
You are someone so inconceivably eminent, I am very happy to
be alive at the same time as you and to be able to listen to you.
In my Viennese home I possess your recording of the Bach A
minor concerto, and whenever I hear the following passages in
which your playing is out of this world, a shiver runs down my
spine:
In the first movement

and so on

In the third movement:

and so on.

Hans Keller drawn by Milein Cosman, with her toes

In tonight's programme, there were two works which I did not particularly like, perhaps I am still too young for them; 1. The Szymanowski, 2. one of your encores which starts as if you were tuning your instrument. But the remainder of the programme! Many, many thanks for all the past evenings and equally for those still to come!!!

With my deepest admiration,

Hans Keller, Vienna.

Compare this with a letter written in 1983 – 47 years on! – dealing with a suggestion of mine that it might be interesting to issue a record of, say, the Beethoven or Brahms Concerto performed on one side by Huberman, on the other by Flesch. I had added that for me the main point of a historical recording was not so much the enjoyment of the music as such as the fact that it had been made by a specific artist whose method of playing one wanted to study in the original or for comparison purposes; or that it might have no special significance, like, for instance, the famous recording of Brahms playing a few bars from one of his *Hungarian Dances* adding at the end with a croaking voice: 'I am Johannes Brahms' – doubtless a priceless collector's item but without any aesthetic attraction whatever. And finally that I had the other day chanced on a wireless transmission of the Beethoven Violin Concerto which I had found outstandingly beautiful; and a few days later on a transmission of the Brahms Violin Concerto which I had considered to be very poor – both, as it turned out afterwards, by Huberman. I concluded that a performance or composition could best be judged in an unbiased way if one did not know their identity beforehand. Hans Keller's reply:[5]

> About the coupled records we totally disagree; at our next meeting, I shall happily demonstrate the fallacy of your argument in favour of it. But when you say that 'you do not listen to a historical record in the first place in order to enjoy the music' I must invite you to speak for yourself, and not to tell me what I do – for I never listen to music for any other reason. You are quite wrong, needless to say [about the advantage of not knowing the identity of an artist beforehand]. As a little child I spotted [Caruso's extraordinary artistry] without the remotest idea who he was. And about the 'absorbing interest' of 'opposing interpretations' 'to a musicologist as well as any student of the violin', you are demonstrably wrong, too. Normally you always have a point in your wrong arguments; this time, and for the first time, you have absolutely none.

Good old Hans! Letters like this were part of his charm. He was streets ahead of me in knowledge and erudition. Further discussion would have been futile – I shall never know in what way I had been

---

[5] Dated 22 April 1983.

so terribly wrong.[6] I greatly valued and admired him. A drawing of him by his wife, Milein Cosman, is a particularly pleasant memento for me. On my remarking how much I liked it, she informed me that she had drawn it with her toes.[7] When I asked the price, she very generously gave it to me as a present; but first she signed it in my presence – with her toes, of course.

Huberman was one of those artists about whom colleagues as well as music lovers in general are frequently at logger-heads. Some venerated, others hated him. Flesch and Keller were, in this respect, at opposite ends of the scale. Keller's reaction to my father's diary entries would undoubtedly have been fascinating; unfortunately, at the time I did not know of their existence. One thing is certain: my father fully realised his prejudice and took it into account. We may therefore regard his privately recorded opinion as genuine:[8]

> Yesterday I heard Huberman play the Mendelssohn and Brahms Concertos with the Baden-Baden Kurorchester. For decades I have been trying to be enthusiastic about his playing (sic!) – but to no avail. But at least I'd like to try to do him justice [. . .].

There follows a detailed analysis which can also be found in his *Memoirs*,[9] But here, too, it is amusing to take a glimpse behind the scenes and to make a close study of how a private expression of opinion is made 'fit to print' – or should I say 'fit for good society'?[10] The diary entry

> His playing represents a catalogue of violinistic, stylistic and general-musical bad manners

---

[6] Except that he had stated in a previous letter (22 March 1983) that when listening to a first-class rendering of a work, one had to banish any thought of comparison; anything else was 'anti-musical'. He was right, of course, if he meant by this that there is no 'absolute best', but I can't see why this should prevent comparisons, for instance, regarding textual accuracy.

[7] See p. 133.

[8] Diary entry for 14 September 1931.

[9] Pp. 176ff.

[10] The German expression 'salonfähig' does not seem to have a full equivalent in English.

becomes, in the *Memoirs*:

> Huberman's technique, though sound, had always betrayed the fact that he left school too early.

What the diary describes as

> Inexact intonation [, . . .] glassy tone quality, disregard of beauty of tone when displaying the rhythmic element

is described thus in the *Memoirs*:

> In tonal respects, too, he follows the tradition of his childhood in as much as he sacrifices smoothness and evenness of tone production, which in our time is an absolute necessity, to extravagant characterization.

The diary's assessment of

> Musically – strictly speaking beyond the pale [eigentlich indiskutabel], wrong accentuation, unscrupulous alteration of the text, arbitrary, not originating from a spontaneous original intuition, but from the waywardness of a pathological condition [Veranlagung]; footling sentiment, artistically overstrained, over-heated

becomes:

> Musically, too, his style gives occasion for serious criticism. The fact that he was left to his own devices at an all too early stage shows in his frequent neglect of elementary rules of articulation, especially in the form of wrong accents. Above all, however, it is the over-emphasis he lays upon his own personality as distinct from the work of art, that characterizes both his good and his bad performances. His personality is self-willed, sensitive, nervous and excitable, passionate and self-assured.

And finally the diary's comment

> In spite of it all, in its way a very considerable individuality, albeit one which I greatly dislike

becomes:[11]

---

[11] In the German original manuscript, but somewhat surprisingly not included in the translation: dare I say that this might be a highly intriguing 'Freudian slip', Hans Keller trying to prove my father's unreasonable hostility towards his idol?

Looked at purely objectively, however – and even in spite of the possible absence of personal sympathy – the suggestive power of his personality, his serious artistic striving and finally his solid albeit old-fashioned technical equipment are beyond question.[12]

The personal relationship between the two was by no means bad, at least, not on Huberman's side:

H. 'phoned me yesterday to invite me to his concert, pretended however, to be somewhat concerned when I accepted, as he was bound to play badly; the fact that I had never heard him when he was in first-class form had been irritating him for years.[13] He explained to me his tendency of being severe against himself, for – 'I am my most ardent follower but at the same time my sternest critic'. Disarming!

Huberman seems to have been a person who was given to tormenting himself and who, at least in his younger years, passed through several crises. Schnabel wrote to my father after a private chamber music evening in 1915 in which he and Huberman played together:[14]

I was again disappointed by Hubermann [*sic*]. He seems inflexible, timid and ponderous. An occasionally beautiful and sweet tone is by no means all that is needed. He is pleasant, zealous and serious and has altogether changed to his

[12] It is perhaps a good thing that my father did not live to read the memoirs of Henri Temianka, one of his favourite pupils (*Facing the Music*, David McKay, New York, 1973, p. 71) in which he writes that as a little boy he prayed every evening: 'Dear God, let me become a second Huberman or, should this not be possible, a second Flesch'.

[13] Diary entry for 14 September 1932. It rather reminds me of a letter from Szigeti to my father (18 May 1937): 'I hope your pupils did not listen to my recent wireless transmision of the Beethoven Concerto from Budapest – I was in atrociously bad form'. Apart from the fact that Szigeti found it necessary to mention the matter at all, it also shows the mental make-up of many performing artists (by no means confined to Szigeti, who was basically a modest man) who regard it as a matter of course – have to, if they want to function successfully – that whatever they do is of the most absorbing interest to everybody: it was, after all, highly unlikely that a young music student living in Germany should even know of or, if he did, wish to listen to a fairly routine radio transmission of the Beethoven Concerto, however prominent the performer.

[14] Letter dated 16 July 1915.

advantage. But he obviously does not compare his own performances with those of others which, however fully appreciated by
him, are measured only against those of other colleagues, never
against his own. Subjectively a very lucky trait! But perhaps I am
doing him an injustice and my assessment is based on an
unfounded imputation.

And a letter written by Robert Perutz,[15] not a high-flyer but a
good solid violinist, professor at the Music Academy of
Cincinnati, and a close friend of many famous colleagues,
gives an insight into Huberman's character:

> Recently Huberman was here. As usual he stayed with me for a
> few days. In between practising and insomnia he cried on my
> shoulder because he feels himself insufficiently appreciated and
> upset also because Ysaÿe was never prepared to let him play for
> him. At the cost of the self-torture practised by him I shall be
> careful not to become a famous violinist; I'd rather do my
> little-publicised concerts and give lessons.

I myself found Huberman a well-adjusted personality, and I
was on good terms with him. In my capacity as his insurance
broker I enjoyed his full confidence, in particular after a serious
flying accident which he and his secretary, Miss Ibbekken,
survived almost by a miracle. I found Miss Ibbeken's description
of this traumatic event quite remarkable.

During take-off Huberman suddenly exclaimed: 'Look, we
are falling!' The next thing she knew was that she woke up in a
field; whether she had lost consciousness during the fall itself,
did not have sufficient time to be afraid, or had simply lost any
recollection of the event, it is, of course, now impossible to
say. But in any case the whole thing was apparently very much
different from what one would imagine it to be.

The anthology of fan letters put together by Miss Ibbekken
does show the magical effect Huberman had on many of his
listeners. It also contains the occasional reply from him which
gives ample proof of his intelligence and originality.[16]

However successful my father's *Memoirs*, he was taken to

[15] See note 11 on p. 68.

[16] See p. 35, for example.

Robert Perutz

task from time to time for dealing with some of his contemporaries unnecessarily harshly and severely. This is a question of principle which deserves being looked at a little more closely.

The basic idea of the *Memoirs* was to provide an expert and objective picture of the persons and events described. No one, however outstanding, can claim to be perfect. Similarly, nobody will wish to deny that the description of an important person's faults and weaknesses is as important as that of his or her strengths if one wants to give a well-rounded portrait. As long as the writer avoids remarks that are pettifogging or not to the point, let alone influenced by personal likes or dislikes, such an objective assessment, warts and all, is surely preferable to meaningless fulsome praise; especially so if the author does not hesitate to mete out the same treatment to himself; and the *Memoirs* are indeed full of self-criticism.

My father demonstrably recognised his own idiosyncrasies, as the case of Huberman clearly shows, and left the reader in no doubt about his basic attitude; I would claim that in the circumstances he fully succeeded in presenting an unbiased picture. The same applies to his assessment of Artur Schnabel, whose actions had hurt him very deeply. In that case, his success in giving an objective and accurate analysis of that extraordinarily complex personality is clearly borne out by the letters quoted in Chapters XV–XVII.[17]

It goes without saying that opinions can differ on whether an assessment is correct or not. Tastes, as well as expert judgements, vary widely. And it would have been a near-miracle if the author of a book as wide-ranging as the *Memoirs* had not committed errors and mistakes now and again. He can't complain about any criticism in this respect even if he feels that it is unjustified or is in its turn subjectively motivated – always provided that there is no imputation of unfair motives.[18]

Is it significant that my father originally stipulated that the book should not be published during his and his wife's life-times? I don't think so. Surely, it depends on his motives. If the reason had been that the book contained gossip or material primarily designed to injure another artist's reputation – a betrayal of former friends or colleagues – then he would have been convicted by his own pen for all to see. But this was not his motive. His stipulation simply expressed his aim of being able to express factual opinions without having to pay regard to feelings of personal friendship. There are certain opinions which convention decrees cannot be expressed to another person unasked.

By the same token no artist will adversely criticise, unasked,

---

[17] See pp. 260–303.

[18] Such an imputation was made against him by Henri Marteau's widow, who protested vehemently against certain passages concerning her late husband and thereby caused some delay of the German edition's first printing (see p. 248, below). (I cannot now recall all the details, nor in particular whether or not her objections were justified in substance.) The efforts of the family to protect a late father's or husband's reputation is fully understandable even if the methods adopted in pursuit of this aim are on occasions somewhat unparliamentary. In my view, a biographer ought to try and avoid saying anything inessential that is personally hurtful. This, of course, does not mean omitting anything essential or important for reasons of principle – but very often it is not.

a colleague's performance to his face. I wonder what Mischa Elman would have said if my father had mentioned to him his opinion that 'owing to the unfavourable shape of his hands his technique [was] limited, though conscientious study [had] enabled him to meet the demands of the repertoire, except perhaps the challenge of certain Paganini specialities'.[19] Or if he had censured Arnold Rosé to his face for his 'habitual orchestral attack, i.e., noisy impacts of the bow at the nut'?[20] The mention of these (and other) adverse features had been preceded by a full description of their undoubted qualities, but clearly his opinion would have been worth very little indeed if he had 'censored' it for personal reasons. With both artists he was on excellent terms; in Rosé's case he organised a successful action enabling him to leave Austria during the Hitler regime.[21] In brief, personal relationships and scientific analysis in a scholarly work are on two entirely different planes. If you believe you have something important to say, should you omit to do so for reasons of friendship? Are only those who are not personally acquainted with the subject of their analysis entitled to refer to adverse features? Or should you have to wait 100 years before painting an objective portrait?

As far as Hans Keller, in his capacity of editor, and I were concerned, we kept rigorously to our intention never to change anything, but on occasion to delete a passage if comparatively unimportant but at the same time potentially hurtful to someone still alive, or to his descendants.

One example is the case of the pianist Bruno Eisner, an intimate family friend. He was a very gifted artist, but there could be no doubt that, at any rate up to the outbreak of the Second World War, he had not achieved the success which one had expected from a man with his undoubted qualities. This fact was clearly expressed in the *Memoirs*, as was the cause – *inter alia*, unceasing experimentation and neglect of certain essentials – but the passage about him ended with the remark that Eisner was still young, 'thus he still has every chance of

[19] *Memoirs*. p. 254.

[20] *Ibid*., p. 51.

[21] See pp. 212–13.

Carl Flesch
with Bruno Eisner

reaching his goal and seeing his struggles crowned by the success he deserves'.[22]

This was one of the cases where I had been anxious to avoid anything that might cause hurt, let alone do damage, and we therefore deleted the following paragraph which we felt was not essential:

> I had recognised the tragedy of this side of his character early on and had tried everything possible to help him, but in vain; the conflict between heart and brain, between feeling and his ten fingers, is still going on with constantly changing results.

No use: Eisner, who had meanwhile reached his seventies, was up in arms, reproaching my mother and accusing my father of having 'spoilt his career'.

Assuming my father had gone ahead with publication in his life time, what would have been his options? Watering down a

[22] P. 270.

friendly yet objective assessment in the interest of a personal relationship? Risking 'the end of a beautiful friendship' in the interest of historical accuracy? Leave out Eisner altogether? All are equally unsatisfactory.

Incidentally, it should not be forgotten that Carl Flesch, dedicated teacher that he was, was geared in the first place to analysing weaknesses and helping pupils to overcome them. Not surprisingly this tendency shows in his *Memoirs* – even if there was no possibility of a useful practical contribution.

I have myself never understood why one should take objective criticism amiss. A few years after my father's death I attended a lecture by Szigeti about the Bach solo sonatas. He and my father had been good friends. But this did not prevent him from criticising my father's edition of these works in the strongest terms. When I happened to meet him a few days later I remarked innocently and truthfully: 'I found your recent lecture about the Bach sonatas very interesting'. The effect was remarkable. He blushed scarlet and started to apologise until I made it clear to him that I did not feel there was anything to apologise for. The real reason for his embarrassment, though, became clear to me only much later when I went through my papers whilst writing this book. He had sent me in 1961, with a few friendly words, the copy of a postcard my father had written 25 years earlier:

> Dear Szigeti,
> Today, for the first time I heard in public the correct phrasing in the 3rd movement of the Bach A minor solo sonata [. . .]. Tonally, too, it was quite outstanding. My heartiest congratulations!

Szigeti obviously had the uncomfortable feeling that he had, in his lecture, not acted in quite the same generous manner. But what of it as long as he expressed a genuinely held opinion in a scientific presentation? Anything else would have been dishonest.

Editing the *Memoirs* and experiencing the reactions of many readers and critics have given me insights which I would not have missed for anything.

---

[23] Dated 26 March 1936.

VIII
CONTEMPORARY MUSIC AND COMPOSERS

'We shall make modern music
our own when it warrants it. It
is its task to convince us.'
WILHELM FURTWÄNGLER

I do not intend to deal in this chapter with the history, let alone assessment, of contemporary music during the period with which this book is mainly concerned. I would neither have the space nor sufficient qualifications to do it justice. On the other hand I believe that I can make a contribution by showing the attitudes and opinions of composers and interpreters at the time, and in particular the opposing viewpoints held by the younger and older generations of musicians. I hope to illustrate this, *inter alia*, by letters from the violinist Alma Moodie, one of the foremost interpreters of contemporary music during the inter-war years.[1]

Everything described is based on papers in my private possession – in particular, letters to and from Carl Flesch, his diary entries, and so on. That they are being published here for the first time would be of little importance were it not for my belief that some of them are of more than transient significance – and that the opinions expressed in them apply no less today than fifty years ago.

Originally I regarded 'contemporary' and 'modern' music as

[1] Strictly speaking the topic 'Artur Schnabel as composer' belongs into this chapter. But I felt that it would be preferable to deal with this particular aspect of his work in context; it will complement what I want to say here (see pp. 276–84). On Alma Moodie, see pp. 171–86.

synonymous, until I found out one day that this was not necessarily so. As chairman of a charitable organisation, 'Self Aid of Refugees' (from Nazi oppression), it was one of my tasks to arrange an annual concert; it had always been my aim to try and offer our audiences something they would not be able to hear in a normal concert. To this end it seemed a good idea to commission a composition specifically bearing on the situation of refugees. My choice fell on Franz Reizenstein, at that time still a comparatively young man. Before the arrival of Hitler, he had been studying composition in Germany and was 'tonally, clearly in the Hindemith mould'.[2]

Reizenstein, kind and helpful man that he was, declared himself willing to contribute a work for our charitable purpose without fee – although, to everybody's profound regret, he died before the plan could be realised. Since, before this tragic event, I had been a little concerned that his contribution might prove somewhat indigestible for our charity-concert audience, I had had the effrontery (not to mention lack of musical culture) to admonish him: '. . . but, Reizenstein, nothing too modern!', to which he replied, laughing: 'But, Flesch, I am already completely old hat!' This surprised me, because to me most of his music sounded very contemporary. But apparently it was considered by the 'real' avant-garde to be already out of date. He realised this but continued unperturbed in his own way, because this was what he wanted and knew how to do it successfully and well.

My father – as usual, the model nearest at hand – had been known, in his younger years, as an exponent and patron of contemporary music. I am convinced that he did not perform any works for the sake of being 'modern'; it depended on the musical value he himself attributed to a composition – or else I would not have come across so many letters from composers whose works he obviously did *not* play. The fact that only very few of the compositions he did perform are still part of the present-day repertoire demonstrates how small is the percentage of works regarded by posterity as being of lasting value – or how capricious posterity is in making its judgement.

[2] Habakuk Traber and Elmar Weingarten, *Verdrängte Musik – Berliner Komponisten im Exil*, Argon Verlag, Berlin, 1987, p. 318.

Numerous letters in my collection clearly demonstrate the enormous difficulties facing composers in getting their works performed. If they do not happen themselves to be proficient on the instrument for which they have composed a certain work, they are entirely dependent on the willingness of interpreters to incorporate their output in their repertoire. And if they have achieved this, their next worry must be whether these artists will do it full justice. One can only admire (and sometimes pity) composers when observing the many ways in which they try to arouse interest and express their pleasure and gratitude in those cases in which they succeed.

Yet I am convinced that they frequently regard interpreters as being beneath them; their flattery can by no means always be taken at face value. They have to learn to accept rebuffs, excuses or even rudeness without showing open resentment. But what other choice do they have? They need the interpreter, but he in turn does not need them – he can perform new works whenever he likes as long as he is prepared to pay the appropriate royalties. The composer's life is, indeed, not an easy one. On the other hand, one must not overlook the fact that nobody likes to tell another to his face that he considers the result of his labours as being without value, however justified this opinion may be. Artists will therefore frequently try to get round this difficulty tactfully by means of vague promises into which composers – wishful thinkers most of them – read more than is intended. My father's archives provide many examples.

Henrich Noren[3] writes in 1920:[4]

I read with great interest in the press that you have of late been applying your art more than ever to the performance of modern violin literature (Suk, etc.).

This gratifying fact gives me some hope that the time is near when you ·will be remembering my Violin Concerto.

You once made the jocular remark – 'When you reach 60, I'll perform your concerto'. Whether it is particularly pleasant

[3] 1861–1928; Austrian violinist and composer. Pupil of Vieuxtemps and Massart.

[4] Letter dated 4 March 1920.

having to state that I have reached that age, is another matter. Suffice it to say – the moment has come to remind you of our conversation.

Cornelius Dopper,[5] wrote in 1906,[6] following my parents' engagement:

I hope you have by now returned to earth sufficiently for you to recall the existence of my sonata which is still awaiting the breath of life from your violin. [. . .] I would be extremely happy if you were to make good your promise – perhaps my second sonata will come off better. If you don't have the time or inclination (which I know can happen) please return the score.

Professor Bernhard Dessau,[7] writing in 1910,[8] suggests that:

It would be of great value both to my publisher and for my future as a composer if you would be so kind as to give your considered opinion about my 'Variations'. I hope you won't find me presumptious for taking up your valuable time [. . .].

R. Gruenberg[9] tells my father in 1912[10] that

I am planning a concert in which my own compositions are to be performed. During our last meeting you were kind enough to promise your collaboration for my 'Suite'. I would be very happy to hear whether this still stands.

Arthur Hartmann[11] asks:[12]

---

[5] 1870–1939, Dutch composer and conductor, for two years with the Amsterdam Concertgebouw Orchestra.

[6] Letter dated simply 'May 1906'.

[7] 1861–1923, violinist and composer; pupil of Joachim and Wieniawski, *inter alios*.

[8] Letter dated 9 October 1910.

[9] It is not impossible that this is a case of mistaken identity, but I believe he is a composer who lived from 1884 to 1964, mainly in the United States.

[10] Letter dated 22 June 1912.

[11] 1881–1956; born in Hungary, he went to America as a child and made a reputation as a violin prodigy. He is better remembered for his arrangements and transcriptions than for his original music.

[12] The letter is undated.

May I enquire whether you would accept the dedication of my cadenza[13] as a sign of my friendship and respect? Naturally, should you ever find it sufficiently deserving – that it is inventive, I have no doubt – to perform it, I would be most gratified. However, please don't feel under any obligation.

Tivadar Nachez[14] writes in 1914:[15]

Permit me to ask you kindly to accept a concerto by Nardini in A major published for the first time. I have arranged it from an non-figured bass contained in an original manuscript for violin and orchestra, and I am hoping that it will meet with your approval. The E minor Concerto by Nardini is being played so often that it should not be without interest to the many Nardini admirers to make the acquaintance of another work by this great master.

I own three Nardini concerto manuscripts and consider the one in A major the most important. [. . .]

In 1912 Otto Neitzel[16] expresses optimism about one of his works:[17]

It seems that my 'Fantasie' for violin (enclosed) is poised to take off. [. . .] Marteau, Busch, Berber have played it, the best performance was that by Dessau [. . .]. I would not submit it to you if I were not convinced in my own mind that it will suit your style. Perhaps you may find the time and opportunity to have a look at the score. I should be very pleased if that one look were to develop into several.

A mixture of naivety and heart-warming frankness is the feature of a letter[18] from Petar Stojanović:[19]

[13] To which concerto is not clear from the text.

[14] 1859–1930; pupil of Joachim and Hubert Léonard, *inter alios*. He wrote a number of violin pieces derived from Hungarian folk songs, but was best known for his arrangements of old violin concertos.

[15] Letter dated 19 May 1914.

[16] 1852–1920; German pianist, composer, conductor and musicologist.

[17] Letter dated 12 June 1912.

[18] Dated 17 March 1915.

[19] 1877–1957; Yugoslav composer. Pupil of Hubay at Budapest and Fuchs and Heuberger at Vienna. His works, in a late Romantic idiom, include seven violin concertos.

I was very pleased to learn of your interest in my Waltz Rondo and I am taking the liberty of enclosing the MS. For the concert repertoire it can be compared, by and large, with the Rondo Capriccioso by St. Saëns. [. . .] You will soon realise that it has been written by a violinist, for it looks far more difficult than it is.[20] It is so easy on the ear that it is even suitable for the American public.[21]

Whether the piece possesses any inner value is for you, the master, to say. Should your judgement be favourable and you were to decide to take it into your repertoire, I could at least exclaim 'A little sunshine at last after so many dark days in this war!'

The tenor of letters from better-known composers – in many cases interpreters themselves – is a little less reverent, but still shows how much it means to them to become known and accepted.

Thus Joseph Szigeti in 1937:[22]

I am giving instructions for my re-arrangement of the Lie[23] song to be sent to you; I should be very pleased if you would show this double-flageolet study and effective 'encore' to some of your students who are already following a concert career. I assume you received the other items already in New York?

Felix Weingartner in 1916:[24]

I can report only the very best about your pupil. He plays my concerto really superbly well. His maturity is astounding.

And a year later he writes:[25]

Before going abroad I just want to tell you how pleased I am about your being prepared to perform my Violin Concerto.

---

[20] The disclosure of a trade secret that may intrigue non-violinists.

[21] An equally startling revelation of what Europeans thought of the state of music in America at the time.

[22] Letter dated 3 July 1937.

[23] Szigeti is referring to a transcription he made of a song, *Schnee* (*Snow*), by the Norwegian composer Sigurd Lie (1871–1904).

[24] Letter dated 14 December 1916.

[25] Letter dated 6 April 1917.

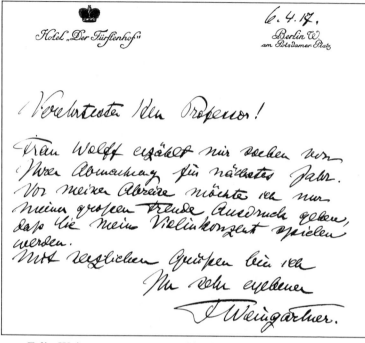

Felix Weingartner expresses his pleasure that Carl Flesch
is going to perform his Violin Concerto

Ernst von Dohnányi[26] reveals that

> I can't tell you how *very pleased* I am to hear that you like my
> concerto so much and how *very disappointed* I am not to be
> able to come to Berlin for the performance. But on the same day
> I have my 55th concert (since October) in Budapest. (I don't
> have to tell you what I would prefer.) [. . .] Apart from this, I
> am hoping for my sake that you will be performing the concerto
> many times and continue to like it. I would be grateful for a few
> lines about the performances in Leipzig and Berlin, their
> reception etc.

Letters from Henri Marteau[27] in which he discusses his

---

[26] In a letter dated 4 January 1921; see opposite page.

[27] Undated, but presumably written between 1905 and 1910; see pp. 154
and 245.

Ernst von Dohnányi apologises for having to miss Carl Flesch's performance of his Violin Concerto

compositions show that he was receptive to constructive criticism, willing to learn from his mistakes and to carry out revisions as necessary:

> Since our meeting in Amsterdam I have revised my second Quartet from A–Z and you can't imagine with what excellent result. It is 50% better. [. . .] I was surprised how much unnecessary material I could delete. [. . .] It will be printed in July and I'll send you the score in September.

> The success of my Violin Concerto in Dortmund was pretty poor. Well, the first part is much too long. I am in the process of re-doing the whole work. This will improve it in the same way as my second quartet [. . .].

The tone of the correspondence with the youthful Erich Wolfgang Korngold is particularly refreshing because the discrepancy in ages (Korngold was about eighteen, my father twice that age) clearly made no difference. Korngold, already a very successful composer, was fully conscious of his status, without allowing it to go to his head. Schnabel and Flesch performed his Violin Sonata a number of times though in later years Schnabel expressed himself in very unfavourable terms

Erich Wolfgang Korngold

about this work.[28] I have really only one complaint about
Korngold's letters: his catastrophically unsuccessful attempts
to imitate Schnabel's famous prowess for inventing rhymed
spoonerisms ('Schüttelreime'), something for which he was
entirely devoid of talent.

In the majority of cases I don't know which of the works
offered to him my father did indeed perform. What I do know
is that he very much liked the *Fantasie* by Suk and played it
whenever the opportunity presented itself. One live performance of this beautiful work has been preserved and forms part
of the Flesch historical CD issue.[29]

Suk was frequently depressed by the lack of public
acknowledgement which did him less than justice. A typical
example is a letter he wrote in 1911[30] on receipt of the news

---

[28] See pp. 274–75. Korngold gave his opinion in a more tactful manner, in an
undated letter: 'Yesterday I heard the (marvellous) [word illegible]. I am
still over the moon with enthusiasm about it. I wonder whether Schnabel's
symphony will turn out equally well'.

[29] See note 2 on p. 16.

[30] Dated 19 May 1911.

that my father would be playing his *Fantasie* under Nikisch in Berlin:

> I read your letter with great pleasure. I have always been upset by the fact that my violin Fantasie is so very little known, so now it is particularly gratifying when an artist of your stature takes an interest in it. It has made the eight years' wait worthwhile. [. . .] The Fantasie is not one of those solo works where one rehearsal is sufficient for conductor and orchestra, and the conductor has to be fully familiar with the score;[31] but, of course, in this regard one can rely on Nikisch absolutely [. . .].

And some months later:[32]

> I have already written quite a number of compositions and nobody outside my homeland seems to take the slightest bit of notice of my new works. Of course, you have to be clear in your own mind about your aims, and I am that, but from time to time one does need a stimulus or something else pleasant, and the news of *your* liking the Fantasie came at just right moment.

He seems to have been one of those people who do not expect success and, are somewhat overwhelmed by it when it comes.[33] What a difference from the unshakable self-confidence of an Artur Schnabel!

But there are attitudes in between these two extremes, as, for instance, in a letter from Arthur Willner[34] in 1928:[35]

> I know that my austere and faithful way of composing is not making life easy for me and that I have to work hard, whereas others, more flexible and pleasing to the ear than I, achieve success far more readily. Yet there are always some like-minded people who acclaim me [. . .].

Correspondence was not always harmonious. Take, for

---

[31] See also pp. 45–47.

[32] Letter dated 9 December 1911.

[33] See p. 176.

[34] 1881–1959; his compositions were performed by Max Rostal, Rudolf Baumgartner, Franz Schalk and others, to moderate acclaim.

[35] Letter dated 1 January 1928.

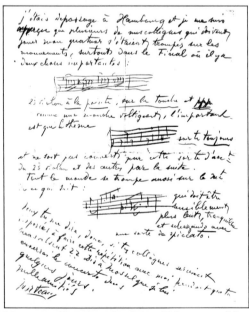

Henri Marteau discusses the fate of his compositions with
Carl Flesch

*Postcard from Korngold: 'The violin part of the IInd and
IIIrd movements you will already have received from
Herr Schnabel. The IVth movement (changed again!) will
be sent tomorrow'*

instance, Hugo Kaun.[36] Apparently the Schnabel-Flesch Duo
had decided – mainly, it seems to me, at the initiative of the
former – not to perform a sonata by Kaun, who thereupon had
written a note that left no doubt about his displeasure. My
father must have been trying to pacify him. Kaun's reply:[37]

> I am sorry if you read any reproach into my recent letter. I do
> know the circumstances surrounding decisions about concert
> programmes – and I blush to discuss them.[38] I am sure you don't
> mean it seriously when you suggest that after all this I should
> still approach Mr Schnabel. I regret that my music does not
> 'suit' you, but let me reiterate that I would never blame
> anybody for that reason [. . .].

Nor did Kaun let it stop him suggesting to my father – as he

---

[36] 1863–1932; composer and conductor.

[37] Letter dated 28 September 1911.

[38] The import of this sentence is not clear to me – except that it is
undoubtedly not intended as a compliment.

did in May 1914 – that my father should perform another of his compositions.

I think most composers accept unfavourable criticism without much ado. For one thing, there is nothing they can do about it, and for another they can always console themselves with the thought that they are ahead of their time and therefore not being understood. Yet I suspect that, if they had a choice, they would still prefer to let themselves go, as did the composer Emanuel Moór, who for some time was highly regarded by some very prestigious artists.[39] For a short time my father, too, became one of his followers and in 1907 gave 'the first and last performance'[40] of one of Moór's violin concertos, which is dedicated to him. Apparently, it was a resounding flop, which Moór was not prepared to take lying down:[41]

I have just been shown the 'Berliner Tageblatt', 'Lokalanzeiger' and 'Norddeutsche Allgemeine'. I myself decided long ago never again to read reviews [an unlikely story!] but a friend and admirer took it upon himself to draw my attention to this extreme loutishness. The same happened last year with my concerto dedicated to Marteau, and now, as you will know, Thibaud and Ysaÿe have taken it up. This time it is not sufficient that you interpreted my work so outstandingly well but you ought to be my *advocate* in this matter: these remarks affect you directly as an artist, because these fools don't credit you with the ability to make a sound judgement. [. . .] You studied and performed my concerto with conviction. [. . .] Mengelberg was enthusiastic and engaged you for Holland etc. It is, in my opinion, your artistic duty to reply in the music press to these attacks by the Berlin papers, drawing attention to the fact that artists such as Casals, Thibaud, Ysaÿe, Mengelberg, etc. etc. etc. have acclaimed my compositions with enthusiasm, and posing the question who is better able to judge – all the more as, in your concert, you had 4 curtain calls, hence clearly a

[39] 1863–1931; his compositions are still highly esteemed by the few musicians now acquainted with them. In 1915 he gave up composing and concentrated on an invention – a two-keyboard piano, the Moór-Duplex Pianoforte.

[40] *Memoirs*, p. 277.

[41] Letter dated 15 October 1907.

success with the audience. This silly ass Schmidt[42] – I'd like to know what he has ever done – his articles are boring and written in bad German. So you and Röntgen[43] did not have the talent to recognise my themes as meaningless! If you write about it, you will be universally applauded and it won't harm you!

I have no knowledge of my father's reply. I seem to remember that he did not think a great deal of Schmidt but I doubt that Moór succeeded in arousing him sufficiently to become involved in polemics.

Most composers react less violently. Ignaz Friedmann was one, although he, of course, had his career as a piano virtuoso to console him:

Yesterday my Quintet was performed for the first time. It was only a moderate success.[44]

Then again, a different reaction from Eugène Ysaÿe,[45] to whom my father had sent the second volume of his *Art of Violin Playing*. After having praised it fulsomely and in detail, Ysaÿe continues, a little tortuously:

Alas! . . . . Why do I in the midst of my eulogy have to express some regrets and a little bitterness!. . . . I came to realise that in your work you have entirely disregarded the composer who has striven during the past ten years to find novel ways of enriching with new elements the basis of our art beyond the state of technique bequeathed to us by VIEUXTEMPS [. . .].

I can't believe that, among my works, you have found nothing worth mentioning. I rather suspect that my publisher (one of my sons) has neglected to acquaint you with the fruits of my labours. [. . .] May I take the liberty of sending you, by the same mail, some material that may interest you?

You well know that I could never entertain the notion of holding a grudge against you. I was just taken aback and felt

---

[42] Leopold Schmidt, a prominent Berlin critic.

[43] Julius Röntgen (1855–1932), prolific German-Dutch composer. His works include twelve symphonies and three piano concertos, as well as a good deal of chamber music. See also p. 302.

[44] His card is postmarked 13 April 1918.

[45] Letter dated 13 October 1929.

that the most honest way would be to express my regret to you.
Now to return to your work [. . .].

And he continued in the same vein in which he had started;
you can't wrap up a complaint more elegantly.

Yet Ysaÿe's compositions were somewhat controversial. A
remark by the pianist and wit Moritz Rosenthal is well-known.
When at the beginning of World War I Ysaÿe escaped by
fishing boat from Belgium – and almost drowned – Rosenthal
quipped: 'When Ysaÿe landed in Great Britain, the calamity
had already happened: his compositions had been saved,
too'.[46]

Hugo Heermann,[47] to whom my father mentioned Ysaÿe's
strictures and who clearly liked to lecture on suitable occasions, commented:[48]

> The fact that Ysaÿe feels slighted as a composer is something I
> can well understand after my own experiences with members of
> that profession who have taken umbrage. What can one say, for
> instance, about Bernhard Scholz[49] and his subsequent bitter
> disappointment, when he triumphantly exclaimed after the
> dress rehearsal of his latest opera – 'How glad I am to have
> safeguarded my family's future for ever!' whereas none of the
> many opera house directors present [. . .] ever had the slightest
> intention of taking the work into their repertoire. Or when,
> after a private performance of the music he had composed for
> Schiller's 'Glocke'[50] he and his expectant family had to listen to
> Brahms, specially invited for the occasion, remarking – 'Well,
> this just proves you simply can't kill a poem as great as this'.

[46] Quoted in *The Memoirs of Carl Flesch*, p. 246.

[47] 1844–1935; prominent German violinist. He gave the first performances
of the Brahms Violin Concerto in Paris, New York and Australia.

[48] Letter dated 9 February 1929. Heermann continues that:

> You may perhaps not be aware of the fact that violinists have to thank
> me for the original version of the Brahms Concerto *not* having been
> altered prior to publication and that subsequently Sarasate and Huber-
> mann [sic] studied the concerto with me in Frankfurt.

[49] 1835–1916; German conductor and composer.

[50] A very long and famous poem by one of Germany's foremost national
poets. It could perhaps be compared – in length, anyway – to Betjeman's
'Summoned by Bells'.

Ignaz Friedman

Opinions on the adequacy of financial rewards can differ enormously. This was powerfully brought home to me in 1973. The Hungarian conductor and composer Aladar Majorossi had, after World War II, first emigrated to the United States but then decided to settle in London as the most likely place to re-establish his position. I made his acquaintance when I heard that he had been the conductor in my father's last Budapest concert in 1942. He was clearly pleased when I suggested that he should write a short composition for four violins and orchestra for a forthcoming concert organised by ESTA to celebrate the hundredth anniversary of my father's birth. It was a charming little piece and performed with much success on that occasion.[51] The event was recorded and subsequently broadcast by the BBC. Since,

[51] See also p. 71. Its playing time, incidentally, is only four minutes and the work would, in my view, be very suitable for school concerts.

considering the quality of performers and audience, most relatively unknown composers would have given their right arm for such an opportunity, Majorossi made it clear that payment was entirely secondary as long as I would pay for the copying and duplicating of the music for all the players – a not inconsiderable expense. However, I did not feel that I should accept his work without payment and sent him an amount which I considered adequate. Quite unexpectedly, I received from him a letter in which he expressed in no uncertain terms his opinion about my stinginess coupled with my complete lack of musical culture and understanding. I could reply only that the amount had been fixed in accordance with a suggestion by Yehudi Menuhin.

A divergence of views of an entirely different kind is mentioned in a letter from H. B. Moser, son of Andreas Moser, Joseph Joachim's collaborator, about the latter's choice of 'the ten best violin concertos':[52]

> Joachim specifically refused to include the Bruch Concerto because he felt it was not in the class of the top ten in violin literature. This caused resentment by Bruch towards Joachim and my father lasting for many years.

Considering that there is a pretty valid claim for including Bach, Beethoven, Brahms, Mendelssohn, Mozart and Tchaikovsky in the top ten, one cannot really blame Joachim (who, as far as I know, did not include his own *Hungarian Concerto*, either). On the other hand, 'rankings' are not the be-all and end-all, as the continuing popularity of the Bruch Concerto clearly shows.

But what about the interpreter's attitude towards contemporary music? It is difficult to generalise; tastes and view points differ too widely. But it should be possible to arrive at certain generally valid conclusions based on opinions expressed by a variety of artists. Similarly, I believe that many letters and notes by my father are typical of interpreters who are no longer young.

Whether or not he likes to admit it, the older the artist, the less he will be attracted to modern music. He may no longer be

[52] Dated 2 October 1931.

*Eugène Ysaÿe, Carl Flesch (partly hidden) the pianist
Alfred Grünfeld, Friedrich Buchsbaum (cellist) and violist
Oskar Nedbal; Bertha Flesch is seated second from the
right, and Ysaÿe's son stands on the far left*

able fully to assimilate a new idiom; and he develops, justifiably or not, a mistrust towards what he frequently feels to be the 'pretentiousness of followers of the modern school'. Musicologists and critics are, by the nature of their calling, expected to keep up with it. And among the older generation of interpreters there are, of course, some artists who feel that they ought to perform modern works, and do. But I cannot imagine that they derive much pleasure from it and, similarly, that young artists whose development has different roots would not find it easier to learn new works and to play them better. It reminds me sometimes of grown-ups anxious to keep up with the younger set lest they be regarded as oldies. More often than not they arouse ridicule. And I should not be surprised if the youngsters were at times to regard such efforts in music actually as an intrusive devaluation of the New; often young people simply *want* to be different from the old ones – in everything. Why should music be an exception?

Joseph Joachim to Carl Flesch:
'Dear Mr Flesch,
I was particularly sorry to be
unable to accept your kind
invitation. Due to a cold I was
forced to avoid concert halls,
and so I could not listen to your
performance of the Beethoven
Concerto, which many friends
tell me was very successful.
    Many thanks for your kindness
in having thought of me; I hope I
shall soon be compensated for my
loss yesterday.
    Yours sincerely,
            Joseph Joachim'.
The letter may not be in Joachim's handwriting, although
the signature is certainly his.

My father's letters, writings and diary entries show this divergence quite clearly. He did not hide his views, nor did he mince his words. He did not have to: hadn't he at one time – as his correspondence with composers amply shows – been a recognised and much sought-after exponent of modern music well into middle age?[53] If some of his opinions sound more caustic and 'old-fashioned' than those of many others, this is because they were not intended for publication but were contained in private papers.

How much he was 'with it' in his younger years becomes clear from an examination of the beginning of his career. He made himself famous at a stroke through five 'Historical recitals', spanning the period from Corelli to his present-day. The fifth concert was devoted to 'contemporary composers'.[54] Reading it, one finds it difficult to suppress a slightly superior smile: that programme with its accumulation of small items! And disregarding Reger, these names, assuming one still remembers them today at all – had they really ever been young and contemporary? Today one feels somehow that they had been old from birth, like Father Christmas. And with *that* you could build a career?

Yes, indeed, you could and did: these compositions were what the public wanted to hear in concerts, and what artists played to satisfy this demand. Of course matters developed. What progress, what a leap, to a Dohnányi, Weingartner, Korngold! Would it not be expecting too much of a musician by then over 50 years of age to take yet a further step towards works by composers belonging to the next generation? At that point in time the fact that one does not – does not wish to – 'keep up with the Stockhausens' is not a flaw, but a natural sign of advancing age, one of the many we have to learn to accept as we grow older.

As already suggested, interpeters who have built up their repertoire by hard work extending over decades may not find it all that easy to bring the interpretation of new works – many

[53] That his positive attitude towards contemporary music generally lasted that long can be demonstrated by his relationship with the conductor Hermann Scherchen; see pp. 332–35.

[54] See pp. 164–65.

IV. ABEND

Dienstag, den 21. November 1905

Abends $7\frac{1}{2}$ Uhr

Von Vieuxtemps bis auf unsere Zeit

PROGRAMM

1. Suite, op. 43 . . . . **H. Vieuxtemps**
   Preludio — Minuetto — Aria — Gavotte   (1820—1881)

2. a) Berceuse, op. 16 . . . . . . **G. Fauré**
                                     (geb. 1845)
   b) Canzonetta aus op. 53 . . . . **B. Godard**
                                     (1849 – 1895)
   c) Havanaise, op. 83 . . . . . **C. Saint-Saëns**
                                     (geb. 1835)

3. Variationen . . . . **J. Joachim**
                                     (geb. 1831)

4. a) Lied des Gefangenen . . . .⎫ **Max Bruch**
   b) Lied und Tanz aus op. 79 . .⎭   (geb. 1838)
   c) Cavatine aus op. 25 . . . . . **César Cui**
                                     (geb. 1835)
   d) Mazurek, op. 49 . . . . . . **Anton Dvořák**
                                     (1841—1904)

5. Phantasie über Motive aus Gounod's
      Faust . . . . **H. Wieniawsky**
                                     (1835—1880)

Während der Vorträge bleiben die Saalthüren geschlossen.

*The programmes of the last two of Carl Flesch's 'Five
Historical Recitals' given in Berlin in 1905*

V. ABEND

Freitag, den 1. Dezember 1905

Abends 7½ Uhr

Zeitgenössische Componisten

PROGRAMM

1. Suite (Ed. Peters) . . . . **Chr. Sinding**
   Presto — Adagio — Tempo giusto (geb. 1856)

2. a) Berceuse, op. 28 No. III . . . . . **Paul Juon**
   (geb. 1872)
   b) Toccata, op. 15 No. 1 . . . . . . **Tor Aulin**
   (geb. 1866)
   c) Romanze aus op. 99 No. I . . . . **E. Bossi**
   (geb. 1861)
   d) Rhapsodie Piemontese, op. 26 . . **L. Sinigaglia**
   (geb. 1868)

3. a) 3 schlichte Weisen, op. 18: Mai-
   liedchen — Reigen — Wenn's
   dunkelt . . . . **Max Schillings**
   (geb. 1868)
   b) Rondo scherzando, op. 16 . . . **J. Jaques-Dalcroze**
   (geb. 1865)

4. Sonate, op. 44 No. I, für die Violine
   allein . . . . **Max Reger**
   (geb. 1873)
   Allegro energico — Adagio con gran
   espressione — Prestissimo assai —
   Allegro energico (Fuga)

5. a) Malaguena aus „Spanische Tänze",
   Heft I . . . . **P. de Sarasate**
   (geb. 1844)
   b) Scène de la Csárda No. III (Hejre
   Kati) . . . . **J. Hubay**
   (geb. 1858)

Während der Vorträge bleiben die Saalthüren geschlossen.

of them not even particularly suitable for them – to the same degree of seemingly effortless perfection to which their public has become accustomed. And it might not even be so easy to convince public and concert promoters of their ability to 'understand' and perform modern works as well as their younger colleagues do. They might even estrange their traditional followers who love them precisely for what they have done – often incomparably well – for decades.

And all this – for what? For the 1% of new works that are of permanent value and may moreover be so much ahead of their time that they have as yet no appeal for the general public?

I know that these views will be regarded by many as philistine, but I reiterate, not by way of value judgement but as a statement of belief: 'Modern music is for the young'.

What of other opinions? Flesch to Artur Schnabel after a musical congress (exactly which I have not been able to establish) in 1927:[55]

> The most intriguing were the political speeches, especially that by Herriot which showed an interest in German music unusual for a politician (or at least his speech writer). You would have loved (?) Stresemann.[56] This quite exceptional orator received enormous acclaim from his audience when he urged German composers to write in a more becoming style and the public, not to be neglectful of classical traditions by allowing itself to be 'seduced by negro rhythm', as he called it. Please take all this to heart!

Admittedly, not much weight has to be attached to utterances by politicians about music. But they do reflect public opinion during a period more than five years before the Nazis seized power, when official attacks against 'degenerate' art were not yet the order of the day, although, as Stresemann's words show, even liberal politicians did not disdain racist remarks.

But my father was not above making fun of his own programmes. As he wrote to Georg Schünemann:[57]

---

[55] Letter dated 13 June 1927.

[56] German Secretary of State for Foreign Affairs. Music was in the family: his son, Wolfgang Stresemann, was for many years manager of the Berlin Philharmonic Orchestra during the Furtwängler and earlier Karajan years. (see also p. 233).

[57] Letter dated 7 August 1928.

A gathering of some of the outstanding names in Berlin's musical life, at a banquet organised by Steinways on 22 June 1926. Among those present are, from left to right (1) Carl Friedberg, (2) Fritz Kreisler's wife, Harriet, (3) Erich Kleiber, (4) Oskar Bie, (5) Emil Bohnke (see p. 167), (6) Bertha Flesch, (7) Louise Wolff (see pp. 43–4), (8) Albert Coates, (9) Gustav Havemann (see pp. 193–6), (10) Fritz Kreisler and (11) Edwin Fischer.

We are slowly beginning to recover from the horrors of the [Baden-Baden modern] musical festival and to prepare our own classical one which will provide well-tried 'numbers' chosen mainly with the thought in mind whether or not members of the audience will gently rock in time with the music.

The following year the modern music festival in Baden-Baden brought many novelties on which he commented to Schünemann in a somewhat more serious vein:

> Between you and me you have not missed much.[58]

> As to my impressions of the 'Lehrstück' by Brecht:[59] I am of the opinion that extreme judgements – 'very good' or 'very bad' – are entirely out of place here. It is an experiment that so far has not come off. On the positive side we have the active involvement of the audience; on the negative, the enormous pretension with which the libretto is spewing platitudes as if they were evangelical revelations. [. . .] Brecht is to be envied for his conceited effrontery with which he presents [. . .] apparently alcohol-drenched literary pranks as divine inspirations. Due to the opposition aroused thereby even in the most unprejudiced listener, you can't do justice to the music, because you don't gain any clear impression of it.[60]

And in a diary entry three years later:[61]

> The other day Furtwängler made a speech during the celebration of the Berlin Philharmonic's 50th jubilee in which he restated his allegiance to classical music. He emphasised rightly – albeit intentionally in a somewhat involved manner – that the modern school has not come up to expectations and has not fulfilled its promises. I wrote to him to say how glad I was that an authoritative personality like him was doing his bit to clear away modernistic humbug [. . .] it had become an unwritten law for every composition to be entitled to a performance irrespective of its inherent value, provided only it was new. Hence the alienation of the great masses from the concert hall. A musician

[58] Letter dated 28 July 1929.

[59] Presumably this refers to the setting of Brecht's text by Hindemith, which dates from 1929.

[60] Letter dated 4 August 1929.

[61] For 10 March 1932.

who has grown up in the tradition of the classics cannot possibly find pleasure in the 'Moderns'. In vain its followers refer to the 'last' works of Beethoven, to Brahms, Schumann, Reger – all of whom at first were not understood. If a valuable work initially provokes protest or even rejection, this does not mean that every inaccessible composition must be automatically of value [. . .].

Sometimes, of course, developments have clearly proved him wrong. In one of his last letters to me[62] he wrote.

Some time ago we heard Menuhin play the Bartok concerto[63] over the radio from London. The transmission was quite a good one, but he could as well have played a composition of his own without anyone noticing it. But in any way it is certainly to be appreciated, that he took the trouble to play and memorize such an enormous work, which is far from being effective.

That the musical world has come to the opposite conclusion I regard as proof of the generation gap in modern music.

But this did not mean that older artists had to be one-sided or in particular uncritical of composers who had been innovators during their younger years, like, for instance, Busoni. In 1937 he wrote from London, again to Georg Schünemann:[64]

Egon Petri is pretty successful here, in particular as interpreter of works by Busoni, [. . .] in my view a rather doubtful pleasure. I can sum up my opinion about Busoni in one sentence: he was a genius, but without talent.[65]

---

[62] Dated 13 October 1944; the letter was written in English, doubtless because of the wartime British censorship.

[63] That is, Bartók's Second Violin Concerto, of 1937–38; the score of the First, which dates from 1907–8, was discovered only in 1958.

[64] Letter dated 3 December 1936.

[65] This statement, obviously, was written for private consumption, possibly in a rather flippant mood. For in his *Memoirs* (p. 155) Carl Flesch expresses himself about Busoni in a rather more guarded fashion:

[. . .] it still seems impossible to pass an objective judgement on the lasting value of his compositions. To me, he seemed to belong, like Franz Liszt, to the class of those Promethean natures whose titanic will

If I did not know that my father was anything but a plagiarist, I would have guessed that this sentence had originated from Artur Schnabel.

Carl Flesch freely admitted to being without talent as a composer, and made very few efforts in this direction, except for a few cadenzas to violin concertos which, however, he himself played but rarely – so seldom, indeed, that I did not know or recognise most of them myself. When an acquaintance who happened to sit next to me during a concert in which a Flesch pupil was performing a Mozart concerto, asked me afterwards: 'Who wrote that awful cadenza?', I replied truthfully: 'No idea, but I'll find out during the interval'. 'You don't know the composer?' the artist exclaimed when I visited him in the Green Room – 'Your own father!' The embarrassment I subsequently caused the original enquirer more than outweighed any hurt family pride.

One can hardly summarise all this better than Furtwängler did in 1949:[66]

> To assert [. . .] that I reject all modern music, is quite ridiculous. [. . .] on the other hand, it is true that I have no wish to hide my attitude to modern works any less than to old ones. If [. . .] I apply myself particularly to the latter, then because it seems to me to be necessary today. We shall make modern music our own when it warrants it. It is the task of modern music to convince us. [. . .] it has living human beings and their interests to back it up. Old music has no such advocate.

---

is inhibited by their earthbound abilities, and whose genius is destined to stimulate other people rather than to perfect their own creative selves.

In more recent years Busoni's stature as a composer has come increasingly to be recognised.

[66] *Vermächtnis, op. cit.*, pp. 48–49.

IX
ALMA MOODIE

'There is only one success – to
be able to spend your life in
your own way.'
CHRISTOPHER MORLEY

To my knowledge there exists no biography of Alma Moodie
(1900–43), a pupil of Carl Flesch originally recommended to
him by Max Reger. Today her name is largely forgotten; *The
New Grove Dictionary of Music and Musicians*, for example,
published in 1980, has dropped the entry on her that was in
the 1954 edition. Part of the reason is probably the absence of
any recordings – surprisingly, because my father considered
her the best female violinist of her generation. In support I
can quote a second, undoubtedly objective, expert opinion –
by no less a man than Arthur Nikisch. In 1925 he replied to a
letter of thanks from my father for the help he was giving her
in furthering her career:[1]

> Your letter has made me almost ashamed. What I have done for
> Alma Moodie has been *a matter of course*. For me, this girl is a
> phenomenon artistically so delightful that I regard it as my
> natural *duty* to promote the interests of this blessed creature as
> much as I am able.

She was Australian by birth. Having lost her parents at an
early age, she had become – and I don't know how that
somewhat unlikely event came to pass – a ward of the Fürst zu
Stolberg und Wernigerode. I remember a visit by the prince in
1921 when we were holidaying in a resort within his princi-

---

[1] Card dated 16 December 1925; see pp. 174–75.

Carl Flesch and Alma Moodie, around 1921

pality. We children were given strict instructions by our
parents to address him as 'Your Serene Highness'; the
German expression is 'Durchlaucht' – a word sounding so
funny to me that I did not dare use it for fear of dissolving into
laughter.

Alma Moodie was a violinist wholly dedicated to her
profession – something not apparent at first glance from her
somewhat insignificant appearance and a personality which
came over as cool and a little ironic. It seems that she realised
this herself, for in 1919 she wrote to my father:[2]

[2] Letter dated 13 September 1919.

Seeing that you probably – and generally rightly – regard me as a cold, and moreover somewhat cynical, fish,[3] I doubt that you fully realise my passion for the violin and the extent to which the perfect mastery of this instrument is my life's aim.

Biographies of interpreters can become monotonous if they deal in the main with the career – and this usually means 'triumphs' – of their subject. If someone is sufficiently important to warrant a book about his or her life, success should be taken as read. There must be other special features to make a biography worthwhile. I believe this to be the case with Alma Moodie. All the same it is not my intention to write her life story, but to concentrate on features that show what made her remarkable artistically: her undoubted flair for the understanding and interpretation of modern works – she inspired composers such as Pfitzner, Krenek, Szymanowski and Erdmann to write for her – and her independent mind and judgement when commenting on compositions, their creators and musical matters in general, including her own feelings and artistic problems.

But of equal if not deeper interest is her defence against the remonstrances by her teacher who considered that she was neglecting the classical in favour of the modern repertoire, and that this was doing her harm. She is clear proof of the generation gap described in the previous chapter.

I believe that her opinions and observations have, even today, validity that transcends the purely personal. The natural, unpretentious and sometimes humorous style of her letters, written in a large and curiously angular handwriting,[4] gave them a good deal of charm. She possessed a high intelligence coupled with a considerable power of critical discernment which enabled her to express her thoughts vividly and well.

During the early 1920s she played a good deal of chamber music with Eduard Erdmann, whose compositions had aroused considerable attention:

---

[3] The German expression 'kalte Hundeschnauze' – literally, 'cold dog's snout' – is untranslatable.

[4] See p. 181.

Arthur Nikisch on Alma Moodie; see p. 171

see p. 171

To collaborate with Erdmann is a wonderful experience. One would never suspect from his somewhat neglected appearance how fastidious he is in his art and how much work he can get done within the space of an hour. Marvellously matter of fact and in addition so free from technical problems that one needs to think of nothing but the work in hand. Apart from this he is pretty impossible and madly funny – an enfant terrible accompli, creates incredible mischief not without burning his fingers now and again, causes me fabulous embarrassment, eats for twenty, becomes fatter by the day, sweats incessantly – but for all that is what I call a 'valuable human being', so absolutely intelligent and decent through and through. One can only laugh and ask oneself in wonderment – what made Nature create a person like him? I hope we can play for you in the autumn – I have a feeling that we have been doing good work.[5]

In 1924, after an important music festival in Prague:[6]

I met Hába,[7] a truly peculiar person. I asked him to explain his

[5] Letter to Carl Flesch, dated 30 July 1921.

[6] Letter to Carl Flesch, dated 5 June 1924.

[7] Alois Hába (1893–1973) was a prolific Czech composer whose reputation

ideas to me in detail; during our chat he admitted to working currently with 12-tone music. Thus a systematic training of the musical ear through which he expects to achieve a relation between ear and any vibration – initially only for himself. [. . .] I can't see what he is hoping to achieve with all this, so much depends on future development. But it is really something to devote one's life to developing a theory without any certainty that it will ever be of practical use. He, of course, believes in it and it is impressive to see how unflinchingly he follows the path he has chosen, recording folk music, measuring it and drawing his conclusions. What must the inside of this man's head look like! Time alone will tell whether he is a fool or a great seer ahead of his time. I incline to the former.

About Szymanowski:[8]

On the 27th we had our first rehearsal. Fitelberg conducted well. Szymanowski was present and declared himself more than delighted. It really does appear that I possess an organ for

---

is largely founded on his experiments in microtonal music. He studied with Novák in Prague and then with Schreker in Berlin; his own composition class at the State Conservatoire in Prague attracted a large number of important pupils.

[8] *Ibid.*

Eduard Erdmann with
Artur Schnabel and the
conductor Fritz Stiedry,
by Emil Orlik

compositions of this kind. I have a feeling, incidentally, that you
will look more favourably on this work than on many others once
you have heard it with orchestra. It sounds so out of the ordinary.
Very delicate sensuous music, violinistically brilliant – but you
notice this only when playing it with orchestra. I don't like his
style, I have no time for anything sentimental, but I find the work
masterly all the same. [. . .]

I [attended a concert] firstly to hear Erdmann's 1st Symphony, unrecognisably improved and creating a very favourable
impression with the audience, and secondly to listen to Szigeti
playing (excellently) a very attractive concerto by Prokoffieff;
during the performance his bridge broke – have you ever heard
anything like it? [. . .]

Now something especially nice for you! Guess who had a
unique triumph – your favourite (rightly!) Suk! A large
orchestral work, 'Ripening' – and how beautiful it was. Such
magnificent mastery and maturity. Everybody acclaimed him –
which just made him blow hard into his handkerchief;[9] he was
the Festival sensation [. . .].

[9] See pp. 152–53. The symphonic poem *Ripening*, Suk's Op. 34, was
composed between 1912 and 1917.

On Pfitzner, whose Violin Concerto she played a few days later at Nuremberg, with the composer conducting:[10]

> Concert in the evening – 1. Overture, 2, Piano Concerto, 3. Me. In the Piano Concerto a flautist miscounts and almost wrecks the performance including Pfitzner's nerves who can't get over it in spite of terrific applause after the Violin Concerto. [She goes on to describe his bad behaviour towards some friends.] I am very depressed. I esteem and like Pfitzner so much that I suffer doubly from all this, and since I did not feel at all well during the past few days[11] – I really had to use all my power and energy for the concert and feel as if I had had to pay for it with a piece of my life – I am a little world-weary. Pfitzner did not say one single word to me after the performance. I know from his wife that he was happy and satisfied, but it would have meant so much to me if he had said something to me, if only the word 'good'. It is all too awful. I myself tend to under-estimate my own achievements, by which I mean in the first place to be alert for what is *not* there, and I did not find the performance as yet anything near to what it should be. I did not feel free, not happy within myself, I'll have to play the concerto a lot more before I am completely satisfied.
>
> If you ask me what the work is like, I am afraid I have to reply that I can't judge it! I am still subjectively too involved. I believe, however, that above all it is very effective, full of virtuosity, excellently well scored, very free and full of humour. I am looking forward to the performance with Furtwängler on October 19/20 – do you happen to be in Berlin on that date? [. . .]

Happily her next letter[12] sounded brighter:

> Before my departure, Pfitzner and I made it up. He considers that I played his concerto incomparably well and planted a fatherly kiss on my head band. Magnanimously, I promptly forgave him all his sins though with reservations, since basically I have a bad character. But I am wholly convinced that it is a

[10] Letter dated 5 June 1924.

[11] She did not have a strong constitution and was frequently in indifferent health.

[12] Dated 14 June 1924.

*Hans Pfitzner tells Carl Flesch that Alma Moodie is going
to play his Violin Concerto – an indication of how much he
valued her playing, even if he could not bring himself to tell
her so to her face.*

most attractive composition with great and immediate audience
appeal. The notices I saw were all quite exceptional. . . .[13]

In a number of letters she discusses her differences of
opinion with my father concerning her repertoire. Regrettably, I possess no letters from him to her, but they can be
easily guessed at from her replies:

Some time this summer I'd like to visit you in order to go
through a few items of the classical repertoire with you, to
discuss Schubert Beethoven Brahms sonatas – I want to study
the Campanella and perform it frequently in order to improve
my technique. I have a great liking for the work, and Szymanowski will write accompaniments to some Caprices for which
he has a wonderful feeling. [. . .]
  However much you are agitated about my 'adolescent aber-

[13] Yet, probably without realising it, she still must have found something
lacking. Twelve years later she writes, after hearing Pfitzner's G major Cello
Concerto: 'Here we have the slow movement that is missing from the Violin
Concerto!' (letter dated 21 November 1936).

rations',[14] they are probably not all that different from those which you yourself went through in your younger years; how else can you explain your inner bond with the composers of *your* time? Perhaps you did not fight as strongly on their behalf as I am doing for mine, but you must have made great personal efforts to understand and come to terms with them; and in the end everybody has to do what he has to do. So there is no need to pity me as yet. I have my feet very firmly on the ground – which reminds me that my foot is very painful [she had pulled a tendon] and it is time for me to go to bed.[15]

Obviously she had had a reply by return:[16]

That was a marvellous answer to my 'book'! [. . .] it was very kind of you to reply so fully and I hasten to reassure your anxious mind.[. . .] Well you see, dear Professor – please don't take it amiss if I speak frankly – I have the feeling that your worries on my behalf are groundless. What you fear and what you have drawn my attention to [. . .] is absolutely correct and fully applicable to musicians in general [. . .] for those *are* the dangers for people who do it [i.e., concentrating on contemporary works] either because they think it is chic or they imagine they can fashion a career only with works of this nature. But those who say this are finished for me, because my first thought is that they *can't* play anything else. What you say about my not being sufficiently 'bourgeois' to work at other compositions is not correct. I am sure you would be much less concerned if you were to look at all my concert programmes over the past 2 years. I have played in public about 120 times and performed in the 'modern section' the Pfitzner Sonata and Concerto, Erdmann Sonata, Suter[17] Concerto, Szymanowski 'Trois Mythes'. That was in 'ordinary' concerts. At modern music festivals I played sonatas by Bartók and Erdmann,

---

[14] German 'Flegeljahre', usually, incidentally, applied to boys, not girls.

[15] This is from the letter of 5 June 1924.

[16] Her letter dated 14 June 1924.

[17] Hermann Suter (1870–1926) was one of the most important Swiss composers of his time. His works include the oratorio *Le Laudi di S. Francesco d'Assisi*, a symphony, violin concerto, three string quartets, a string sextet, and a quantity of vocal music.

Jarnach,[18] Wellesz[19] Suite and Szymanowski Concerto.[20] I did
not play these works in my other concerts. On the other hand 40
times Beethoven, 25 Brahms, 10 Bach and (usually in the same
programme) Mozart, 10 Mendelssohn, in addition Bruch, Lalo,
Paganini, Nardini. In recitals Händel, Bach, Biber, Nardini,
Mozart and an unending string of small genre pieces which,
however, I am not over-fond of.

My Study Bible consists of 3 'Fathers of the Church': Ševčik,
Paganini Caprices, and Bach solo sonatas, which I feel an inner
need to master. No, my dear Professor, you are wrong if you
want to type-cast me as a modern violinist!!? I admit, though,
that I made a mistake in bringing to you only those [modern]
works, but I believed in my youthful enthusiasm that it would
be more amusing for you to hear something for which you
normally have no time instead of those which you have to listen
to every day of the week. Of course I am ambitious, very much
so in fact, and it is my wish to leave something behind before I
die, and this will be, for me, to have introduced and popularised
a few good compositions. [. . .]

If during the past few months I busied myself a little more
than usual with modern works, this was quite incidental, and if
you could hear me now struggling with Paganini's Tremolo
Caprice in order to bring it up to concert standard, your heart
would jump with joy. As a 'world premiere' I am studying
with terrific enthusiasm – Viotti 22!![21] In spite of Kreisler![22]

---

[18] Philipp Jarnach (1892–1982) is now best remembered for his completion
of *Doktor Faust*, the last of the four operas of Busoni, with whom he studied
and whose ideals he upheld in his own compositions.

[19] Egon Wellesz (1885–1974) was an eminent Austrian composer and
musicologist (he was an authority on Byzantine music). When the Nazi
invasion of Austria compelled him to leave Vienna, he joined the Music
Department of Oxford University. His work includes nine symphonies, two
concertos and several other pieces of orchestral music, six operas, four
ballets, and a wealth of chamber and vocal music.

[20] I.e., Szymanowski's First Violin Concerto, of 1915–16; his Second was
not completed until 1933.

[21] The 22nd of the 29 violin concertos of Giovanni Battista Viotti (1755–
1824) enjoyed a considerable popularity in the nineteenth and early
twentieth centuries. Brahms was among the admirers of Viotti's music.

[22] Since to the best of my knowledge Kreisler neither recorded nor edited
this concerto, she is presumably referring to the fact that he apparently
played it particularly well.

*Part of a letter from Alma Moodie, showing her curiously
angular hand-writing. She writes about the performance of
the Beethoven Concerto by Carl Flesch that had moved her
to tears; see p. 185.*

The tragedy is that if you play one solitary new work, you are
type-cast and whole concerts are disregarded – at any rate some
of mine in Berlin.

To sum up – you are right in what you say in general, and you
would be even more right if I in reality placed the emphasis on
the 'moderns' and it is really terribly kind of you to worry so
much about me and I am most appreciative and to give you a
pleasant surprise, I shall study some virtuoso items, 2 in
number (additional ones) which I shall then play to you nicely.
Strictly speaking, my technical work this summer is concentrated on my right side. I have to improve my whole right arm
and to this end I am playing Ševčik exercises. I am also trying
for more liveliness in certain details of my interpretation –
something which I find difficult but which I can see with my
inner eye.

In 1927 she got married:

[. . .] since last Saturday I entered the haven of marriage at full
speed [. . .] you can imagine that it is a very happy person who
is writing you today. [. . .] Through my marriage I hope to
achieve what you have always found so desirable for me – a

discipline and steadiness which will [. . .] enable me to work with greater regularity.[23]

But the births of two children sapped her strength and she began to restrict her concert activities, especially as she developed an aversion to travelling and subsequently also to appearing in solo concerts. Possibly this is another explanation of the fact that she is so little known today. Violinistically she did not deteriorate: she was very critical of herself and would not have hesitated to say so – but she equally shunned false modesty when she felt she had done well:

> At the beginning of the month I had a shortwave broadcast concert in Berlin. Afterwards I listened to the tape. I liked my playing very much and feel that if I were to retire from the concert platform today, nobody could say that I did so because I was playing less well than formerly. In fact I have never heard myself perform better.[24]

> There is no doubt that I have developed an entirely different style of playing, which I regard as a definite improvement [. . .] my successes are enormous. [Yet she goes on to confess that] I play solo as little as possible, the aversion is chronic.[25]

She started concentrating on chamber music – a trio with Erdmann and the cellist Carl-Maria Schwammberger.

Her letters also contain quite a number of interesting comments on other artists:

> During my last vist to Berlin, I heard Adolf Busch play Beethoven with Klemperer and was bitterly disappointed notwithstanding the regard I have for his playing on the whole. Qualitatively his tone has made great strides and is moreover astonishing big, but I have never heard, from a first-class violinist, so many unbearable glissandi and, more serious, so many wrong accents and consequently unmotivated phrasing. With a man who himself composes, this arbitrary way of playing, for which there was no discernible reason, was incomprehensible to me. Already a year ago when I heard him play Brahms I had

[23] Letter dated 21 December 1927.

[24] Letter dated 31 October 1936.

[25] Letter dated 21 November 1936.

Alma Moodie with one of her children

the impression, which has now grown even stronger, that he should be much more seriously critical, because musically his repertoire items just don't seem to be working. If he interprets them in this way, one has to reject him.[26]

She writes rather less directly about another artist for the simple reason that at the time of writing she had never heard him play. Her letter shows that she was fully aware of her human traits ('weaknesses' would not be the right word here) and for that reason obviously felt entitled – somewhat amused at herself – to express an opinion without reserve:[27]

On Monday Milstein will be playing here. I am very curious albeit a litle prejudiced, because some conductors have been saying already that they can play with *nobody* else. Well, I shall have my ears and my critical faculties in very high gear. 'Nobody' is a damned big word!

[26] Letter dated 8 July 1928.
[27] Letter dated 11 December 1931.

Unfortunately there is no record of her opinion on his performance – I am certain it would have been both interesting and absolutely honest, as she was about Stravinsky's Violin Concerto:

> 8 days ago Stravinsky was here. The reception at our home went off very well – as a human being he is simply enchanting. He did not feel under any obligation to 'talk', but he could be, and was, himself and showed that he possesses a degree of loyalty and kindness which surprised and touched me. His Violin Concerto is not my cup of tea. I believe I am able to judge it. I followed it with the score during both the first and the dress rehearsal. The work is not difficult – neither to understand nor to perform, since it is somewhat conventionally predictable. It is well made – he has far too high an artistic standard and sense of responsibility ever to write anything inferior – on the contrary, it is almost too carefully groomed for my taste – one feels somehow that it was a commission which he was anxious to execute well. (Borowsky whose acquaintance I made yesterday evening claims that the Englishman Fairchild forked out $25,000 for it.[28]) I don't think one can get very much more out of the concerto than Dushkin did. He lacks any personality (about which I don't think Stravinsky is particularly sorry) but it was very neat playing with the exception of tenths, which he can't get right either – but I have no doubt that he realised Stravinsky's intentions.[29]

---

[28] According to Boris Schwarz (*Great Masters of the Violin*, *op. cit.*, p. 514), the commission had come from the violinist Samuel Dushkin. But Eric Walter White (in *Stravinsky: The Composer and his Works*, Faber and Faber, London, 1966, 2nd edn. 1979, p. 368) confirms that the Concerto was commissioned by Blair Fairchild (1877–1933), an American composer (not English, as Alma Moodie claims) who was Dushkin's adoptive father.

[29] Letter dated 11 December 1931. Compare it with a diary entry by Carl Flesh dated 25 October 1931:

> The day before yesterday, Dushkin gave the world premiere of Stravinsky's Violin Concerto with the composer conducting. [. . .] Dushkin's protector is said to have paid out 5000 dollars for D. to have a monopoly on performing it for a year. Dushkin, a sold violinist without personality, good technique, small tone, small format generally.

Thus far teacher and pupil are in complete agreement. But the diary continues:

She was equally candid about one of the best-known figures of her day:

> I am curious about Furtwängler's new violin sonata, I hear it lasts 55 minutes and is somehow connected in style with the young Brahms. Not a very exciting notion.[30]

In one of her last letters (if not, indeed, *the* last – some are undated) she congratulates my father on a radio transmission of the Beethoven Concerto – the same over which Casals enthused,[31] and which has found its place in the CDs of Carl Flesch's playing.[32] Her letter[33] shows the warmth of her personality and, equally, the pain the political situation caused her:

> [. . .] I was simply shattered. How marvellously well you played! With what elan and warmth [. . .] an entirely successful performance in every respect [. . .] which I shall always regard as one of the most glorious memories of my life. [. . .] Alex [her husband] had to lend me his hankie during your playing. If I remember that I moved to Germany on account of you – and now have to rely on the wireless to hear you! I envy you your faith and enthusiasm. I have lost mine entirely. What remains is such a sad skeleton that I can no longer take part. Perhaps the time will return one day when I regain my capacity for enthusiasm, for then I too could play in a way to touch the hearts of others [. . .].

As far as I know this moment never came. She died, far too early, in 1943, ostensibly from a heart attack, although it has

---

Next day one read detailed reviews in all the papers, about the concerto's content, style, form, etc. I myself did not understand it at all and could not, in all good conscience, have written a single line about it.

What a difference from Alma Moodie who found the concerto 'not difficult to understand'. It is convincing proof of the part played by age in the assessment of contemporary music (there were 27 years between teacher and pupil).

[30] Letter dated 11 March 1937.

[31] Postcard dated 3 January 1937; see p. 301.

[32] See note 2 on 16.

[33] Dated 4 January 1937.

also been suggested that her marriage was unhappy and that she committed suicide. In spite of the obscurity into which her reputation has fallen, I have no doubt that the enthusiastic opinions of Nikisch and her teacher were justified.[34] The principal loss to posterity is the absence of recordings of her performances of works by her contemporaries; their authenticity would in many cases permit insights into their musical thoughts and intentions which are now lost for ever.

[34] Joachim W. Hartnack (in *Grosse Geiger unserer Zeit*, Atlantis Musikbuch Verlag, Zurich, 1983, p. 283) mentions that critics of the day regarded her as one of the leading members of her profession.

X

ART, POLITICS AND ECONOMICS

'Aggressiveness is the greatest
obstacle to cultural progress.'
SIGMUND FREUD

When one thinks of the effect of politics (and to some extent
economics) on art during the first half of this century, the
mind automatically turns to the Hitler regime, which, Soviet
Russia apart, certainly has had the most devastating impact
both on world history and individual lives. But before dealing
with that particular period, there were other events – in
particular the 1914–18 conflict and the inter-war years – that
produced important repercussions, too.

Artur Schnabel predicted in 1914 that the World War would
cause a reduction in cultural activities only initially and that
after a short time the need for art would, if anything, be
stronger than before.[1] He had foretold with equal perception
that not a few charity performances would be organised during
the war by certain people and organisations mainly as ego trips
not related to their ostensible purpose.

Amongst my father's papers I discovered an anonymous
sketch parodying this tendency. (It is undated but must have
been written early in the War: people had more pressing
worries later on.) Unfortunately, it is not of a sufficiently high
standard to warrant quoting here, but clearly many people
were spending a lot of time trying to dream up new 'charitable'
causes. This sketch, for instance, deals with concerts for the

---

[1] See pp. 266–67.

provision of funds to buy skat playing cards[2] for the men in
the trenches or for employing fifty manicurists in the front line
on the grounds that well-groomed hands would increase the
soldiers' morale. However far-fetched and overdone, there is
no smoke without fire.

Like all artists not on active service, my father was frequently called upon to participate in 'genuine' charity concerts. I
possess a letter over the signature of the German Reichskanzler, Graf von Hertling, expressing his personal thanks to my
father for having played in such a concert in neutral Holland.[3]
I consider this a historical document, not, of course, because
of its contents, but solely on account of its date: 20 September
1918. Historians can draw their conclusions about a mentality
which made a leading member of the German government
waste even one minute's time and effort – less than two
months before the final German collapse – on an event of such
supreme unimportance as that concert. Fiddling while Rome
burns (if I may be forgiven the pun)? Utter incomprehension
of the prevailing situation? Conscious or unconscious main-
tenance of good manners whatever the circumstances?
Complete inability to distinguish between the important and
unimportant? Who can tell?[4]

There is another intriguing letter (a copy this time) amongst
my father's papers. I don't know the identity of the writer – it
is simply signed 'Leo'. What makes it so remarkable is not only
an extraordinarily vivid description of conditions at the front –
in a style reminiscent at times of Erich Maria Remarque's *All
Quiet at the Western Front* – but even more so the apparent
reason for writing it: that families at home frequently did not
seem to have the remotest idea of what the men who were
fighting were having to go through. Reading the letter one
almost gets the impression that mothers were in the habit of

[2] Skat remains even today, in spite of bridge, a very popular German card
game, played mainly by the male population. Richard Strauss was very fond
of it.

[3] See opposite.

[4] I have verified the signature as far as I am able and have been told that it is
authentic. But even if the letter had been signed only on the Chancellor's
behalf, the incident would not lose its point.

Der Reichskanzler.   Berlin, den 20. September 1918.

            Sehr geehrter Herr Professor F l e s c h !

        Der Kaiserliche Gesandte im Haag hat mir berichtet,
    daß Sie an dem so wohlgelungenen Konzerte zu Gunsten
    deutscher Kriegswaisen, das am 25. August in der dor-
    tigen Gesandtschaft stattgefunden hat, mitgewirkt und
    den erheblichen Ertrag der Veranstaltung dem angekün-
    digten wohltätigen Zwecke zur Verfügung gestellt haben.
        Jch möchte nicht verfehlen, für den selbstlosen
    Dienst, den Sie durch die Darbietungen Jhrer großen
    Kunst der genannten guten Sache geleistet haben, Jhnen
    meinen aufrichtigen Dank zum Ausdruck zu bringen.

                                    Graf von Hertling

*Near the end of the First World War the Reichskanzler finds time –
inexplicably – to thank Carl Flesch for a charity performance*

debating the question among themselves – almost constructing
'league tables', as it were – as to which of their sons was
stationed in the most dangerous section of the front. And,
worse still, that they seem to have put the disputes to their
boys on active service. One can only guess at what the
recipients must have thought of that, though the letter gives a
hint. The surprising thing is the respectful tone it still
maintains.

I appreciate that there is no direct connection between the
subject of this book – music – and that letter. Yet I found it so
striking that I could not resist preserving it from oblivion.[5]
My 'justification' is that more than 95% of the papers in Carl
Flesch's files deal with music or at least came from musicians.

[5] It is reproduced as Appendix VIII on pp. 370–73.

It is therefore a near-certainty that the writer was a musician's son. (And even if I am wrong, the fact that my father kept the letter shows that I am not alone in having been so strongly impressed by it.)

It is well-known that after the First World War and during the years of rocketing inflation German musical life was in a very bad way and many artists suffered severe hardship. This decided my father to form a charitable organisation, the 'Hilfsbund für deutsche Musikpflege' (roughly translated, 'Self-aid for German Musicians') with the aim of interceding in at least the worst cases – a drop in the ocean, perhaps, although the Hilfsbund did give practical help to quite a number of musicians in distress. The circumstances surrounding my father's withdrawal from this charity, something which had become unavoidable during the Hitler period, may be worth recounting.

Early in December 1933 he wrote his letter of resignation, which was acknowledged in a reply[6] concluding with the sentence: 'You may rest assured that the Hilfsbund will always remember with gratitude your warm interest and your self-sacrificing devotion'. This triggered off correspondence, the most remarkable feature of which is that it was still possible – one year later it would not have been.

Carl Flesch to the Hilfsbund:[7]

> I am constrained to comment in some detail on the content and form of your letter; someone not in the know would deduce from it that my relation to the Hilfsbund was that of an ordinary member acting more or less actively for its benefit. I feel therefore that I should jog your memory a little and briefly recap the events leading to the Association's formation.
>
> Deeply perturbed by the ever-increasing hardships experienced by the musical profession during the inflation, I resolved in 1920 on my own initiative to instigate a vigorous campaign to try and deal with the problem on a long-term basis. By means of a charity concert in Holland which produced a net profit of approx. 2,400 Dutch guilders – which was to form the initial capital of the Association – I managed to create a solid financial

---

[6] Dated 7 December 1933.

[7] Letter dated 10 December 1933.

basis for my plans.[8] That done, I called a meeting of a number of prominent German musicians in which I set out my plans and asked for their collaboration in realising them. You all asked me at the time to accept the chairmanship – which I declined on the grounds that I did not think it fitting for a German-Hungarian citizen to be at the head of a purely German enterprise. However, I accepted the post of vice-chairman.

These facts – fully minuted at the time – make it clear that the Hilfsbund owes its existence exclusively to my personal initiative. I attach some importance to recording this fact vis-à-vis possible later attempts to cloud the issue. I am not interested in formal recognition – anything good I have done I did for its own sake. And in the present case I am quite satisfied with being able to take some pride in having founded an Association which during the past 12 years has been instrumental in assisting colleagues in dire straits. I do hope that the Association will continue to pursue the aims which we all had in mind at the time of its inauguration.

And the reply:[9]

The Board of the Hilfsbund für deutsche Musikpflege e.V. has in its session of the 15th inst. noted your letter dated 10th inst. The Board is fully aware of the facts enumerated in your letter both about the formation of the Association and your activities as a Board member. They will not be forgotten, all the more so as they have been fully recorded in the files and publications of the Hilfsbund.

The Board would like to reiterate its thanks to the founder of the Association.

My father had made his point, but the formal style, without reference to any concrete facts, which it was considered prudent to adopt, makes its own sinister point.

Whatever the financial circumstances of individuals, there can be no doubt that from the mid-1920s until shortly before the mid-1930s Berlin could again be classed as one of the main music centres of the world. The ever-changing and frequently

[8] Reading that figure, one has to remember that the year was 1920.

[9] Letter from 'Prof. Dr. Georg Schumann, First President', dated 16 December 1933; see also note 24 on p. 197.

unfavourable conditions in the United States during part of that time may have contributed. A few observations by Robert Perutz, a former Flesch pupil who was Professor in the violin section of Cincinnati University, are enlightening:[10]

> People in Europe don't seem to know how enormously difficult it is at present to succeed in the USA even half-way. [. . .] There is no let-up of competition anywhere. I recently read the report of an interview with Mischa Elman in which he bewailed the difficult times: 'Today a 10-year-old little boy has only to play the Mendelssohn Concerto to be immediately hailed as a great virtuoso'.[11]
>
> These days every pupil reminds me of a piece of raw meat over which a pack of hungry dogs are fighting. [. . .] I hardly feel a gentleman when accepting money from my pupils instead of advising them to do anything else rather than play the violin. [. . .] The 'living monuments' appearing in concerts have all of a sudden become very human and are passionately wooing for every public appearance. The times when the artists' room was firmly closed to the public have gone. The doors are wide open and the Giesekinder, Horowitzes and Masturbis [Iturbi] will soon beg people to ask them for their autographs. All the same, it is still possible to made a modest living in this country. [. . .]
>
> Heifetz played before an entirely empty hall. [. . .] Hubermann [*sic*], Tertis, Bauer and Salmond did not fare much better. They all played very well.

And an entry in Carl Flesch's diary in 1932:[12]

> [Discussed with Piatigorsky] the material conditions of present-day concert life. The conclusions were devasting. In the USA especially, expenses amount to 60%–70% of the fees. [. . .]

But elsewhere artists experienced equal difficulties, as is shown in a letter[13] from Karel Hoffmann, a member of the famous Bohemian String Quartet:

[10] As usual with Perutz, this letter was not dated.

[11] There are no prizes for guessing which ten-year-old virtuoso Elman was referring to!

[12] Probably for 7 September 1931.

[13] Dated 15 March 1928.

We no longer undertake long tours. [. . .] Concert conditions
have become much worse. New quartet ensembles abound and
audiences are not sufficiently numerous – the middle classes
have become impoverished, especially in Germany, where
formerly we had most of our engagements.

Nevertheless, a look at the official Berlin concert programme
(*Führer durch die Konzertsäle Berlins*),[14] say, for the first half
of March 1932 reveals – for those few weeks alone – names
such as Busch, Furtwängler, Klemperer, Patzak, Rosé,
Schlusnus, Tauber and Walter. In addition many others,
comparatively little known to the general public now, but at
the time undisputed first-raters; Elinson, Ivogün, Kern,
Osborn, Roswaenge, Vecsey, Wittrisch, and others. Anti-
semitism in the shape of declining audiences for concerts by
Jewish artists was – before Hitler, of course – not noticeable.
Indeed, almost the opposite was true: the regularly sold-out
Huberman concerts on the (Protestant) 'Day of Repentance'
('Busstag') were an old-established Berlin tradition although
nobody could have been in any doubt about Huberman's
Jewish origin.

On the other hand it is indisputable that even before the
Hitler revolution anti-Jewish intrigues were anything but
unknown at the Berlin Hochschule für Musik although frequently not under an overtly antisemitic flag and not yet as
pronounced as at some provincial music academies. At that
time many people were already clandestine members of the
Nazi Party and proudly displayed their swastika badges on the
very day of Hitler's access to power. Since they assumed –
rightly, as it turned out – that the issue date of the membership card might be significant but at the same time that
complete inactivity in racial questions before Hitler's accession
would not make them favourites with the powers that then
were, they started early to take up their positions with an eye
to the future.

A typical case was that of Gustav Havemann, a Joachim
pupil, and like my father Professor at the Berlin Hochschule
where they met daily and were on amicable terms. Yet that did

[14] 'Guide through the Concert Halls of Berlin'; one might say that the
problem soon became the Führer *in* the concert halls of Berlin.

not deter Havemann in 1931 from writing an 'open letter' in a music magazine accusing my father – by twisting his words in a convenient if transparent manner – of aiming at 'forcing Jewish sound quality on German violinists'. The consequent newspaper polemic is not sufficiently interesting to merit reproduction here.

Havemann represented a peculiar but not entirely unusual mixture. I myself had always regarded him as a clandestine – perhaps not even that clandestine – Nazi. Others – for instance, the composer Berthold Goldschmidt – found him 'friendly and unprejudiced'.[15] His attitude can be briefly illustrated by recounting the case of Franz Schreker. It was typical of the methods followed by many right-wing personalities at the time who, although not – or, at any rate, not at first – joining in the blind uncompromising National-Socialist antisemitism, made no secret of their dislike of the Jewish race. But their ploy was first to attack Jews and then to add something on the lines of: 'Basically we admire the Jews. If only they were to behave decently, the whole Jewish question could be resolved in no time'. From this it was only a small step to tacit toleration of National-Socialist excesses; in this way those who were not outspoken Nazis still played into their hands.

Franz Schreker, Director of the Hochschule für Musik since 1930, lost his position in 1932; he may have been one of the first victims of the 'cultural revolution', even though his dismissal dates from before the Nazi period and he was permitted to exchange his directorship for the post of professor at the Akademie der Künste in Berlin. My father who at that time no longer had any illusions about Havemann, wrote in his diary:[16]

> The papers report the news of Schreker's resignation as director of the Hochschule following a vote of no confidence by the body of teachers. One recognises Havemann's unmistakable scrawl.[17]

---

[15] Quoted in Traber and Weingarten, *Verdrängte Musik – Berliner Komponisten im Exil, op. cit.*, p. 49.

[16] Entry probably for 13 June 1932.

[17] An untranslatable pun: 'Klaue' also means 'claw' or 'talon'.

Franz Schreker
by Emil Orlik

He must have contacted him about this and similar cases (in particular, that of the pianist Leonid Kreutzer, another of Havemann's bêtes noires) for Havemann's reply[18] is vitriolic:

> No successor to Schreker has as yet been named, he is on leave until January when he will take over a master class at the Akademie. [. . .] Schreker applied *voluntarily* for a transfer to the Akademie after I had convinced him that *the whole of Germany* was rejecting him as Director. I am glad for him that he can now devote himself entirely to composing. The *Berliner Tageblatt* has, however, commented by distorting the facts, alleging that we did not want Schreker for political reasons. It would be far better if the Jewish press were to desist from making knowingly false statements – we would be able to overcome the Jewish question, which formerly did not exist in Germany, far more quickly. You will say that in former times Jews were not regarded as first-class citizens either. That is correct but the same applied to the middle-classes: the

---

[18] Dated 22 July 1932.

> aristocracy had feudal rights [. . .]. The German hatred
> towards Jews originates from the time when Eastern Jews began
> to spread themselves in our country. [. . .]
>
> Art must and should be or become impartial. The Jews are
> strong as a people and Zionism sees to it that this position is
> maintained. But we claim the same right for ourselves. [. . .]
> We value the good Jewish traits far too highly not to wish to
> educate our people in a similar way.

I believe that expressions of opinion of this type, representing
as they did a mixture of cynicism, hypocrisy, mental confusion
and – it is fair to add – some opinions genuinely held, provided
antisemitism with what one might call a 'liberal' underpin-
ning. They can be more informative than whole volumes of
learned theories.

As a matter of interest, Havemann himself fell subsequently
foul of the authorities and never reached the goal he had set
himself (which, I believe, was to become Director of the
Hochschule; it is intriguing, moreover, that Havemann's
professorship there came to an end in 1945).

If Schreker had not been Jewish, he would almost certainly
not have been treated in the way he was. To be fair, however,
one should not omit to mention an opinion held by a number
of people and shared by Carl Flesch:[19]

> Schreker was, however, as unsuitable for the post as can be
> imagined [. . .]. What a tragic fate for this man. Paul Bekker[20]
> has him on his conscience; he ruined him by exaggerated praise
> in his early years.[21]

I possess a letter from Schreker, dated 10 June 1933, which
is no less than a cry of anguish. He obviously no longer knew
which way to turn and was helplessly disorganised:

> [. . .] Do you think one could get cheap housing in Baden-
> Baden? Possibly my wife could open a pension there. [. . .] I
> would accept *any* position abroad, even if it offered only a

---

[19] Diary entry, probably for 13 June 1932.

[20] Well-known critic and musicologist (1882–1937); he regarded Schreker as
a potential successor of Wagner.

[21] A literal translation from the German would be 'lauded him to death'.

minimum living wage. [. . .] 4 weeks ago my nerves were completely shattered and – urged by everybody around me – (I could no longer get any sleep, not even with Veronal) I entered a sanatorium. I have in these 13 Berlin years gone through too much, it was a *martyrdom* about which I shall write one day. Already in the 3rd year I wanted to go back to Vienna and could have done so, everything was arranged – and then I allowed myself to be persuaded to stay. I was an ass!

I possess an interesting letter from dear colleague Havemann dated 1920 at a time when I was the first to engage him. His son-in-law Höffer was my student (he was nothing and knew nothing when he came to me) and then I gave him a job at the Hochschule. It is all a mountain of meanness through which I had to eat my way. I did it and now I am suffering from indigestion. Now, as you so rightly say, it is a question of not losing one's nerve. I possess a collection of letters from prominent musicians all over the world, including the German gentlemen Strauss, Pfitzner, Furtwängler, Schillings,[22] Mottl,[23] G. Schumann[24] and others. Strictly speaking I would need to do nothing else but to publish a selection of these letters, but I shall never do so. The main reason why I have been eliminated is that I am too good at my job and have become a nuisance to the crowd of mediocrities.

This catastrophe, as well as his subsequent dismissal from the Akademie der Künste, led to a stroke from which he never recovered. He was one of the many tragic Nazi victims and a great loss to music.

Interesting in a different way is a letter from Paul Schwers, the editor of the *Allgemeine Musikzeitung*;[25] in it he discusses the question of foreign students at German music academies, a

[22] Max von Schillings (1868–1933) was a well-known German composer and conductor. He was Intendant of the Berlin State Opera from 1919 to 1925.

[23] Felix Mottl (1856–1911), an Austrian, was one of the most outstanding conductors of his day. He was especially renowned as an interpreter of Wagner.

[24] Georg Schumann (1866–1952) was a German composer and choral conductor (he was Director of the Singakademie in Berlin from 1900 to 1950). Ironically, he was elected President of the Akademie der Künste in 1934. See also p. 191.

[25] Dated 12 November 1930.

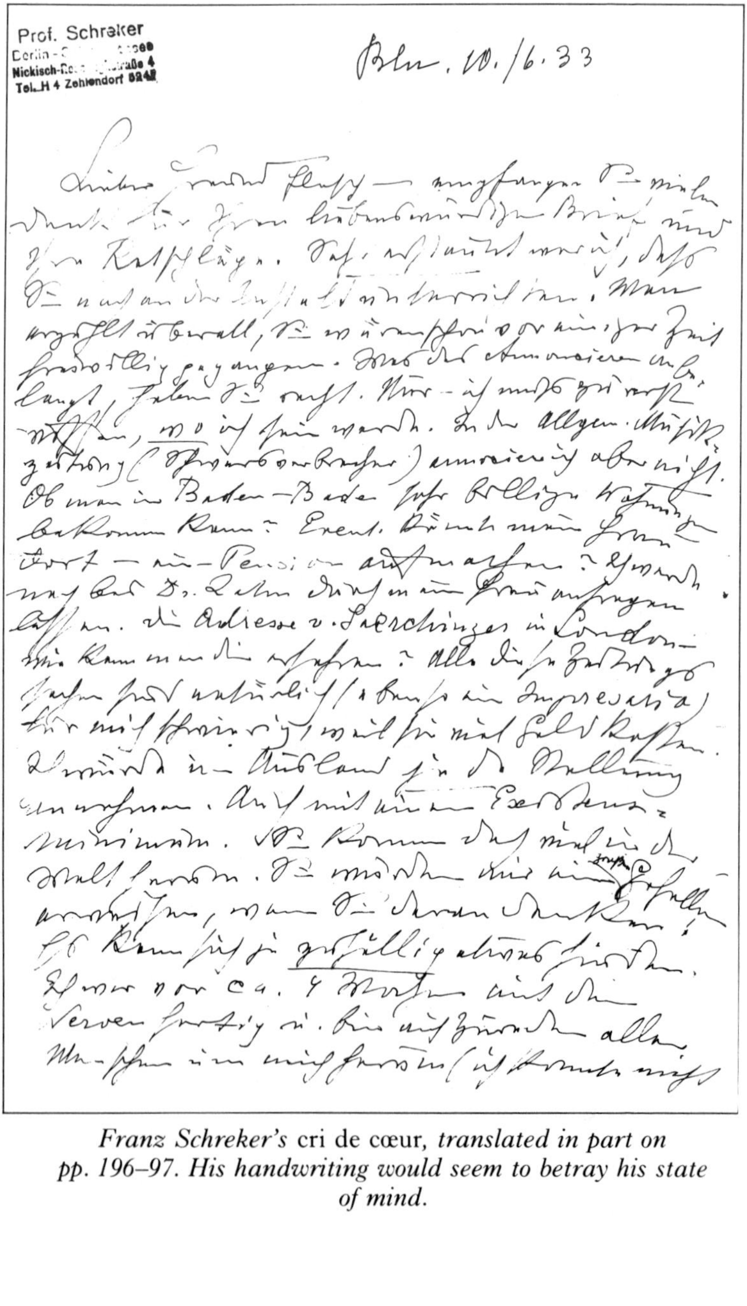
Prof. Schreker
Berlin-...
Nickisch-...straße 4
Tel. H 4 Zehlendorf 5242

Bln. 10./6.33

Franz Schreker's cri de cœur, *translated in part on pp. 196–97. His handwriting would seem to betray his state of mind.*

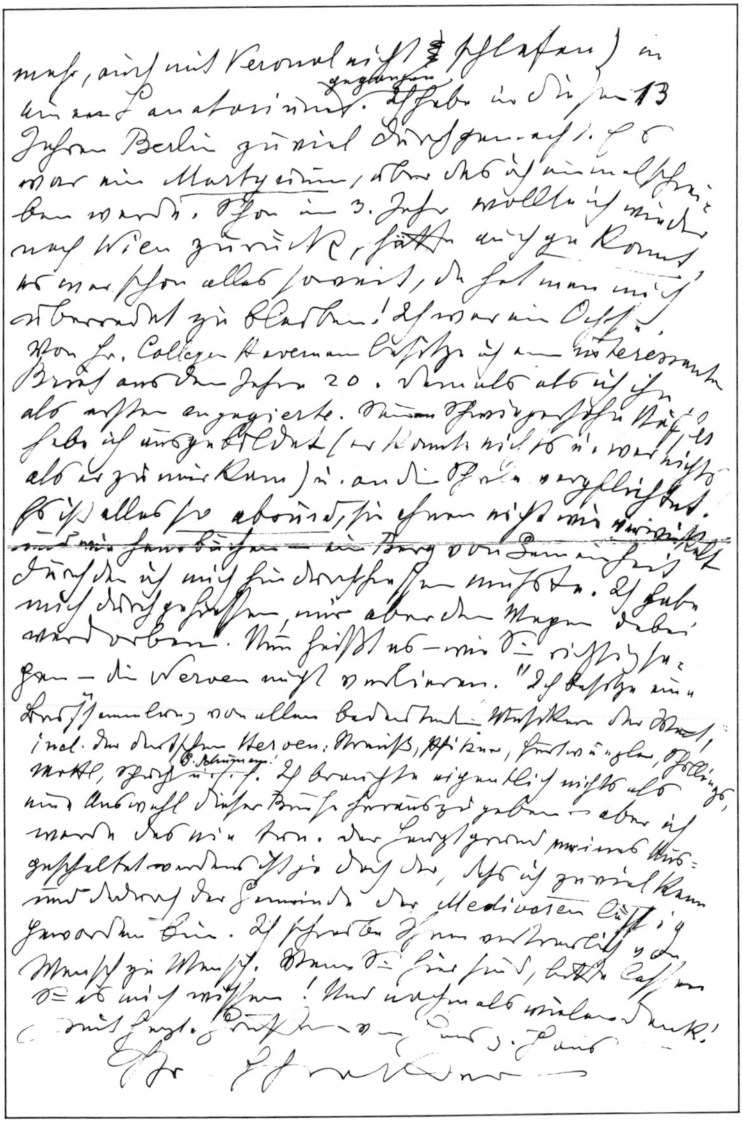

mixture of political, cultural and purely financial reflections
equally typical for the German mentality at the time.

It would indeed be a good thing if the question of foreign
students at our state teaching institutions were to be seriously
considered. I am of the opinion that it would be definitely
desirable to reserve a certain percentage of places for foreigners.
We are all interested in these students subsequently becoming
ambassadors for our German cultural values. Of course, I have
in mind primarily those countries whose attitude towards us is
no longer hostile or devoid of understanding, and who are at the
same time in a position to send us pupils who can afford our
fees. This means in the first place North and South America
and USA with their dominions [*sic*!]; Scandinavian countries,
Holland, possibly Spain. Not to forget Japan which is showing
itself just now one of the main friends of German musical
culture.[26] As far as France, Belgium and Italy are concerned, I
think we don't have to make great efforts, partly for political
reasons, and partly because these countries never showed any
great interest in German teaching institutions for their young
musicians. Moreover, it is of course a fact that these countries
have a very strong musical culture of their own which we on our
part can and must respect. On the other hand, I am strongly of
the opinion that pupils belonging to countries of the so-called
Little Entente, i.e., Czechoslovakia (as far as it concerns
Czechs) and Poland should not under any circumstances be
admitted to our state institutions as long as they continue
openly to preach contempt and hatred towards everything
connected with German culture and – in particular Poland – to
adopt a politically unacceptable stance towards ourselves.

Russia does not permit its students to travel abroad. Moreover, we would get from that source only paupers and starve-
lings anyway – of whom we have more than sufficient in our
own country.

Switzerland poses special questions; during the past few
years it has shown a highly chauvinistic attitude towards
anything and anybody coming from abroad, in particular
Germany, wishing to be active artistically. One has to keep a

---

[26] A remark which underlines that the Japanese interest towards Western
music dates back rather longer than is generally assumed today. Although
many Japanese composers studied in Berlin I can remember only a single
Japanese Flesch pupil, whose talent, incidentally, was not above average.

strict eye on people from Switzerland so as to prevent them obtaining posts in Germany whereas Switzerland on its part virtually bars Germans. On the other hand, Austrians should be treated no different from Germans. [. . .]

Incidentally, I am by no means averse to the idea of a special academy for foreigners, but of course it would have to be on a basis quite different from last spring's badly thought-out 'seasonal' undertaking which the Americans rightly regarded as a mere tourist trap. The amateurish idea of providing Americans with 6–8 weeks' German musical culture should under no circumstances be revived. Such undertakings and their effects are highly counter-productive.[27]

The changes wrought by Hitler's access to power occurred not in one fell swoop but gradually. For the time being, my father retained his teaching post at the Berlin Hochschule. To this end he had to apply for membership of the 'Reichsmusik-Kammer', which was granted to him. During the following years the position became, of course, more and more difficult, and in 1936 he finally turned his back on Germany.

It has been held from time to time against prominent personalities – and my father was no exception – that they did not leave Germany immediately or, at least, much earlier than they did, rather than trying to accommodate themselves to the prevailing conditions. A good point if one had been able to foretell the future. But who could? Even those who were to become the Allied Governments could not. Matters appeared nothing like as clear-cut as, with hindsight, they do today. Of course, the decision to leave Germany – although, tragically, it often failed to guarantee the possibility of doing so – was simple and unequivocal for those who had been immediately ruined professionally or were in constant danger: they had no choice. But for others – the majority – the situation contained

[27] In view of today's abundance of (often highly successful) courses, seminars, etc., of even less than six weeks' duration, this is one of several misjudgements, in a letter which also lacks any reference to Great Britain (unless, of course, Schwers regarded it as one of the 'USA dominions' he mentions!). If, as is likely, he just forgot about Britain, in a letter written off the cuff, it still shows how little importance Continentals attached to British musical life and culture of the 1920s.

so many imponderables that it was practically impossible to arrive at a fully reasoned decision.

This was even more true in my father's case. The Hochschule did all it could to convince the authorities of the importance of retaining him on the staff. This is evident from, *inter alia*, several letters addressed to him by Professor Fritz Stein, the new Director of the Hochschule:[28]

> I have yesterday emphasised to the Ministry the necessity of holding you at all costs. [. . .] even Prof. Havemann[29] agrees [. . .]. Please don't do anything further in this matter for the time being and should you be asked by anybody, state categorically that you are not on leave but are staying on as Professor at the Hochschule.

A little later Stein wrote again:[30]

> I heard a rumour that you had been invited by Mussolini personally to conduct a teaching course in Rome. Is this correct? If so [. . .] this would be an important fact [. . .] which I would want to pass on to the Ministry [. . .].

And finally on his sixtieth birthday, 9 October 1933:

> We are thinking today with gratitude and respect of your successful life's work [. . .] and hope and wish that you may continue to work for a long time for the good of our art with undiminished vigour – ad multos annos.

It would have been difficult to react to all this in a negative way, particularly in view of some purely practical considerations: Carl Flesch was in his sixtieth year; he had lost all his money a few years earlier in the American crash and in fact still owed his bank a considerable sum; he had long ago decided to retire from concert life at 60 and to devote himself entirely to teaching; and for the major part of his life Germany had been his main base. Is it really surprising that he could not

[28] Letter dated 1 June 1933.

[29] The 'even' is highly significant, and gives some idea of the position and power of this man at the time.

[30] Letter dated 21 June 1933. As far as I know, the teaching course in Rome was mooted, but the project was never pursued.

lightly abandon all this and start afresh abroad – with all the difficulties about labour and residence permits, local competition and so on, that such a move implied? Had he been younger, his attitude might well have been different: he was sufficiently realistic to persuade me to leave Germany as early as 1933 – rightly so, but as I felt at the time, against my 'better' judgement.

There was the initial optimistic opinion held by very many people – most of them not in my father's untypically favourable position – that the situation would 'normalise' itself within a comparatively short time. One cannot repeat sufficiently often that very few people could even begin to imagine, let along foretell, what was to come. I myself, for instance – a law student, interested and quite well informed in political matters – vividly remember the day the Nazis officially achieved power. I had – today one can hardly credit it – a feeling of relief: 'Thank God, now there is no longer this uncertainty; now we can begin to see the light at the end of the tunnel'. A Nazi regime had become inevitable, sooner or later, but it was bound to be of short duration. We would just have to sit it out.

And this optimism was shared by many people with a life's experience in the highest ranges of the economy and politics. The most striking example remains for me a remark by Georg Bernhard, chief editor of the *Vossische Zeitung* (a paper comparable to, say, *The Guardian*).

First, a few remarks about Bernhard may be helpful. He was also a German MP and lecturer at the Handelshochschule, the Berlin equivalent of the London School of Economics, and thus occupied a prominent position in Berlin social and political circles. From time to time he organised private concerts at his salon, in some of which my father played, not only out of friendship, but also because he was interested in some of the people, in particular prominent politicians, whom he met on those occasions. An ironic entry in Carl Flesch's diary:[31]

House concert at Georg Bernhard's. It is amusing to observe

---

[31] Probably for 25 November 1931.

how German politicians succumb to the German 'original sin' –
the fascination with everything French – and dance attendance
on the French ambassador who treats them with disdain.

And about Bernhard himself:[32]

> Peculiar mixture of clear thinking and adventurous fantasising
> (very noticeable in his bidding when playing cards). If he were
> not to act the proletarian in such a pronounced – and to many
> people convincing – way, but showed more dignity, exchanged
> the role of the 'son of the earth' for something more fitting for
> his position, he would by now be Chancellor of the Exchequer.

I cannot say whether or not this assessment was correct,
except for his adventurous bidding at cards. When husbands
arranged an evening of skat, their wives frequently went out
together to a theatre or cinema. Bernhard lost at cards with
monotonous regularity and, shortly before the ladies were due
back, used to make sure that the score was settled. Thereafter
play continued with everybody having a clean sheet. On the
wives' return Mrs Bernhard would ask her husband: 'Well, are
you losing again?', whereupon he could prove to her how
much she was misjudging him.

On his fiftieth birthday his staff issued a 'private edition' of
his paper dealing, of course, entirely with him. One
advertisement has stuck in my memory: 'Will any clairvoyant
who has so far *not* been consulted by a gentleman with greying
hair and a lighted cigar kindly contact the editorial office of
this paper'.

But with all that he was a highly intelligent, experienced
professional politician and journalist on whose editorial desk
all kinds of information were converging. And this brings me
back to his extraordinary remark. When, after a concert given
by my father, we all had supper together at a Berlin restaurant, we heard the news of the Reichstag being on fire, almost
certainly a deliberate arson instigated by Hitler which
strengthened his hand no end. The news, however, prompted
Bernhard to utter six words (seven in the English translation,
to be pedantic), which certainly were and I suspect will
remain the most misguided prediction I have ever heard and

[32] *Ibid.*

which for this reason I shall always remember: 'This is the end of the Nazis!' If someone like him could make such a blunder, we ordinary mortals have no reason to be ashamed of our own misjudgements.

My father had left Germany in time, had refused – in this instance guessing developments correctly – a teaching post at the Austrian Mozarteum and eventually settled in London where he succeeded after some time in obtaining a permanent labour permit. He remained in touch with former colleagues and thereby managed to keep abreast of developments at the Academy. News, of course, had to be retailed in a very veiled manner; for instance in a letter written on 23 March 1936 by Professor Max Strub, a former pupil: 'The man with the special talent for examining pupils on their knowledge of tonality keys (the one with the parson's voice) has applied for voluntary retirement'.[33] This is how you had to write at that time in order to avoid trouble, since many letters were being opened by the censor.

Others preferred to wait until they were on a tour abroad before opening their hearts, like Georg Kulenkampff, who in a letter dated 10 July 1938 lamented that he felt 'more and more like working in a vacuum'. As one of the foremost remaining violinists in Germany, he feared 'the risk of standing still owing to lack of competition and the absence of "artistic friction"'. For this reason he had decided to give a concert in London in the following year – 'notwithstanding the prevailing sentiment – cold showers are good for metabolism'. The outbreak of war frustrated this project.

In this respect – and only in this – artists who had managed to establish themselves in countries that were as yet musically somewhat under-developed, fared better by facing a challenging task. The violinist Diez Weismann, for instance, who had found refuge and a teaching post at the State Music Academy in Guatemala, writes:[34]

The violin students who have to undergo a course lasting 8–9

[33] Strub's reference has eluded identification, which suggests that the obliquity may have achieved its goal.

[34] Letter dated 8 September 1935.

years, have so far been tormented with a method [. . .] which required them to play nothing but studies. [. . .] When I gave my first lessons, hardly any of them were able to perform a normal piece of music. [. . .] They are just beginning to grasp the fact that they are supposed to become musicians, not étude-playing automatons.

At the outbreak of World War II my parents made the mistake of moving to Holland, where my father happened to have a number of engagements and which he anticipated would remain neutral, as it had in the First World War; an expectation incidentally, shared in the highest circles of the Dutch government – another instance of child-like naivety in high places.

Initially the German occupation did not produce any far-reaching changes; for instance, Jewish artists were not immediately forbidden to play in public. Some concert promoters decided nevertheless to anticipate developments, as, for example, the management of the Kurhaus Scheveningen where my father had appeared literally hundreds of times during his career. I found a copy of the letter he wrote on that occasion:[35]

It has sometimes happened in the course of my career that concert promoters were afraid that I might *not* play; it has been left to the Maatschappij Scheveningen to produce the first and only case of a promoter fearing that I *would* play. [. . .] Considering all the circumstances, making your U-turn in racial questions a painful surprise not only for myself but for many others, I hereby inform you that I regard it as being below my dignity to hold you to your contract.

This, of course, was only the first of many painful surprises. Matters became worse by the day. As my mother later wrote to Artur and Therese Schnabel after the War:[36]

We were in constant danger of deportation. Twice we were arrested but released both times although the second time we were already in prison prior to being transferred [. . .] to a

---

[35] Dated 25 June 1940.

[36] Undated; part of the letter appears to be missing.

concentration camp [. . .]. A third time we were picked up in a
so-called 'random police round-up' ['Wilde Razzia'] when we
were already in bed, but since this was not a specifically
personal arrest we managed to get rid of the three policemen.
What they did to all of us in Holland is indescribable. One was
no longer permitted to do anything. There were restrictions in
every sphere merely in order to give the authorities an excuse to
arrest or deport people on account of having violated them. We
ourselves were still treated comparatively lightly, but you can't
begin to understand the sadism, the crafty and cunning meanness of the regulations and decrees, and the sadistic pleasure of
those whose job it was to enforce them. Later on it was not even
necessary to transgress any rules in order to suffer deportation.
You were just picked up and that was that.

After my father had received a visa for the USA (still
neutral at the time) but had been unsuccessful five times in
obtaining a German exit permit,[37] he asked to be admitted to
the Court of the Belgian Queen Mother, an enthusiastic
amateur violinist whom he had met on the occasion of his
membership of the jury at the first Ysaÿe competition in
Brussels in 1937. With her my parents would presumably have
been comparatively safe. I have two letters from the Queen
Mother's secretary in 1941 in which he writes that she would
be delighted to see him, but at the same time he draws his
attention to the fact that it would be up to my father to
obtain permits for the journey there – and back. This gentle
put-down killed the idea at birth.

In August my father received, at the suggestion of Ernest
Ansermet, the offer of a post at the Lucerne Conservatoire,
but again an exit permit was refused. Meanwhile my parents
had lost not only their German, but also, for purely technical
reasons, their Hungarian citizenship. This made them 'State-
less Jews', a category in greater danger than any other. Luckily
Ernst von Dohnányi and the violinist Geza Krész succeeded,
against all odds, in getting their Hungarian nationality re-
instated, whereupon the German authorities graciously
granted them an exit visa to Hungary. Once there, it took
them another three months to obtain permission to proceed to

[37] See the letter to Furtwängler on pp. 258–59.

Switzerland, where my father was able to teach and give concerts until his death in 1944.

In Holland and the United States my parents had many faithful friends – too numerous to be mentioned by name – who did for them everything they possibly could. But, of course, they were powerless in resolving the really vital problems. The four men whose intervention – independently of one another – almost certainly saved their lives were Furtwängler, whose letters my father could produce to the authorities; Ansermet, through his intervention in Switzerland; and Dohnányi and Krész, through their successful efforts to regain for them their Hungarian citizenship. To them as well as all the others the family's deep-felt thanks are due.

I am certain that these experiences shortened my father's life. Indeed, during the trip from Holland to Hungary, which took them over devious routes through war-torn Germany, my father suffered a slight heart attack – with no immediate consequences but almost certainly the beginning of his terminal illness. But one cannot be sufficiently grateful for the fact that my parents were spared the horrifying fate of so many other Jews.

XI

CARL FLESCH THE MAN

'One had the gratifying and
reassuring knowledge of being
in the presence of a complete
human being blessed with what
Goethe has called the greatest
gift – personality.'
DR PAUL EGER,
IN HIS MEMORIAL ORATION
FOR CARL FLESCH

I have already mentioned in the Introduction that however
frequently Carl Flesch's name appears this book is not meant
to be a second biography. Rather, it presents information and
impressions gleaned from correspondence and other documents, as well as recollections and conclusions of my own. At
the same time, I wanted to clarify, in the appropriate context,
a number of misconceptions. This I hope to have done. What,
I think, is still missing is a personal sketch of Carl Flesch as a
private individual. His *Memoirs* concentrate on professional
matters; personal details show gaps that can probably be filled
in only by members of the family – as, for instance, his role as
a father.[1]

To understand him, one has to bear in mind three strands in
his mental make-up: he kept professional and private life
strictly separate; he combined in himself – like most of us – a
goodish number of contradictory traits; and he was able to
summon unusually strong will-power and self-control. The
latter could sometimes make him appear cold and unfeeling to

[1]I have described it in chapter XII, pp. 223–42.

outsiders, but this impression was misleading: he was, in fact, a warm if somewhat restrained human being who was best able to express his feeling through music.

His views and life style were thoroughly liberal. There is a remark in his diary that he had had 'no reason to complain about lack of affection from the opposite sex',[2] although I have already stated[3] that female students were taboo – certainly in theory but, as far as I am aware, also in practice, at least in his later years.

He had a wide circle of friends and acquaintances who liked him enormously and enjoyed his company. There was hardly a colleague with whom he was not on amicable terms; many of the younger generation who had not been his pupils sought and received his advice and help with all kinds of professional problems. That he sometimes expresses very critical opinions in his *Memoirs* should not be regarded as a contradiction, but on the contrary as proof of his distinction between the professional and the private sphere. He did not spare himself – his striving after absolute objectivity did not stop short of referring to his own inadequacies.

His undisputed reputation as a teacher meant that many colleagues, violinists and non-violinists alike – Burmester, Dohnányi, Enescu, Huberman, Kreisler, Marteau, Mengelberg, Monteaux, Persinger, to name but a few – referred pupils to him whom they considered either very talented or who were in some cases posing problems with which they felt they were not qualified to cope.

He was always ready to assist colleagues who had fallen on hard times mainly by trying to interest wealthy patrons in their plight. It was this that caused him to found after the First World War, the Hilfsbund für deutsche Musikpflege,[4]

---

[2] Max Dessoir, in his *Buch der Erinnerungen* (*op. cit.*, p. 259), even goes so far as to assert that 'women found him extraordinarily attractive and easily fell for him' ('flogen ihm zu'). I must confess that I believe this to be somewhat exaggerated view of a philosopher and aesthete who was not necessarily fully conversant with the ways of the world in less spiritual questions.

[3] See p. 89.

[4] See pp. 190–91.

which did much to help impoverished musicians. Other instances are his concern for Busoni's widow (as mentioned in a letter to him from the sculptoress Annette Kolb[5]), for Henri Marteau, and in particular, his efforts for Arnold Rosé during the Hitler regime. In this particular case his attitude was certainly different from that of many others. Some of the letters he received give an interesting insight into the reaction of certain people on these occasions. He had, for example asked friends and colleagues in a circular to identify for him some well-to-do music lovers who might be regarded as potential contributors. Not everybody complied with the request, but a few of those who did stipulated that when making an approach to would-be contributors he should not disclose from whom he had received their names and addresses. This, of course, is understandable considering the incessant requests for charitable contributions, particularly in those days. But less comprehensible is the attitude of some people who could well afford a substantial gift but declined or restricted it to a minimum for very unconvincing reasons. A letter from a wealthy business man famed for his undisputedly valuable work for music, for which he had received much publicity and honour (later, in Britain, he was knighted), is significant:

> [. . .] Judging from your circular, Rosé is going to be pensioned and from the further contents he has not put by any savings. Far be it from me to say anything unkind about a great musician like him, especially when he is in this most unfortunate position, but I do feel very strongly that men like him who have had a chance of saving money during a long and successful career, must take the consequences, and personally I feel much more like supporting younger people who have had nothing like the chance of making a career and have had no chance of making any money. It is for these reasons that I enclose a very small cheque – I do not want to say 'no' to anything coming from you.

A letter from Rosé explains the 'unfortunate position':[6]

> [. . .] As you rightly surmise, I have now, after 57 years opera,

[5] Reproduced on p. 80.

[6] Dated 24 March 1938.

56 years quartet and 44 years 'Hofmusikkapelle', been unceremoniously pushed into retirement. I think you know me well enough to believe me if I say that vanity is not part of my mental make-up, but to be written off all of a sudden is inconceivable. I am hoping to receive my full pension from 1 May onwards, but so far I have had no official notification. My few assets have melted to nothing during the inflation, so that I shall have to reduce my standard of living to a more than modest level.

I am in my 75th, my wife in her 70th year – thus one may hope that the pension will be sufficient for our few remaining years. My wife has been in poor health for some considerable time which sadly affects me too, particularly now, but I myself am in good nick and don't even suffer from the notorious tremor,[7] Ho, Ho.

And then, later in the same year:[8]

I am now forced through reasons entirely beyond my control and very much against my own inclination to write to you and tell you that my future living standard will have to be more than modest. [. . .]

If your generous initiative would make it possible for me to receive DM 500 per month, this would indeed mean a relatively carefree existence for my wife and myself. The nursing care essential for her requires great financial sacrifices. If I were to earn additional money by teaching, my pension would be reduced, otherwise I could still work a good deal. [. . .] Please accept my very heartfelt thanks even if your efforts should be in vain.

This does not sound like a man who had squandered his resources. Rosé did not know at the time, of course, that this was only the beginning. But he managed, partly with my father's help, to leave Austria in time. His daughter Alma, on the other hand, had been trapped in Holland by the German invasion and, on 7 August 1942 wrote a farewell letter to my father:

There is no other way of saying goodbye to you – this tells you all. I am going, trying to reach freedom, otherwise I shall perish.

[7] The more descriptive German expression is 'Tatterich'.

[8] Letter dated 9 July 1938.

Alma Rosé's farewell letter to Carl Flesch

At this moment I want to tell you once more – I know that only you made it possible for my father to be living in a free country – nobody in this world could have done more for me [. . .] and I don't have to describe once again what I feel for you. [. . .]

Shall we meet again in this life? God bless you both!

I am told that she was killed in Auschwitz.

My father was a surprising mixture of business sense and naivety. His appearance did not conform to what one expects a member of the artistic profession to look like – strangers would probably have guessed his occupation to be that of a successful banker. But appearances are deceptive: he lost his and my mother's money twice over – once in the German inflation that followed the First World War and then again in the American stock exchange crash of 1929 which moreover, left him with a considerable debt to Mendelssohn & Co., one of the most prestigious German merchant banks. It was way beyond what he could possibly hope to repay; the only way out was to relinquish his Strad in part-settlement. The firm's senior partner, Franz von Mendelssohn, a long-standing friend of the family, declared himself willing to accept this solution. He was, incidentally, himself an excellent amateur violinist (except that he had never learnt how to produce vibrato).[9]

Von Mendelssohn was a banker of the old school – a good business man with a distinguished and highly cultured personality. A hand-written letter to my father shows the interesting combination of all these traits and is, I think, worth preserving for the way in which he tried to do justice to both his firm and a friend in need. I don't know precisely what my father had proposed, but I would assume from the reply that it was the outright sale of his instrument at a higher price than that which Mendelssohn felt able to pay. He therefore suggested a different solution:[10]

My Dear Mr. Flesch,

I have been extremely sorry to note how badly you have been hit by the present crisis, and I can well understand your desire to resolve this difficulty in some way. The suggestion which I want to make in reply to yours is perhaps more suitable under present-day conditions. It has to be anticipated that, if we purchase the violin at the price you are asking, we shall have it on our hands for a very long time, since it is on the cards that prices of old instruments will be adversely affected by the current economic situation in the same way as everything else.

I believe therefore that we should agree to purchase the instrument for $37,500 with the proviso that you retain the right to repurchase it – should it still be in our possession – for the same sum plus notional interest from date of purchase by us. Should we sell it meanwhile for more than $37,500, we will pass to you our whole profit less, again, notional interest. We

---

[9] The family played a prominent part in Berlin musical life. My father's pleas to help an impecunious musician never fell on deaf ears. Von Mendelssohn's daughter Lilly had been a Flesch pupil; she subsequently married the composer Emil Bohnke (see p. 167). A few years later both she and her husband were killed in a motor accident. A letter from Artur Schnabel (17 May 1928) clearly shows how acutely the loss was felt:

The terrible end of the Bohnkes [. . . is a] destruction, a devastation of something for which the future seemed to hold only mellow ripening and no hardship. [. . .] Lilly will be irreplaceable [. . .]. There was no young woman of her background more gifted, ardent, bound up and familiar with what is noble in music. Musical life has lost a most important supporter [. . .].

[10] Letter dated 25 August 1931.

*The wedding of Carl and
Bertha Flesch in 1906*

shall, incidently, be very accommodating when fixing the rate of interest.

In this way you will receive at least $37,500 for your instrument, but in fact any better price which we – or you – could achieve. At the same time we ourselves would not run the risk of acquiring an instrument at the very highest price obtainable under present market conditions, and moreover would not necessarily forgo interest for the period between purchase and sale.

Unfortunately there was no question of re-purchase – my father had to emigrate and make a new start; the instrument was destroyed during an Allied air raid on Berlin. What would be its value today?

My father's diary entry on the loss of his Strad:[11]

It will probably hurt me badly having to part with this inspired piece of wood, for during 25 years it has been my faithful companion, went through many vicissitudes with me and has shared good and bad days. In return, however, I shall now be able to sleep better. Tomorrow I am playing it for the last time.

[11] Dated 5 August 1931.

This was, if memory serves me, also one of the last concerts with Artur Schnabel – the end, for my father, of an epoch.

Since, in spite of his capital losses, my father's earnings did not suffer, he was able to maintain his lifestyle more or less unchanged. In particular, he made sure at all times that his family had everything it needed. As far as I am concerned, he assisted me most generously whenever necessary – in particular at the start of my business career when I, like most refugees, encountered considerable difficulties.

He never showed his worries, always appearing as a man sure of himself and fully in control. I was therefore considerably surprised to find the following entry in his diary around that time:[12]

> For the last 10 years everything I have touched has gone wrong. Market speculation à la hausse during the inflation, practically complete ruin. Through my lucrative contract with the Curtis Institute I succeed in getting back on my feet, but then comes the German stock exchange crash in 1927, and the American one in 1929. I manage to keep my head above water, make a deal with Mendelssohn to pay the majority of my debts by sacrificing my Strad – and now, to crown it all, my daughter's husband is ruined [he was bankrupted by the devaluation of sterling].
>
> I have lived through terrible days. Professionally I am not happy either – most people have other worries than to take violin lessons. My reserves are infinitesimal – I am curious how I shall manage to get through these 'great' times. I shall still be satisfied if I can retain my good health and continue to work. Of course, the dream of a care-free comfortable old age is vanishing before my very eyes. I shall have to toil until the end of my days.

This prediction came true, but I doubt that he regarded it as a hardship; rather the contrary. Apart from finding – as he wrote to me himself – his renewed concert activities at least as successful as previously, he was an impassioned teacher, and it was his declared intention to create a new generation of young Swiss violinists. And I believe, he would have done so if he had been spared. He loved work and used to say that idling on

[12] Dated 6 October 1931.

*My father's Stradivarius,
sold to the bankers
Mendelssohn and Co. in
1931*

holiday got on his nerves – a trait I have inherited from him and which I could well have done without.

But his needs went deeper:[13]

> If I do not have the feeling at the end of a day that I have made progress in some way, I don't feel happy within myself. The illusion of doing it, or becoming, better is an absolute necessity for my mental equilibrium. Whether or not my feeling is justified is beside the point.

The diary bears witness to some other, perhaps less important, matters that occupied him; for instance:[14]

> When one loves beauty as much as I do, it is a misfortune to be ugly oneself. But on the other hand it is fortunate that one only realises this when one sees onself in a mirror – on the wall or in the eyes of another who does not return one's love.

[13] Diary entry, probably for 27 September 1931.

[14] *Ibid.*

In this respect he seems to have suffered from a certain inferiority complex early on. With advancing years this became more and more unjustified, for he could be called attractive and impressive-looking. In his youth, on the other hand, I am bound to say that his fears may well have had some substance.[15]

I have an amusing letter dated 1907 from a Lausanne concert promoter; apparently this man had asked for photos and my father had sent him a selection, probably accompanied by a few humorously 'apologetic' remarks about his looks:

> Dear Friend, the pictures have arrived. Don't take the matter too much to heart – your looks are not your fault and the committee will overlook the matter this time – although our contracts with soloists contain a clause to the effect that they have to make the Lausanne and Geneva finishing school girls fall in love with them.

I wish to state my belief, purely for the sake of my family's honour, that, had it come to the crunch, my father would most likely have been able to comply with this condition to everybody's satisfaction – in spite of his looks.

By and large he was not a friend of publicity and in this respect, if anything, somewhat inept with it. I remember, for instance, a Berlin radio station in the 1930s announcing a broadcast by my father as 'Violin Recital by Carl Flesch'. I drew his attention to the fact that, in contrast to his own, wireless concerts by other artists were often announced under the far more intriguing heading 'Mischa Elman (or whoever) plays!' I suggested that he insist on a similar billing, which he did successfully; but it would never have occurred to him without prompting.

He felt a certain contempt for colleagues who were particularly skillful in this sphere. I heard him remark for instance, with some astonished disbelief in his voice, about Joseph Szigeti: 'You know, he has an address book which contains the names of his acquaintances all over the world. When he knows that he will be appearing in a certain city, he alerts those living

---

[15] The photograph on p. 105 may or may not confirm this. At any rate, he seems at the time to have had no lack of success with the opposite sex.

Ginette Neveu and Carl Flesch

there of his coming beforehand'. He was of the opinion that it was for the public to seek out artist; not vice versa.[16]

He possessed a very strong sense of loyalty. In the early

[16] I must confess that I cannot agree with him. I see no reason that an artist should not follow normal business practice in the pursuit of his profession. My father's views on the subject do him credit but were, to my mind, unnecessarily stringent. But these differences – never discussed, to my knowledge – did not affect the friendship between the two men.

My parents with my wife around 1937

1930s his friend Georg Bernhard[17] was involved in a sensational libel suit with the head of his paper's proprietors, the very powerful Ullstein Verlag; he consequently had a very bad press. His reply[18] to a letter from my father allows its contents to be easily guessed:

[17] See pp. 203–5.
[18] Dated 27 July 1930.

You can't imagine how good it feels to get a letter such as yours at a time like this. One realises that one still has one or two friends left after all. It is hard to credit (I have got used to it and can laugh about it now) how even close friends become worried and prefer for the time being to observe developments from a distance. All the more pleasing that you are one of those who in addition to intelligence and friendship possess also the courage of their convictions.

And a letter from the conductor Ernst Kunwald, who left Berlin in 1912:[19]

[. . .] your note was the only sign of sympathy I received on my departure from the literally hundreds of soloists whom I had accompanied in concerts [. . .].

He was an excellent raconteur, not least of humorous anecdotes against himself. Whether it is true that – as Max Rostal alleges – he occasionally suggested an improved version of a joke someone else told him, I do not know; it never happened to me, anyway. Perhaps he did it only in the case of pupils, extending, as it were, his urge to teach from the professional into the private sphere, much though he usually kept the two apart.

His manifold activities did not mean at all that, as far as his time allowed, he neglected his role as a family man or was not assured of his wife's and children's love and affection. This is evident with moving clarity from letters which my mother wrote to me during the first year after his death:

Of course, my real life is over. You know yourself what he was to me and how my whole life revolved around him. But I really believe that he himself it was who gave me the strength to bear the present situation.

The knowledge that his death was peaceful and without suffering is my greatest consolation. We must be grateful that he was able to fulfil his tasks and live his life so successfully and well, spreading happiness among all who knew him and living on in their hearts.

I miss him more every day. [. . .] you can't imagine the loneliness his death is causing me. I was always used, in

---

[19] Dated 16 May 1912.

everything I did, to think of him first – and now I can't do anything for him [. . .] ever again.

On every walk I have the feeling that he is next to me and it is still impossible for me to come to terms with the fact that I shall never see him again.

However, I am glad that I can look back on a life that I am sure was happier and more beautiful than that of most others.

These are not the words of a wife who was neglected by her husband. It shows that with all his peculiarities and faults – and who could claim to be without them? – he was, in the last resort as successful in his personal relationships as in his art. As far as I am concerned, I can fully confirm this.

XII

CHILDREN OF FAMOUS PARENTS

'When we have finished
praising famous men, we
should think of mourning for
their children'
D. J. ENRIGHT

'I am sure you must be very proud of your father.' This is one of the well-meaning remarks frequently made to children of famous men, as, with obvious modification, to those of famous women. I was never quite certain how to react: 'Yes' might have sounded conceited, 'No' disloyal towards the father and impolite to the speaker whom one might have caused embarrassment. Moreover it would have been untrue – of course, one was 'proud' but, not necessarily in the sense the questioner presumably had in mind; for one was used to accepting parental fame as a matter of course.

I myself am in no doubt that a famous father will usually have an unfavourable effect on his children's development in later life.[1]

Whilst the children are young, their father's position is distinctly pleasant for them and moreover frequently carries

---

[1] Or, more accurately perhaps, 'more unfavourable'. Children of non-famous parents frequently have their difficulties, too. Philip Larkin has stated the problem accurately and concisely, even if perhaps not in words commonly associated with a poet of national standing:

They fuck you up, your mum and dad.
They may not mean to, but they do.
They fill you with the faults they had
And add some extra, just for you.

'This be the Verse', *High Windows*, Faber and Faber, London, 1976.

with it certain advantages. The snags show up only later, rather like having eaten too many sweets as a child. Very tasty but more often than not bad for teeth and figure; and possibly even triggering off an addiction.

Surprisingly little seems to have been written about this subject, disregarding biographies by offspring about their famous forbears. But these, for obvious reasons, usually concentrate on one person only and are frequently pretty one-sided – some in a positive, others in a negative sense.[2] This is not what I have in mind here. I would like to try to look at the subject as objectively as I can, and in some depth, basing my opinions on my own experience. First, however, there are some problems of definition.

Let us take the father first. Famous in what sphere? As a well-known author, actor, musician, leading industrialist – i.e., in a profession where his position is not normally subject to sudden and marked fluctuations? As a pop star whose meteoric rise is usually followed by an equally rapid decline? As a sportsman who has literally to fight for success every time? As a politician whose job and reputation notoriously can be subject to decisive changes and ferocious attacks? All these cases are completely different, but they have one common denominator – they are outside the norm.

Nor is there any uniformity in the make-up and character of the children. Some develop into intolerably puffed-up self-important pests; others go to the other extreme and withdraw into themselves; if they possess very wealthy parents they may develop into money-snobs or come to the conclusion that they don't have to make an effort, since there will always be abundant money available; politicians' children may become their father's fanatical followers or opponents – in brief, the possible variations are practically unlimited.

But at the same time we should not forget that many of these children are normal, well-behaved and destined to mature into successful, well-adjusted adults. I once asked Igor Oistrakh what effect his father's fame had had on his career.

---

[2] Probably more often the latter, at least in the opinion of Bernard Levin, who summed up his views in the title of one of his *Times* articles: 'Why bare these old bones?'

I expected the customary moan – 'Terrible, everything was twice as difficult for me as for others!' Instead, he replied: 'Marvellous; it helped me no end'. This made me realise that circumstances are not always as clear-cut as one might think.

Since what I am writing about is based on my own childhood, I can obviously deal with only a strictly circumscribed area of the problem: a father in a secure position, which all the same depended to some extent on his *ad hoc* performances as well as public opinion; and a son (myself) endowed, if my own assessment is half-way correct, by and large with a fairly normal, modest character and average intelligence who never intended, nor was subjected to the least pressure, to follow in his father's footsteps. Thus mine is a limited, but in its way not untypical, case which in addition to some purely personal experiences has led me to a few conclusions which I believe to be of more general validity.

The unfavourable influence of famous fathers on their children's future development does by no means necessarily prove that they have been 'bad parents', certainly not in the sense of the children having suffered any material deprivation – money is, in these families, usually no object. It is the psychological aspect that is more interesting. One has to admit, of course, that nobody seems as yet to have discovered what are in fact 'good' parents. An experienced psychologist once told me: 'We have learned by now how to avoid certain education errors and mistakes, but so far we don't know how to bring up our children *correctly*'. If this applies to 'normal' parents, how much more to famous ones?

I personally am convinced that for a number of reasons a damaging influence is the almost inescapable result of parental prominence.

As long as we are babies or very small children we regard our parents as all-knowing and all-powerful. Gradually we begin to recognise that there is more – or should I say, less – to it than we originally assumed and that they, too, have their own peculiarities and faults; if we play our cards right we may even outwit them on occasions. The next phase is puberty with all its difficulties and conflicts, and thereafter, if we are lucky, a relationship of genuine affection on equal terms.

With children of famous parents development frequently takes a different course. The small child's belief in its all-knowing parents persists for far longer, because it is not only continuously being confirmed but even strengthened by outsiders. And this does have a basis in reality because, after all, the parent in question happens to be above the norm. Sons usually start at an early age to compare themselves with their fathers, trying to emulate them. If the father happens to be (in the widest sense of the word) a 'superman', the comparison is frequently sufficiently daunting for the child to arrive at the conclusion that there is no point in competing with so superior a being; it would be better and easier to give up the unequal struggle from the outset. If this attitude were confined to the relationship with the father, it would be bad enough but it can easily extend to all the child's activities, with sometimes near-catastrophic results.

During puberty, a period beset with an abundance of complications at the best of times, this state of affairs can become more acute – or it may change into the very opposite. This is fertile ground for the development of difficulties. Although their roots are basically in the child's own nature, they are augmented by the practical effects exerted on family life by the father's professional situation.

He has a public position of higher-than-average distinction. The more important it is, the more time and energy it is bound to consume, and these commodities are not inexhaustible. This poses a dilemma: how to divide them between family and profession? In most cases, the answer is a foregone conclusion.

Of course, there are no firm rules on how much time a father should 'expend' on his children; this depends on many factors which vary with individual circumstances. Too much can be as bad as too little. It is not easy to find the correct mean, but we may safely assume that with a prominent parent 'too little' is the norm.

Here, of course, we encounter a complicating factor I have already referred to.[3] There are quite a number of professions

[3] See pp. 52–55.

Flesch, father and son, around 1921

potentially far more important, more responsible, more labour-intensive than that of an artist – not least that of a medical man. But curiously enough, the conflict between family and professional life is in these cases usually (not always!) less marked. There is, to my knowledge, no clear-cut answer to this apparent contradiction. I suspect, however, that it may lie in the amount of public limelight surrounding the respective professions.

There is yet another facet whose existence I realised only when reading one of my father's diary entries: 'My feelings for my pupils are those of a father, and *like him* [my italics] it is not given to me to show them openly'.[4] This inhibition was something which, curiously enough, he considered normal for fathers. One might regard this as a strictly personal trait – and indeed, as I have mentioned elsewhere, he did find it difficult to show his feelings, except through his music. But might this not have a more general application to artists? If you have, as part of your job, to show your feelings publicly to an abnormally large extent, you may not have 'sufficient' left over

---

[4] Entry probably for 18 September 1931.

for, as it were, normal consumption; in other words, affection and feelings, or rather their outlets, may be limited in the same way as time and energy. The apparent contradiction in many actors (and politicians) wearing their hearts on their sleeves does not necessarily disprove this theory: their job is uttering 'words'; these represent their public image (which does not have to correspond to their true nature). A musician's image is conveyed through his music which he cannot express in words.

My father's difficulty in showing his feelings did not, of course, strike me as in the least unusual at the time. Demonstrative affection was up to my mother and simply not expected of him. In no way was it regarded by us as lack of love. To be with him was almost invariably a pleasure, because he had a lot of interesting things to say and a marked sense of humour.

He exerted a strong natural authority and hardly ever found it necessary to so much as raise his voice. Corporal punishment even in its mildest form was unnecessary and therefore unknown (and, of course, it might have damaged his hands!)

Educational questions as such were, again, my mother's or, in our early youth, our governess' department. His own (very rarely applied) educational methods could sometimes be called a little eccentric. Everybody knows the story – hopefully entirely untrue – of the father who asks his son to jump off a high wall; he would catch him. The son jumps but the father makes no effort to keep his promise, in order, so he says, to demonstrate to his son that no-one should rely on anybody but himself. On one occasion this 'principle' seemed to appeal to my father though happily in a form rather less dangerous to life and limb. Since I had acquired a knowledge of shorthand and typing at an early age, I frequently acted as his secretary and from time to time submitted an 'invoice' covering the agreed remuneration. Once, in order to save time, I submitted the bill already receipted, upon which my father declared that he would not make any payment in order to teach me not to trust other people so easily. It took quite some persuasion to disabuse him of his glorious idea.

Sexual matters were not discussed with us children. When I was thirteen years old and my father started spending several months in the United States every year, he felt it incumbent upon himself to acquaint me with the facts of life. But the task was obviously embarrassing for him. He asked me to accompany him on a walk and talked at length about the dangers to young men 'going with strange women'. I realised, of course, what he was driving at and his difficulty in getting to the point. He could have saved himself the embarrassment, for like most boys of that age I was, through talks with my school-mates (schools at that time offered no other form of sex education), already quite familiar with these matters. On the other hand, I felt that confirmation of what I had learnt, coming from such an authoritative source, could do no harm; moreover, I was sufficiently modest to visualise the possibility of my still having to learn one or two minor details. I therefore eventually interrupted him, asking innocently: 'But Daddy, how does one actually do it?' His reply, for all its practical value, belongs in my opinion in the Lie-back-and-think-of-England class: 'Nature will tell you at the right time'. This said, we turned for home, he with the satisfied feeling of a difficult job well done, I of having been slightly let down.

The diary that he kept for about eighteen months is interesting in this connection: it mentions family and private matters only twice, once when my sister's husband, a banker, went bankrupt on account of the sterling devaluation, and the second time when our little dog had been taken to a bitch in heat but had not managed to perform his allotted task (Nature had told him at the right time what to do, but he had been too excited to apply this knowledge successfully).

So, in the midst of quite a number of original and profound opinions about art, modern music and colleagues, there is a report about the impotence of a little dog. Talk about a contradictory character! In fairness, I should mention that he added a thought which today sounds commonplace but at the time may have been more novel: 'Could it be true that in lovemaking, too, technique is of surpassing importance?' This still leaves the question of the virtual non-existence of references to his family. Yet there was some logic behind it: the virtual disregard of domestic matters was an expression of his propensity not only to keep private and professional life strictly apart, but also to regard the former as a matter of course and therefore usually not sufficiently interesting to be specifically referred to. The same tendency shows in his *Memoirs* which contain next to nothing about his family, with the exception of his parents, to whom he devotes several pages, though I think mainly in order to demonstrate the development of his own character. The only mention of us children can be found in a quotation from a letter from his friend Julius Röntgen on the occasion of my and my twin brother's birth: Röntgen commented on my father's particular aptitude for double stops. Apart from this we once served as publicity material: during his first American concert tour in 1914 there appeared a long illustrated article in a New York paper about the world-shattering fact that three famous violinists had produced twins – Kubelík, Kneisel and Flesch.[5] Apart from this I can't remember a single instance in which the family played any part in his professional life.[6]

The distinction between profession and family occasionally took somewhat extreme forms. During the first months of the war, for instance, I received a letter from Holland, at the time still neutral, in which he expressed his surprise, indeed consternation, that my sister and her husband, who at that time were living in Paris, should have visited Jacques Thibaud in the Green Room after one of his concerts. Thibaud was one of his oldest friends. They both had studied with Marsick and, although we children knew him only slightly, he had been our house guest in Berlin a number of times. One would therefore have thought that a Green Room visit by a member of the Flesch family would be a fairly self-evident courtesy; I am certain that my father would have welcomed it in the reverse case. Nor had he ever shown any signs of wishing to keep his family away from his colleagues. But in his subconscious mind Thibaud apparently belonged into an entirely different compartment, which he was accustomed to seeing entered only in his presence. Before I could write to him about it – for

---

[5] See p. 232.

[6] Max Rostal, in a speech during his centenary celebrations, called him 'the Freud of the violin' (see note 21 on p. 86). I wonder what Freud would have made of his psychological make-up?

Enescu, Thibaud and Flesch playing the Vivaldi Concerto for Three Violins at a rehearsal for a concert in memory of their teacher, Martin-Pierre-Joseph Marsick, in 1933

the matter really intrigued me – Holland was invaded by the German army and we had more pressing problems.

His peculiar attitude in this case certainly did not denote any lack of concern for us – quite the contrary. Immediately after the Dutch armistice one of his first letters was to an Italian pupil asking her to give us the message that both my mother and he were alright, but that they were very anxious for news about us. Our well-being was more important to him than his own.

However famous the father, sooner or later the son has to adopt a profession of his own. If it is the same as his father's, open comparisons are unavoidable and go all too frequently – rightly or wrongly – against the younger generation (people seem to love to say: 'Well, of course, there is no comparison with the old man!') But even in a different profession there is the possibility of an in-built substantial handicap, because usually the son's job does not entail any public acknow-ledgement, something which played such an important part in

*The Flesch family around
1913, the author on the
left knee of his father*

the father's activities. It can lead to the son regarding his
own profession as inferior by comparison. He has the shining
example continually before him but – at least in his own
estimation – always tantalisingly out of reach. This can be
most discouraging even if the son, in his own sphere, does
excellent although 'unsung' work. Whatever he undertakes is
subjectively devalued. The path towards release from this
feeling, if it leads anywhere at all, is long and stony.

Of course, there are exceptions, but the number of cases in
which children do not equal their famous parents' successes,
but achieve 'only' average marks – or less – is far larger. I once
toyed with the idea of conducting systematic interviews with
my (what shall I call them?) 'fellow sufferers', with a view to
publishing them. I soon discarded the plan. You cannot
possibly ask other people – some of them friends – to reveal
their innermost feelings with the declared intention of demon-
strating that they are or were inferior, even if only in their own
eyes!

Hence I restricted myself to occasional researches as a
private hobby. In almost every case my preconceived notion

was amply confirmed. I have already mentioned Igor Oistrakh, one of the exceptions. Another is Wolfgang Stresemann, with whom I once had the opportunity briefly to allude to the question. There can of course, be no doubt that the position of his father as one of the most important and controversial German inter-war statesmen must have caused him enormous problems in his youth. But he was one of the cases whose own career as manager of the Berlin Philharmonic Orchestra brought him real satisfaction, honour and success.

Many instances are known of famous parents' children starting on a downward path, becoming junkies, crooks or simply drop-outs. But I doubt that their number is larger than that of offspring of 'normal' families. Presumably they just have more news value and their cases are therefore more readily taken up by the press.

Another significant point is the fact that at some time you can become so absorbed by the father's profession that you begin to attach comparatively too little importance to your own affairs and interests. You no longer regard yourself as an independent personality but merely as the 'son of'. You live as it were second-hand. Here again the danger is that you take this attitude into later life when it becomes disproportionally difficult to kick the habit. I experienced an amusing example of this with my life-long friend Karl Ulrich Schnabel, like his father a pianist, and a very good one. (Please note that I have avoided the expression 'son of Artur Schnabel'!). He once presented me to some of his friends with the words: 'May I introduce the son of Carl Flesch'. We were, at the time, both pushing fifty and both our fathers had been dead for a long time.

At this point I would like to make a plea on behalf of all the offspring of parents who were prominent in the fairly distant past, so that their names are no longer generally known to the present generation. My request is addressed to those who introduce us to acquaintances of theirs and then feel constrained to add: 'Son of the famous. . . '. The recipient of this information frequently does not have the faintest idea who 'the famous' is or was let alone why he should have been famous at all. He will desparately try to hide his ignorance in order to avoid seeming impolite or disclosing a serious gap in his education. It would often be funny were it not at the same time so very embarrassing for all present, most of all of course the 'son of the famous. . . '.

What can you do to save the situation? Since for me this way of being introduced to strangers is always unwelcome, irrespective of whether the name means anything to them or not, I use the same ploy in either case: 'Not any merit of mine. I am only the son. At least, as far as I know'. This remark, in the worst possible taste and an entirely unjustified slur on my late mother's reputation, usually leads to relieved laughter, enabling everybody to skate over the embarrassing situation.

A man who obviously knew the problem and dealt with it in the humorous manner typical of him, was the pianist Moritz Rosenthal.[7] My sister had, as a young girl, an autograph album entries to which were restricted to contributions from really important people. It contained a number of very intriguing items and it is a real pity that it got lost during the War. But Rosenthal's entry has remained in my memory: 'For Miss Hanni Flesch, the daughter of the famous violinist – and herself'.

But even if you are not introduced as the 'son of. . .', awkward situations can arise – if, for instance, you have achieved a venerable age yourself. So it happened to me once that a man to whom I was being introduced expressed his pleasure at making my acquaintance with the words: 'Very honoured to meet you, Sir; you are a legend in your own lifetime!' He was obviously under the impression of having my father before him. Despite my in-born tact, this did go too far! Deeply hurt, I drew his attention to the fact that I had not yet reached the age of 114, whatever my looks.

It is well known, though, that we ourselves are the last person to realise how old we have become: in England because policemen are getting ever younger; elsewhere that others start talking more and more softly. If you don't notice it yourself, kind friends are not slow to draw your attention to it. Some years ago I· contributed a prize to the Carl Flesch Violin

---

[7] Once he alleged that a man had been arrested at a concert for snoring too loudly. 'But surely, that's no crime?' somebody objected. Rosenthal: 'True, but he kept the audience awake'.

Competition in London. The programme called it 'Prize donated by Carl Flesch jun.' 'Who is Carl Flesch jun.?' was the immediate question from a long-standing acquaintance.

The most emphatic manner in which my age was brought home to me was when a mutual acquaintance said to me: 'I met Mr. X. the other day. He asked to be remembered to you.' 'Oh, is he still alive?' I asked, not having seen him for quite some time. Short pause, then: 'That is precisely what he asked me about you'.

I have already explained that children of famous people often consider the affairs of the latter as far more important and interesting than their own. Unquestionably, I was a case in point. As I have said, my father frequently made use of my secretarial skills, usually on Sunday mornings. This substantially curtailed my free time although that did not bother me in the slightest. And I am certain that money, though welcome, was a secondary consideration. My remuneration was one pfennig per type-written line; shorthand came free. (I must admit, though, that my letter contained more than the normal number of new paragraphs: half-lines were paid in full.)

At the same time I proof-read the whole of Volume I of my father's *Art of Violin Playing*, which was first published in 1923. The day on which I started this job is significant: Christmas Eve. We children had just received our presents (which in Germany are given on the evening preceding Christmas Day) when my father asked me to come with him to his study. Once there, he took from his desk the first proofs, which had arrived the same morning, and started with my help to compare them with the original manuscript.

One might assume that a twelve-year old boy would have liked, on this day of all days, to examine his presents or leaf through his new books. No way! The idea that I might prefer this occurred neither to me nor to him; he did not even ask whether I was willing to help – he considered it a matter of course.

And this is, I believe, characteristic of the majority of prominent people. They regard their work less as a profession than as a calling which has priority over everything else. And the family goes entirely along with this – not from any pressure but from conviction. In a 'normal' household one would have expected the mother to take the father to one side reproving him, with something like 'For goodness' sake, stop working and, if you can't, at least leave the boy alone today'. But this did not occur to anybody, nor would I have welcomed it. For I was most happy to do the work and even remember how hurt I was when a few years later proof-reading for the second volume was transferred to my sister who had, on leaving school, attended a commercial college. I may be wrong, but I can't remember that I ever received, or expected, any payment for this task.

I am certain that this attitude is not an isolated case, but typical of many 'artists' children'. I can offer an example which is very unimportant in itself but I think highly significant in this context. Many years later, as an adult and long after my father's death, I had occasion to go to the Green Room to congratulate a very famous artist after his concert. On entering I saw his son, of about the age I must have been in 1922, engaged in putting his father's violin back into its case. His facial expression, his whole demeanour made me think of a sacred act carried out by a devoted priest. Immediately and automatically I was able to enter into that boy's train of thought as if it had been my own: there was nothing more important than helping the father in his work; it put everything else in the shade.

But there was more. With surprise and amusement I suddenly realised that, for a split second, I had been intensely jealous of that boy: *I* had never been allowed to put my father's violin away; all I had been permitted to do was to carry it occasionally in its case. Why this preferential treatment? The unshakable dogma of the famous father's activities surpassing in importance everything else becomes so firmly embedded in the child's mind that it remains fixed in the subconscious and surfaces when one least expects it.

This perception of the importance of the work of one's parent and his (or her) unconditional concentration on it is something with which, in principle, I can't quarrel even today. There are things which only he is able to do – this is after all the reason for his outstanding position. Matters concerning daily life which others can deal with just as well if not better, or which offer less dramatic material, are delegated; and this often includes, whether one wants to admit it or not, dealing with the children, unless there are some really important problems to tackle.

Needless to say, this view is usually indignantly refuted by the parents concerned. Politicians in particular think they have to prove that they are, on the one hand, very special, but on the other that they have exactly the same interests as 'ordinary' people – their voters – and that they therefore possess first-hand knowledge and understanding of their everyday problems and activities. So Mrs Thatcher allegedly prepares breakfast every morning with her own hands; President Truman – even less believably – washed his own socks every evening because this was what he had been taught at his mother's knee; other statesmen build sandcastles with their children at the seaside, etc., etc. The wife of Harold Wilson, when he was Prime Minister, said to him on an occasion when he was helping her with the dishes: 'I hope you'll do this in future even when there are no press photographers about'.

Why all this hypocritical cant? You feel tempted to say to these people what you usually want to reply to a policeman (but rarely do) who is about to book you for having parked on the wrong side of the road: 'Haven't you anything better to do?' For policemen the answer may well be 'No', for important people it is usually 'Yes'. They have, whether they want to admit it or not, a duty-conflict which is insoluble in their situation. If they want to perform all their paternal duties, i.e., devote more time to their children, they will usually have to forgo becoming or remaining famous. There are precedents for this, but usually in the case of mothers: famous actresses, for example, interrupting their careers until they have safely brought up their children. That the situation never seems to apply to fathers appears to me to be significant.

The fact that I noticed my schoolmates' parents taking a more active interest in their children and their friends did not change my views. Possibly I was, without consciously thinking about it, even surprised that these fathers had so much time at their disposal for these comparatively minor matters. Clearly, they did not have anything else very important to do. In other words, far from feeling neglected, I looked down, in all innocence, on parents who showed more interest in the day-to-day affairs of their children.

I remember a school friend who occasionally visited me at home. One day he explained to me that he would rather not come to me that afternoon because he was having a violin lesson and would therefore be having his fiddle with him. 'I would not like your father to ask me to play something for him.' The idea that my father would do this – or in fact appear anywhere near the scene – struck me as extremely funny. I was able to reassure him that this simply would not happen; it seemed to surprise him.

One phrase my father sometimes used has remained with me from my earliest childhood: 'In case of fire, first the violin, then the children'. Of course, it was quite clear to all of us that this was meant as a joke and that, if it ever came to it, there was no doubt who was going to have priority. But I could well imagine that my father would have himself taken the violin and have called out to my mother: 'You look after the children!' This, too, we considered self-evident; after all, we had legs, the violin had not, so that we would be able to move under our own steam should the need arise. But whenever I retailed this saying to acquaintances, I noticed to my surprise that they did not see the joke at all but found my father's remark rather strange.

I think I have made it clear that in my opinion famous parents' children do not consciously suffer from neglect in their youth. Hence this, in isolation, cannot be the reason for any later difficulties. Moreover, the situation offers sufficient advantages providing ample compensation for any possible feeling of neglect: the possibility of impressing one's friends, for instance, or the contact with famous people who visit the parental home. This, incidentally, is not being regarded as anything special. I have mentioned elsewhere my brother's contemptuous remark on an occasion when we were told that we would not be allowed to be present at supper one evening because there was going to be a dinner party: 'But who is coming after all – just Kreisler, Schnabel, Furtwängler. . . '.

Had I been endowed with more foresight, I would no doubt have kept a diary into which I would have entered all the interesting pearls of wisdom which incessantly fell from the

A letter to Carl Flesch from George Enescu in which he presents, and praises, a young violinist, Arlie Furman. The postscript promises a copy of Enescu's Third Violin Sonata as soon as it is published

lips of those celebrities. But perhaps the omission is not entirely my own fault. These people, disregarding, of course, their special gifts, were rarely more weighty than their less famous contemporaries. In most cases, therefore, I am sorry to say I can't lay claim to remembering anything particularly profound.

The only thing I recall of a visit by Enescu, for instance, is his knack of reproducing the 'Ride of the Valkyries' by means of rather rude noises produced with his hands. I never heard him play the violin except on the wireless. Yet I know from report by Norbert Brainin, first violin of the Amadeus Quartet, that a phenomenal memory enabled him to play new compositions by heart after one single hearing, and similarly that he could spontaneously transpose most Beethoven quartets for the piano.

Of the American conductor and arranger Sam Franco I recall a present to my parents in the shape of a particularly beautiful corkscrew whose grip consisted of an elephant tusk with a silver plaque engraved with an ornate 'F'. We were all very impressed by this largesse until my father remembered that they shared the same initial.

Of a well-known musician – no name, for obvious reasons – I recall the reply to my father's question 'Did you come per pedes?': 'No, on foot'. The fact that he had a lisp made his answer – 'Nein, zu Fuss' – doubly amusing.

I remember one of my father's well-known colleagues – I genuinely can't recall his name – visiting us in Baden-Baden; it was almost impossible to convince him that it would be quite safe to leave his violin at our house instead of taking it on a three-hour walking tour. And I recall a get-together of musicians who decided to play quartets with instruments exchanged. My father failed dismally with the cello, whereas Piatigorsky acquitted himself well by means of playing the violin like a viola da gamba. None of this can lay claim to the least importance.

I would not like to omit, though, mention of a Heifetz visit which was to have an important effect on my own future. There was to be private quartet playing, with Max Rostal and his first wife, the excellent cellist Sela Trau, as participants. Events of this nature always took place strictly *en famille*, and excluding any strangers, so that the participants should not feel under any constraint. Chamber music with Heifetz was something special even in our home and I asked for permission to invite a young lady in whom I was strongly interested. 'But, Carl, surely you know – family only'. There was nothing for it – we had to get engaged. For me it was the best possible result of a chamber-music evening: our marriage lasted for almost 49 years until my wife tragically succumbed to a long illness.

I have often been asked whether the fact that my father

One of the last pictures of Carl Flesch,
taken in Lucerne in 1944

devoted more time and care to his pupils than he expended on his children made me jealous. Possibly I am in this respect different from other artists' children, but I can truthfully answer this question in the negative. Almost the contrary: I identified his pupils with himself – they represented an important part of his work and an outstanding student was an indication of his success. Their training was something which – other than his children's education – he could not leave to anybody else. The fact that I myself had no ambitions to become a violinist may have played its part.

For the same reason I do not suppose that his pupils regarded me as their competitior either. Anyway, I was on good terms with those whom I knew personally. They no doubt felt that it could not hurt to maintain cordial relations with their teacher's son. This could have led to interesting developments with female pupils. Unfortunately I was in no doubt about the probability of most such approaches being made not on account of my own charms, but for more worldly reasons. At this particular point identification with my father ceased. Today, having lost part of my idealism, I could kick myself when I think of the opportunities I missed.

Negative effects of my father's position were very few in my youth – although there was possibly a certain amount of worry that my parents might look down on my friends because many did not come from families as prominent as mine. I believe that my fears were groundless if only because my parents did not evince much interest in my friends anyway.

Unfavourable concert notices would undoubtedly have been traumatic for me, but the simple fact is that I just can't remember any. Those I read were by and large always excellent, though I recall one occasion when at the end of a chamber-music concert I heard a listener make a derogatory remark about my father's playing. I was deeply surprised and quite shocked – a sign of how very much this sort of thing was outside my experience.

In brief, then, I regard famous parents as a pleasant experience for young children but as a definite pain in the neck in later years. Usually the children simply are not their father's first priority. But this is an unavoidable result of the parent's prominent position – a fact of life.

When I became a father myself, I decided to bring up my children in such a way that there would not be the slightest risk of their personal development being adversely affected by my appearing as anyone special. I intended that they should see me from their earliest youth onwards as the person I was – someone with his full share of faults and weaknesses. In this way I hoped to spare them the difficulties to which I myself had been exposed.

I am glad to be able to report that my and my wife's efforts in this respect were crowned with success exceeding my wildest expectations. They never suffered in the slightest from the 'famous-parent-syndrome' – rather, if anything, the opposite – and in consequence grew into well-adjusted, successful adulthood. And after all, who could wish for a better result of his educational endeavours?

XIII
ARTISTS' WIVES

'There is no higher praise of a
wife than not talking about
her.'
CHINESE PROVERB

I should like to offer a few comments about artists' wives, but,
since it is my intention to write only on matters within my own
experience, I shall be silent about female artists' husbands – a
situation entirely outside my personal knowledge.

Most wives of busy and successful men regard it as one of
their main tasks, even if they are professionally active themselves, to spare their husbands mundane, day-to-day problems
so that they may concentrate on more important issues, and to
give them what moral support they can in the face of
occasional unavoidable vicissitudes.

Many will do more: they look after the social side with a
view to advancing their husband's professional career, or even
work in the spouse's business themselves. It is in this respect
that they are decisively different from artists' wives: although
the latter can offer hospitality to important and powerful
people, there is one thing they cannot do – 'help in the
business'. Of course, they can see to it that his wardrobe is
always in tip-top condition, with well-pressed tails and clean
shirts readily available, and arrange for plane tickets, hotel
reservations, passports. But when it comes to the public
performance itself, they just have to grin and bear it. They
cannot contribute, not even by influencing public opinion; the
husband has to rely entirely on his own efforts.

This enforced passivity can result in attitudes which differ
between individuals, but most artists' wives have one thing in

common: an over-reaction to what (for want of a better word) I am tempted to call their 'impotence'. This often takes the form of fierce and unconditional loyalty and over-protectiveness, which is sometimes regarded by outsiders as overdone, even annoying or ridiculous. As long as the husbands are at the top, this matters little even if some wives allow their spouse's success to go to their heads. But there are few, if any, artists who do not from time to time strike a critical patch; even a Kreisler could occasionally be at the wrong end of a devastating press review.[1] Moreover many interpreters simply cannot remain at their peak indefinitely. New names, new 'sensations' appear, threatening to over-shadow the existing ones. These are the predicaments that have the most marked effect on their wives.

It does not necessarily make any difference whether the adverse situation is real or imagined. The enthusiastic praise of another artist may already be perceived as an indirect attack. This can sometimes develop into an exaggerated aversion towards all 'competitors'.

These wives – nuisance though they may be on occasions – deserve sympathy rather than the opposite. For their attitude is in most instances the underestandable reaction to their enforced passivity. But in extreme cases they are accused of having 'spoilt their husband's career'. Of course, it can happen that wives make their husbands unhappy (and vice versa) and even that this affects the injured party's professional life – but in the case of artists, to a lesser extent, I believe, than in many other walks of life. For since wives can do so little to influence their artist husbands' careers beneficially, there is no reason to suppose that they can do it much harm either. Moreover, a musician has the advantage of being able to take refuge in a place to which his wife cannot follow him: the concert platform, facing his public – whom she can hardly ever influence, however unreasonable her behaviour.

A typical example on which to demonstrate this seems to me to be the case of the wife of Henri Marteau. Opinions about him are divided. Most experts seem to hold the view that he

[1] See pp. 326–27.

Henri
Marteau

deteriorated as a violinist comparatively early;[2] an assessment shared by my father but violently attacked by Joachim Hartnack[3] as '[. . .] Carl Flesch's malevolent deprecatory opinion [. . .] another example of his unfortunately all too frequent precipitate and wrong judgements'. I can only assume that Hartnack did not peruse the chapter in the *Memoirs* about Marteau very carefully, or even finished reading it (at least the English edition). It contains passages such as this:[4]

[2] For instance, Boris Schwarz, *Great Master of the Violin, op. cit.*, p. 324.

[3] *Grosse Geiger unserer Zeit, op. cit.*, p. 113.

[4] P. 90.

*My mother (far right of seated row) and sister (second from
left), in New York after my father's death, with a group of
former pupils and their wives. They include Max Rostal
(third from left), Stefan Frenkel (centre, foreground) and
Szymon Goldberg (centre, at back).*

The dispassionate estimate of a great artistic career has to take
account of all the phases through which it passes. Whoever heard
Joachim after 1890 or Ysaÿe after 1910 cannot give these two
giants their full due. In my memory the young Marteau certainly
lives as one of the most distinguished violinists of his time. [. . .]
His stimulating influence during a for me highly critical period
has contributed much to my development.

If this is 'malevolent', I wonder what Herr Hartnack regards
as 'benevolent'?[5]

I have read several letters from various acquaintances to my
father after Marteau's death in which it was alleged that his

[5] I would like to add, incidentally that these highly personal, subjective –
and (dare I say it?) precipitate – expressions of opinion are one of the
features that make Hartnack's book so interesting and stimulating. Whether
or not one necessarily agrees with them is another matter.

second marriage had been a disaster. Whether or not this was true on a personal level I have, of course, no means of knowing, but I do not think for one moment that it had anything to do with his alleged premature artistic decline. For as I have pointed out, this can hardly ever be caused by the artist's wife. On the other hand it is beyond question that she was suffering from a severe case of 'Artist's-wife syndrome'. She must have been uncommonly jealous of some of her husband's colleagues and have managed to convince him of their hostile attitude towards him: he broke relations with many of them, including my father with whom he had been on terms of personal friendship.[6] But, particularly if it was true that his fame was in decline, her attitude is understandable.

In a letter to me[7] my mother has described her only encounter with Mme Marteau:

> I have never seen her, except her back, incidentally before she was even married to Marteau. It was during a tea party at the home of a concert agent named Salter. I attended it in the company of Mrs Kreisler. When she was introduced to us and heard our names, she turned her back on us. Mrs Kreisler asked in a loud voice – 'Who is this unpleasant person?', and I explained to her that she was Marteau's girl friend.

My mother could not resist a slightly malicious comment:

> I have never forgotten the incident, because it was so funny. [. . .] What poor Harriet [Kreisler] did not realise was that she herself was known as an 'unpleasant person'.

Marteau's last letter to my father is dated 17 December 1930. He was at the time only 57 years old, but his hand writing was that of a much older man. The letter shows anything but animosity: he asks my father for a few biographical details since he had been commissioned by the Swedish publishers of a 28-volume dictionary, to deal with the history of violin playing: 'For you, the editors have permitted me 36 words – rather insufficient for a man of your importance'.

---

[6] I should add that I have not been able to find any letters from Marteau testifying to his changed attitude – rather the contrary. See also p. 151.

[7] Dated 27 March 1961.

I have an amusing letter from Thibaud, dated 21 November 1909 – presumably at a time when Marteau was already on bad terms with many of his colleagues. Thibaud accepts an invitation by my father and writes how much he is looking forward to it: 'Nous disons le plus de mal possible de Marteau! Dieu qu'on va s'amuser!!' Grist to Herr Hartnack's mill, no doubt; even though I am sure it was a joke among intimate friends, both of whom had a good sense of humour.

Incidentally, after Marteau's death my father made enquiries about his family's financial position with a view to arranging help if necessary. Similarly, the violinist Robert Perutz, who at one time had been Marteau's pupil (which he subsequently greatly regretted), made enquiries of my father in similar vein. It all shows that Marteau was basically well-liked by his colleagues even if he obviously did not appreciate it. The idea of financial help, incidentally, was not followed up.

When the German edition of the Carl Flesch *Memoirs* was about to be published, Mme Marteau objected to several passages dealing with her late husband which were, at her request, modified. This caused a certain amount of inconvenience to the publishers and myself, but I see no reason to take it amiss, irrespective of whether her objections were justified or not. I regard it merely as a sign of her desire to protect her late husband's name with all the means at her disposal. It is a well-known fact that an artist wife's loyalty towards her husband does not cease with his death. Neither, for that matter, does any other wife's but the difference lies in the public position the artist-husband occupied during his life time. The widow will do all she can to keep his memory fresh and to re-awaken public interest whenever the opportunity presents itself. A case in point was, I gather, Franz Lehár's widow who seems to have done, rather unnecessarily, more than her fair share in this direction. The Viennese dubbed her, very unkindly, 'die lästige Witwe'.[8]

---

[8] A pun which unfortunately completely loses its point in the English translation: instead of *'merry* widow', it is *'irritating* widow', whereas all it needs in German is the change of one single vowel, from 'u' to 'ä'.

There can be, incidentally, the additional aggravation for some wives of being dropped by former acquaintances after their husband's death. Sometimes they are left in no doubt that it was not they but the late spouse who had been the attraction, and that they are of no further interest in themselves. But even if people do not behave in this unforgivably tactless manner, it must be very painful to realise how quickly an artist is forgotten as the public transfers its allegiance to someone else who, in the opinion of the widow, probably bears no comparison.

My mother was in a somewhat happier position inasmuch as my father had produced a large number of pupils through whom his name lived on. But she, too, was by no means free from 'Artist's-wife Syndrome'. As I sometimes jokingly (and, of course, exaggeratedly) remarked: 'For my mother there are only two kinds of violinists: my father's pupils – and all others'.

But I am doing her memory less than justice. An obituary in 1971 in the German-language *Aufbau*, published in New York, gives a true appreciation of her life and character:

[. . .] She was a mother figure to her husband's pupils [. . .] an intelligent and lively woman with charm and humour whose invariable helpfulness and kindness will be gratefully remembered by many.

XIV
WILHELM FURTWÄNGLER

'Present-day mechanisation,
carried to extremes, seems to
be pushing into the background
the higher musical values that
are after all the main reasons
why we make, and listen to,
music.'
WILHELM FURTWÄNGLER

For many of the German inter-war generation Furtwängler
was an almost legendary figure. As I remember them, his
Subscription Concerts at the Berlin Philharmonie were invariably sold out. For us young people this meant 'unreserved'
only at the public dress rehearsals which, in fact, were
fully-fledged Sunday Morning performances preceding the
concert proper on the next night, and none the worse for that;
indeed, in our youthful arrogance, we considered the Sunday
Morning audiences to be more musical and therefore
'superior'.

'Unreserved' meant waiting at the doors until they were
opened and then sprinting 200 yards or so for the best possible
standing room. (Queuing was, at that time, unknown in
Germany, for anything: the efforts to reclaim your coat after a
concert or theatre performance were dubbed 'cloakroom
battles' – 'Garderobeschlachten'.)

I must confess to an occasional unfair advantage: my
parents had a permanent invitation to the box of the proprietor
of the Philharmonie, the so-called 'Landecker Loge', from
which one had an unimpeded view of the stalls. My mother
would spend the first half of the concert – though, hopefully,

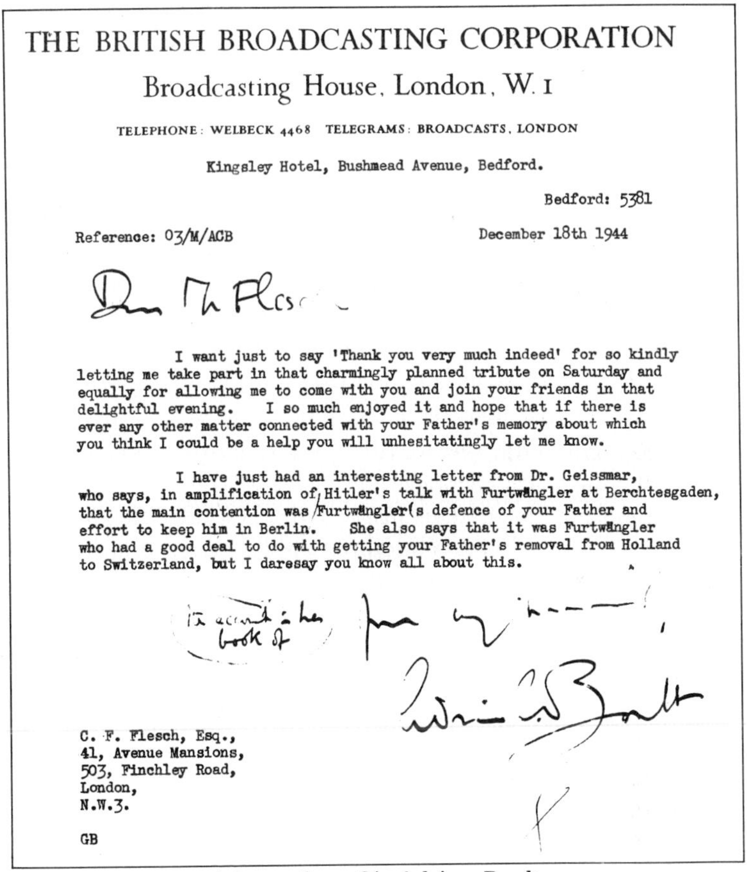

THE BRITISH BROADCASTING CORPORATION

Broadcasting House, London, W. 1

TELEPHONE: WELBECK 4468 TELEGRAMS: BROADCASTS, LONDON

Kingsley Hotel, Bushmead Avenue, Bedford.

Bedford: 5381

Reference: 03/M/ACB   December 18th 1944

[handwritten salutation]

      I want just to say 'Thank you very much indeed' for so kindly letting me take part in that charmingly planned tribute on Saturday and equally for allowing me to come with you and join your friends in that delightful evening. I so much enjoyed it and hope that if there is ever any other matter connected with your Father's memory about which you think I could be a help you will unhesitatingly let me know.

      I have just had an interesting letter from Dr. Geissmar, who says, in amplification of Hitler's talk with Furtwängler at Berchtesgaden, that the main contention was Furtwängler's defence of your Father and effort to keep him in Berlin. She also says that it was Furtwängler who had a good deal to do with getting your Father's removal from Holland to Switzerland, but I daresay you know all about this.

[handwritten closing and signature]

C. F. Flesch, Esq.,
41, Avenue Mansions,
503, Finchley Road,
London,
N.W.3.

GB

A letter from Sir Adrian Boult

not entirely – trying to locate the rare occasional empty seat. If successful, she would whisper its precise location to me during the interval, and I was able to spend the remainder of the concert in more comfort. Not that it made much difference at that age: it was the performance that mattered.

My father has described his first meeting with Furtwängler in his *Memoirs*:[1]

In 1910 I had played the Brahms Concerto in Lübeck with a young conductor by the name of Wilhelm Furtwängler and had

[1] P. 271.

formed the impression that he was the 'coming man'. This was the first position Furtwängler held, the first time he had accompanied a soloist, and only the second concert in his life. From that day dated a friendship which has survived all vicissitudes.

Nor, as I know from his widow, did Furtwängler forget this meeting:[2]

> My husband has told me that Carl Flesch was his first soloist in Lübeck, how they had an immediate sympathetic understanding and how pleased he had been to receive his valuable advice.

My father has described Furtwängler in his *Memoirs* (written before the Hitler period) as a man with 'inner uncertainty [. . . ,] the childlike naïveté [of] ·the true artist [. . . ,] honest through and through'.[3]

To complete the picture, here is one of my father's diary entries – certainly not intended for publication;[4] in it he deals with Furtwängler's (as he tactfully describes it) 'Don Juanesque restlessness':

> The other day I heard after some time Furtwängler conducting. Nearing as he does, his 50th birthday, there are signs of lustful passion being superseded by greater serenity. At present both are roughly equal, resulting in a harmonic equilibrium, a balance between Dyonysius [*sic*] and Apollo. He belongs to that category of artists where artistic and sexual activity are running parallel, substitute for each other, where the one stimulates the other, a varied expression of a single emotion.

His inner uncertainty showed itself – surprisingly, and how unnecessarily – in occasional jealousy of other conductors' successes. My father remembered meeting him at an opera performance conducted by Toscanini. 'How did you like it?' my father asked him during the first interval; whereupon Furtwängler went into a relentless and devastating panning of Toscanini's performance without a single redeeming feature. In the second interval they met again: 'Well, what did you

---

[2] Undated letter (February 1988) from Elisabeth Furtwängler.

[3] Pp. 272 ff.

[4] Dated 26 May 1932.

Bruno Walter, Thomas Mann and Arturo Toscanini,
photographed at the 1935 Salzburg Festival by Lotte
Lehmann

think of the second act?' Furtwängler, towering over my father
(who was rather short), bent down and replied, in all serious-
ness: 'The first act was better'.

My personal recollections of Furtwängler are, I am afraid,
of scant historical interest, unless you count the fact that he
seems to have placed little value on sartorial elegance. I recall
his arriving at my parents' house for lunch, having changed
into a lounge suit after conducting one of his Sunday morning
'dress rehearsals'. Under his arm he carried a tightly rolled-up
brown paper parcel; it contained his tails. His photo, too,
would hardly be a suitable advertisement for a high-class
tailor.[5]

I am not qualified to comment on Furtwängler the musician; nor is there any need to add to the abundant existing
accounts. But I do recollect, a story told by the leader of a

[5] See p. 255.

string quartet – unfortunately, I cannot recall who he was. For some reason or other, Furtwängler happened to be present at one of the quartet's rehearsals and, after a time, started 'conducting' it, probably without knowing what he was doing. To the surprise of the members of the ensemble themselves, the effect on their interpretation was magical – a sign of his remarkable ability to transmit his musical ideas and intentions 'without really trying'.[6]

What I can write about with some authority is his attitude during the Hitler regime. I possess a number of his letters to my father written in the 1930s. I feel that these – if no other material had been available – would have been sufficient to vindicate him. I am only sorry that I did not know of their existence when his activities were being investigated after the War. Since Furtwängler, indirectly, saved my parents' lives during the German occupation of Holland in 1942, my attitude is bound to be subjective, but it is identical with a more objective judgement of his sentiments which are amply documented by his letters during the Hitler period before the war.

Initially, my father had turned to him for advice and help when, shortly after the Nazis' access to power, his position and livelihood were being threatened by colleagues who had been – or suddenly turned out to be – long-standing Party members. There was, however, no question of my father assuming the role of a 'supplicant'; their relationship continued unchanged, for it was based on full mutual understanding and equality. Even at that time my father could afford to express his views to him as bluntly as he liked. This is borne out by a letter from

---

[6] There were – and no doubt are – other conductors similarly gifted. I remember a charity concert by a pretty mediocre amateur orchestra where Hepzibah Menuhin had agreed to play a Beethoven piano concerto on condition that Sir Adrian Boult – regarded by many artists as the best accompanying conductor of the time – was to take charge of the orchestral part. The difference in quality between that item and the remainder of the programme, in which Sir Adrian was not performing, was quite astonishing. Anybody listening without seeing the performers could have been forgiven for thinking that two entirely different orchestras were concerned. Some conductors are obviously able, on occasions, to get more out of orchestral players than is actually in them.

Carl Flesch and Wilhelm Furtwängler in Baden-Baden, c. 1930

Furtwängler's secretary, dated 26 June 1933, written at his request during his absence on a concert tour, in which he refers to my father's disapproving remark that he had chosen, for a Philharmonic concert, a soloist of obviously inferior standing – but a Party member. The reply states that

Furtwängler had never contemplated engaging that particular artist, 'especially as he has no need to include in his programmes composers and soloists "immunised by Aryan great-grandmothers" as you write'.

Furtwängler intervened on my father's behalf with the then Minister of Culture and even stated to have written to the 'Führer'.[7] He genuinely tried to safeguard the position of the Jewish leaders of the Berlin Philharmonic Orchestra, Szymon Goldberg and Nicolai Graudan, and felt clearly hurt when, apparently not appreciating his efforts, they eventually decided to resign. But he bore no grudges. In a letter written on 22 May 1935 he says: 'I wish [Goldberg] well in his solo career. I fear, however, that in many respects his artistic achievements will not be recognised and appreciated in the same measure as during his time as leader of our orchestra. Please give him my kind regards should you see him'.

Two more passages deserve mention here, because they cast a revealing light on his state of mind. The first, dated 4 June 1933, from Paris: 'I am glad to be rid of Berlin for a fortnight, in order to forget'. And in the second, dated 25 September 1935, he asks my father to make sure that they meet in London: 'I usually stay at the German Embassy, perhaps you could drop me a line there so that we don't miss each other'. Clearly, he did not hide his views nor care who knew them; in 1935 there was a near-certainty of his correspondence being intercepted and scrutinised by the appropriate Embassy staff.

Leaving all personal matters aside, however, I think that the most significant letter is one illuminating his motivations in general. It will be remembered that he was severely taken to task by the international art world for having remained in Germany instead of going abroad. It was suggested that he was profiting from the persecution of his Jewish colleagues.

I think it can be shown conclusively that this was not the case. For one thing, he had been, long before Hitler had come to power, probably the most acclaimed conductor in Germany. Since he was notoriously disinterested in politics, there was no improvement in his standing in Germany to which he

---

[7] See the letter from Sir Adrian Boult on p. 251.

could have aspired. Remaining in Germany could not have gained him any material advantage. Nor did it; his ups and downs with the regime are well documented. If, on the other hand, he had chosen to emigrate, he would no doubt have had the pick of any positions or engagements going – probably at a higher fee than obtainable in Germany, and with a hero's welcome to boot.

But there is no need to surmise. This letter, dated 28 April 1934, is significant in that it was not written with any intention of posturing. Far from defending his attitude, he in fact accused others – and Jewish artists at that – of not recognising, and helping him to achieve, his artistic aims and principles, a viewpoint that aptly illustrates my father's assessment of his 'child-like naïveté' but which was undoubtedly genuinely held:

> Unfortunately, Goldberg could not be dissuaded from his decision to resign. I regret this very much indeed and, much as I appreciate his reasons, cannot think it right that *he leaves the work to which I apply my efforts, namely to preserve for German musical life performances and quality of the highest standard.* Goldberg, in his argumentation, has intimated that you are supporting his views, which does not mean, dear friend, that I am blaming you. *All I can see is that in the long run living and working in freedom is becoming more and more difficult for musicians who are transcending average* [my italics].

Is there anything to add? One thought, perhaps: what would have been the reaction of his colleagues – who, having been forced to emigrate, were struggling to rebuild their existence – if he, too, had left Germany? My guess is that, far from welcoming this step, they would have resented it on the grounds that he was taking the bread out of their mouths, although he could have stayed in Germany with impunity. And, for that matter, wouldn't they have had a point? Furtwängler was in the unenviable position of facing two virtually impossible alternatives.

As I have said, there can be no doubt that my parents' friendship with Furtwängler saved them from deportation and almost certain death. I would like to conclude with an extract from a letter addressed to Furtwängler by my mother shortly after the War.[8] From its context it seems clear that it had been written at his request – but this does not alter the facts in any way whatever.

As you will know, my husband obtained, in 1940, a professorship at the Curtis Institute, Philadelphia; this enabled us to get an entry visa for USA. Unfortunately the German occupation authorities refused 5 times to grant us an exit permit, in spite of your very kind efforts to help us in this matter. When after America's entry into the war the US consulate was closed down, we tried to go to Cuba, but again were unable to obtain a German exit visa. At the request of my husband you sent him a letter to Dr. Bene, a high German official in Holland, asking him to grant us a travel permit to Cuba. Unfortunately it was not possible for this letter to be delivered: there was nobody with the so-called courage to pass on a message concerning a Jew. In this way we missed the chance of emigrating to Cuba. However, subsequently we did find someone prepared to pass on your letter to Dr. Bene; although it could no longer serve its original purpose, my husband hoped that it might give us a small measure of security if Dr. Bene knew at least of our existence.

When in September 1942 we were arrested and transferred to prison in Scheveningen, my husband handed to the policewoman at the reception desk, together with our passports, a photocopy of your letter in the hope that it might help us out of this dangerous situation.

It does appear that that young woman who had initially informed us that we would be transferred next morning to a Dutch concentration camp where we would be told 'what would happen to us next' was somewhat taken aback. It seems that she contacted Dr. Bene's office where she was told to release us. Clearly it was your letter that brought about our delivery from this desperate plight.

I would like to add that at a time when it was already quite dangerous for you to use your influence on behalf of a non-Aryan, you always stuck to us and did what you possibly could to help us. My husband and I have never forgotten the debt of gratitude we owe you.

[8] Dated 21 July 1945.

Furtwängler's towering artistic achievements were matched by an outstanding personality, an intensely human one with all its strengths and weaknesses – the former far outweighing the latter – and with the courage of his convictions, which he placed at the disposal of his friends without reservation when it was a question of helping them in adversity.

XV

ARTUR SCHNABEL
THE MAN AND ARTIST

'The notes I handle no better
than many pianists. But the
pauses between the notes – ah,
that is where the art resides.'
ARTUR SCHNABEL

On 26 May 1935 Carl Flesch wrote to Georg Schünemann
about his *Memoirs*, which during that period occupied a good
deal of his time:

I am just beginning an analysis in depth of Artur Schnabel – a
very difficult undertaking, for his character is as complicated
and contradictory as those of a dozen other men rolled into one.
But since none of his contemporaries know him as well as I do,
the effort is certainly worthwhile.

The opinion about his intimate knowledge – family, of course,
excluded – was at that time undoubtedly justified. The
Schnabel-Flesch collaboration had begun as early as 1908.
During the following two decades they appeared at hundreds
of sonata and trio concerts which meant extensive travelling in
each other's company; they issued editions of classical
chamber-music works; and, quite apart from their professional relationship, they were close friends who held each other
in high esteem.

In his *Memoirs* my father has attempted a detailed description of Schnabel as an artist and human being and of their work
together. But since the *Memoirs* are mainly intended for
violinists and other specifically 'violin-orientated' readers,

whereas this book is addressing itself to a wider circle of music lovers, a few brief excerpts may not be out of place:

> The personal and artistic contradictions of Schnabel's life made him a riddle to most of his contemporaries. According to their own outlook, or their experience of him, people loved or hated Schnabel but never understood him. In a less pronounced personality, the contradictions of his character would have cancelled one another out. With him, however, they freely existed side by side, to come into action at need.[1]

> He loved contradiction since it gave him the opportunity to busy himself dialectically [. . .].[2]

> I freely acknowledged his unparallelled artistic gifts, his spontaneous musicianship [. . .] and his wonderful ability to realize it. The secret of our perfect ensemble was that, coming from opposite directions, we met in the middle.[. . .] Our collaboration thus held much attraction for either party. We stimulated each other, and our rehearsals satisfied us far more even than our concerts.[3]

> When in Beethoven or Brahms, Schubert or Schumann, the holy spirit came over him [. . .] it was given to him to reach heights [. . .] hardly ever scaled by others.[4]

> He certainly remains one of the most remarkable musicians of our time. [. . .] I would not for anything have missed [his] influence on my artistic development.[5]

I believe these remarks to be very much to the point. It is a

---

[1] P. 259.

[2] *Ibid.*

[3] Pp. 261–62.

[4] P. 220. On the other hand, my father thought little of Schnabel's interpretations of contemporary works. In his diary (9 November 1931) he mentions a concert tour in the course of which Schnabel was to have played eighteen different piano concertos, but which came to naught: 'Artistically, this may be a blessing for him. I feel certain that his reputation would have suffered, for I don't think that he plays the moderns at all well' – an interesting view, considering Schabel's then hyper-modern compositions (see pp. 276–84). I myself cannot remember ever having heard him play a contemporary work.

[5] Pp. 262–63.

An early photograph of the Schnabel–Flesch duo

pity that there exists no reciprocal assessment of my father by Schnabel, since, because it would have been based on an equally intimate knowledge, it would have been highly interesting and revealing. But in his series of lectures entitled *My Life and Music*[6] he refers to him only very briefly indeed. I believe this is due to a repression that can be traced back to their estrangement.[7] Curiously enough, an obituary of

[6] Longmans, London, 1961.

[7] See pp. 285–303. In this context a recollection by Peter Diamand (in conversation with me), as a young man his private secretary and occasional

Schnabel in *The Times*[8] did not refer to his chamber-music activities with even a single sentence.

I can add a number of observations – a few personal recollections, some entries in my father's diary, but in particular excerpts from letters, none ever published before, which offer insights into the working and thinking of this giant among pianists – Artur Schnabel observed from close by, as it were.

One of my father's diary entries from 1931, a time when their artistic partnership was almost at an end but their personal relationship still unclouded, at least on the surface, deals not with Schnabel the artist – whom, as we have seen, my father admired almost without reservation – but with the man himself. Of course, it is not expressed anything near as 'elegantly' as in the *Memoirs*, but for this very reason perhaps all the more informative:

> About Artur, who visited me yesterday, one could write volumes. A man whom one has to love and hate at the same time, full of the most hair-raising contradictions, idealist and materialist, naive and wily, impulsive and finicky, but above all a born dialectician. His great passion: talking, himself, listening to himself talking. [. . .] One knows that from habit and inclination he will mount an attack on any view expressed by someone else, even if (or just because) it agrees with his own. [. . .] In spite of it all – fascinating. In reality, inwardly torn – basically an impulsive personality [. . .] which [. . .] unsuccessfully strives for absolute intellectual control [. . .] Hence this amazing dualism [. . .] making him appear angel and devel in turn.[9]

To assess whether or not this opinion, coming from a man whose own character was no stranger to ambivalence, hits the

---

chauffeur, is noteworthy. Not far from Tremezzo, where the Schnabel family owned a house, there was a castle in which, over the years, Schnabel and my father had given a number of sonata recitals. Whenever he passed this building, Schnabel never omitted to refer to these concerts in a clearly nostalgic mood.

[8] 17 August 1951.

[9] Entry probably for 25 October 1931.

Artur Schnabel by Eugen Spiro

target, we have Schnabel's letters to my father to help us, an often absorbing read, full of originality and surprises. It mirrors his character: clear and judicious – or muddled and misconstruing real situations; cool – or impulsive, at times even unrestrained; uncommonly idealistic – or highly materialistic; self-assured – or almost over-modest; and much else besides. Reading these letters one could sometimes almost suspect that they had been written by two different persons. Occasionally this can be quite droll:

There ought to be *no* concert without a Mozart work.[10]

I would suggest a slight change in the programme and would ask you to agree to the D minor Trio by Mendelssohn instead of a Mozart work.[11]

I don't know my father's reaction. I expect he agreed, with an indulgent smile. It would have been much more interesting if he had reminded Schnabel of his previous letter; I am pretty certain that Schnabel would have proved with compelling logic that there was no real contradiction. For, however differing his utterances, they represented his honest opinion at the precise moment at which he pronounced them. He had the precious gift of being able to convince not only others, but also – and in particular – himself that his views and actions were right at the time, even if they were entirely at variance with the principles expounded on another occasion (which he might not even recollect). This habit caused some people to accuse him of gross insincerity[12] – but this, I think, fails to appreciate his particular trait.

His earliest letters in my collection date from the beginning of the 1914–18 War, well after the start of their collaboration. Since both artists lived in Berlin at the time, written commu-

[10] 3 September 1929.

[11] 1 May 1930.

[12] A judgement which at times could be expresseed in venomous terms. From a letter dated 27 July 1936, from one of Schnabel's former friends: 'I received a letter [from Schnabel] which had ideological hypocrisy and twaddle dripping through the envelope – before I had even opened it.'

Somewhat hilarious but no less significant for his reputation with some colleagues is a sentence in a letter from Leonid Kreutzer, an excellent pianist who had an unfortunate tendency to construe every utterance by others as an attack on himself – something to which his own demeanour not infrequently contributed: 'Here [at the Berlin Hochschule] everything is very peculiar. Schnabel is scheming against me, but probably does not know it yet himself' – a remark so profound that one could ponder over it for hours.

nication was normally unnecessary. But when war broke out, we happened to be on holiday in Holland, my mother's native country. Schnabel, like most citizens of nations at war, was swept along by the prevailing wave of patriotism, not, of course, by the idea of war itself, but by the dominant atmosphere and propaganda.

> Here in Berlin things are going along aplendidly. The predominant feeling is that of quietly confident animation [. . .]. Wonderful (and as a matter of fact very unexpected), suddenly to be amongst an inspired crowd of people for once not thinking mainly of themselves seeing that formerly the masses consisted of uninspired egoists [. . .].
> Don't believe any news from Paris or London![13]

On the other hand, both were very thankful for having been found unfit for active service, thereby escaping the danger of permanently ruining their hands. My father was exceptionally shortsighted and Schnabel had a hammer toe – 'two praiseworthy defects worth preserving', as he put it.

He was better able than my father to analyse, clearly and with vision, the situation and its inherent difficulties without being able to refer to precedents. And he was capable of expressing his views graphically and forcefully thereby giving them even more strength and conviction.

The outbreak of war resulted in a flood of panicky concert cancellations by promoters. Schnabel was never in doubt about the importance of taking a firm stand:

> It would be folly and madness for us to accept [these cancellations. . . .] We must not agree, on principle, to any such deprivation of our rights; we must, for the time being, not accept defeat. [. . .] Moreover, and this is the salient point, it is at present still far too early to make any decisions, to tie oneself down. [. . .] What can one say, for instance, about the Philharmonic Association of Bremen cancelling the contract for a concert on Good Friday next (2.4.1915). This is quite obviously nonsensical.
> And now I want to say to you that I do not at all share your

[13] 25 August 1914.

> pessimistic expectation of the coming season having no vitality. If anything, I hold the opposite opinion. [. . .] It is after all very likely that in 5–6 weeks' time we shall be experiencing a strong demand for matters spiritual. I feel we ought to play in any event regardless of whether we gain or lose. Just now we must not allow timidity to make us desert our fellow men. [. . .] At worst, tickets will remain unsold. But we *must* play. [14]

Today, after two world wars have demonstrated the hunger for art in all its forms, Schnabel's opinion is generally accepted, but at the time he expressed it, it was entirely untested, original – and right. Even on the very first day of the German revolution in 1918 they played to a full house.

In the same letter Schnabel continues:

> I am strictly against the idea of announcing concerts as being for charitable purposes. If we wish to give some of the proceeds to charity, there are sufficient institutions worth supporting who would accept our offer with alacrity. I am prepared to pass any potential profit from our concerts to them, but under no circumstances do I want to have a charity link-up in our advertising. We want people to come to our concerts because they want to listen to us or to Beethoven sonatas. If you saw the many second-rate people already trying to jump on the charity band wagon in order to pad out their skinny bodies, I am sure you would agree with me.

Admirable, both in form and content.

Honestly though these idealistic sentiments were being held, a somewhat dissonant note is sounded in a letter from Oskar Nedbal[15] who clearly had a strong voice in deciding which artists the Vienna 'Tonkünstler-Vereinigung' was to engage for its concerts. It was in 1916, the third year of the war; my father had apparently mentioned to him reprovingly that Schnabel was, at that time, not being considered for engagements with the Association. Nedbal wrote:[16]

---

[14] *Ibid.*

[15] 1874–1930; Czech composer and conductor. A composition pupil of Dvořák, from 1891 to 1906 he played viola in the Bohemian String Quartet (with Karel Hoffmann, Josef Suk and Hanuš Wihan). He was conductor of the Vienna Tonkünstler–Orchester from 1906 until 1919.

[16] Letter dated 14 April 1916.

You know that at the outbreak of war artists – in the first place you *yourself* – were very accommodating towards us in the question of fees. We have offered Schnabel the highest amount at our disposal, 800 Kronas, but Mr Schnabel insists on 1000 Kronas, or else he won't come!

Nedbal then asked my father to intervene and appeal to Schnabel's better nature.

The significance lies in Schnabel's contradictory attitude – on the one hand his intention, no doubt wholly genuine, to play without a fee, and on the other his insistence on an additional 200 Kronas, of whose justification he was very probably convinced although the Association's current financial difficulties must have been obvious to him.[17]

Who was 'right', Schnabel or the Association, is quite a different question. After all, looked at purely in economic terms, playing the violin or piano is a profession like any other; to remain viable, it has to feed and clothe the artist and his family. Payment, again like in any other profession, is governed by supply and demand. And of course, lots of people try all the time to get a professional – in this case artistic – job done for nothing or at least at a reduced price. Doctors and solicitors face somewhat similar problems, but a pianist who is asked at a party 'to play a few notes' cannot react in the same way as the doctor whose advice on a medical matter is being requested at a social gathering by a lady whom he has never met: 'OK, let's have a look. Take your clothes off'. All he can do is refuse or, in the case of a professional concert, insist on his original demand. It is up to either party whether or not to accept.

In most cases, anyway, although not according to the old story attributed to Fritz Kreisler – probably wrongly, for he was anything but a snob. A wealthy American society hostess had planned a soirée combined with a private concert for which she intended to engage him. She was so unwise as to announce this as a *fait accompli* before terms had been agreed. Kreisler, annoyed, decided to teach her a lesson: he asked for

---

[17] I should emphasise here that Schnabel liked to play at house concerts of friends, and often did – without any fee whatever.

*Artur and Therese
Schnabel*

double his usual fee and would not give way despite all her entreaties. Since his appearance had already been announced, the lady eventually had to agree willy nilly so as not to lose face. She did so, but not without adding: 'Alright. But playing only; on no account do I want you to mingle with my guests'. Kreisler: 'But my dear lady, why didn't you tell me before. If I'd known, my fee would have been much lower!'

Nedbal's case is not all that dissimilar, for his letter concludes: 'I admit that Mr Schnabel, if he does not give in, will get his 1000 Kronas from us, for the simple reason that we shall be celebrating our 10th anniversary next year and simply don't want to do without his name on the programme'. So Schnabel was right after all, at least if one doesn't know his previous views; and neither perhaps, those he expressed on a subsequent occasion:[18]

> I have been touring Russia for a month. It is a great *beginning* and, as always in these situations, a pleasing honesty is apparent. My main motivation for going there is the possibility once more to provide some sustenance – before they have finally had their day – for the spiritually starved members of a class who have been brought up with higher cultural needs.

[18] In a letter to Carl Flesch dated 5 March 1925.

Thus speaks Schnabel the idealist. Now for the materialist, in the same letter:

> I have given seven concerts in Russia. To date I have not received a brass farthing.[19] But I assume this is merely due to inefficiency.

So far we have seen Schnabel the self-confident, positive-thinking artist. But he also had his darker, extremely pessimistic moments which lured him into expressing somewhat quixotic opinions. Earlier in this same letter he had written:

> Furtwängler told us a good deal about America. [. . .] What advantages for a conductor compared with ourselves! From the outset he is appointed to a top position. Money is no object. [. . .] How different the conditions for the likes of us! Who, if he is not a trafficker in artists looking for fresh victims to exploit, would at present introduce a pianist to the American public? Usually you have to offer yourself to a manager, entreat him to take notice [. . . ;] the pianist is seduced into using instruments of inferior make, because in this way he can increase his income (but is bound to diminish the quality of his performance). Whilst the conductor [. . .] immediately has a large and comparatively well-educated audience at his disposal, the pianist has to scrape it together painstakingly, by cadging and resorting to God knows what degrading ruses in order to lure people into concerts.

Although this was written during a slump in American musical life,[20] I venture to doubt that the majority of conductors and pianists saw matters in quite the same light. But it gets even better. There is an unintentional punchline to this letter:

> I have no illusions about the importance of my absence from America. I am not needed [. . .]. I shall be playing in London on April 22nd and May 5th. You have to try everything.

With hindsight, and considering Schnabel's subsequent successes particularly in the United Kingdom and United States,

---

[19] In German a typical Schnabel pun which, like most, is untranslatable. The German expression is 'keinen roten Heller', i.e., 'not a red farthing', which, of course, has a neat double meaning.

[20] See p. 192.

this remark is an amusing illustration of the vagaries of concert life. And it also shows the inability of even the most intelligent artists to assess their prospects with any degree of certainty. Unfortunately, more often than not, they are over-optimistic and apt to be disappointed; it is good to know that in this case the disappointment was far more pleasant.

But what about his opinions on matters not strictly musical? From the same letter:

> Europe has only a tiny islet left to save its life. Perhaps it will soon be inundated by the combined waves – Asia and America. Europe has become unnecessary. It has fulfilled its task and is solely permitted to continue its existence in the role of vendor (who of course has to be given the possibility of obtaining sufficient means to pay for his purchases). It is in a state of transition. [. . .] Here we have a great *ending*. And as always in these situations, an intolerable dishonesty. But at the same time we have to fight against the death of Europe until we have been swallowed up or butchered.

This was written more than sixty years ago. So far his fears have not materialised. Perhaps he was further ahead of his time than he realised himself. I can't presume to judge, except to say that six decades seems a somewhat lengthy ending.

If this seems a depressing picture, it is, as always with Schnabel, only one side of it. He was a man blessed with real humour and a sparkling wit. In his presence something usually happened to cause mental stimulation and frequent laughter. He loved plays on words. Unfortunately, almost all those I know require a knowledge of German since they are not amenable to translation. I am therefore forced to relegate some examples to a footnote.[21]

---

[21] He invented 'professions', such as 'Donauwalzer' and 'Bettvorleger'. He was also famous for creating rhymed spoonerisms (Schüttelreime), for instance:

Am Anfang war der Schnabel nur
Das Ende einer Nabelschnur.

Erst scherzt' ich mit dem dreisten Lieschen,
Dann schmerzten mich die Leistendrüschen.

Von jedem Schund e bissel,
Das nennt man Bunte Schüssel.

There was usually something going on in the Schnabel household, and for the occupiers of the flat below, rather more than they cared for: Artur played the piano, his wife sang, his older son, Karl Ulrich, was a budding professional pianist, and when they did not practise, they gave lessons. They all had managed so to distribute themselves around their home that they did not interfere with one another. But this did nothing for the hapless tenants below whom this arrangement left without any peaceful corner in their own flat, except when a member of the Schnabel family happened to be operating outside the home. On Sundays the younger generation liked to give noisy table tennis parties. But these resulted in severe complaints from long-suffering neighbours who felt that at least their weekends should be respected. A drastic curtailment of that particular activity became necessary.

I know comparatively little about Schnabel's attitude towards colleagues. I believe it varied. On the one hand, he collaborated with them at house concerts in the fullest harmony. I have a letter written in 1915 in which he discusses in a very objective way the merits (or otherwise) of a number of

---

(A 'Bunte Schüssel' was a selection of cookies, an essential German Xmas gift for children).

During the height of the currency restrictions afflicting most countries, he thought up a fairly elaborate one:

Ob wohl der Papst, der weise Christ,
Den Ausweg aus der Krise weiss,
die, wie Ihr all' im Kreise wisst,
Um manches Land's Devise kreist?

And finally his reply to the conductor Heinz Unger who complained to him about the attitude of the Berlin Philharmonic Orchestra. During a rehearsal the players, at the stroke of one, had put away their instruments in unison in order to have their lunch break. Schnabel:

Mein lieber Heinz Unger,
Das Orchester hat um eins Hunger.

The musicologist Peter Stadlen tells the story of Schnabel's son, Karl Ulrich, having had a serious argument with his teacher Leonid Kreutzer. Schnabel suspected that in this instance his son was in the wrong and felt it incumbent upon himself to try and re-establish diplomatic relations on his son's behalf. When leaving his flat in order to accomplish this task he sighed: 'Jetzt muss ich zu Kreutzer kriechen'.

musicians with whom he had been playing.[22] On the other
hand he could make merciless fun of colleagues, even friends,
as, for example, on the occasion of a concert in which a work
for four pianos with orchestra was being performed, the
soloists being pianists of the first rank though not as successful
as he was. He called them the 'cabinet des refusés' and
suggested fixing a red light to each instrument which was to
come into operation at the appropriate moment so as to
indicate which of the four happened to be playing (I must
admit that, since the artists seated behind their instruments
were practically invisible to the audience, he had a point). On
the other hand I remember a Furtwängler concert in which
Rachmaninov himself performed his Third Piano Concerto to
considerable acclaim. Schnabel, whom I happened to encounter in the interval, criticised his playing in a manner which for
pungency and venom – whether justified or not – went way
beyond what was called for.

Generally, of course, one does not want to take these
matters too seriously: musicians love to make fun of one
another if they see an opportunity of doing so in an ingenious
manner. Schnabel himself could be the butt of these jokes.
Since, for instance, composers like Chopin were not his forte,
some colleagues dubbed him 'Chopinhauer'.[23] And his unfit-
ness for active war service was ascribed by Moritz Rosenthal
not to his hammer toe but to quite a different defect: 'stiff
wrists'.[24]

Schnabel, of course, gave as good as he got. In the case of
the pianist Jan Smeterlin, who apparently had the reputation
of a know-all, he composed the only English 'Schüttelreim' of
his known to me:

What the men of letters mean
Who to noble matters lean,
All that knows Jan Smeterlin.[25]

---

[22] Huberman was one instance; see pp. 137–8.

[23] 'Hauen' is the German verb 'to hack'.

[24] Quoted in Henri Temianka, *Facing the Music*, *op. cit.*, p. 145.

[25] Most enjoyable, though regrettably again untranslatable from the original

He edited both on his own and in collaboration with my father a number of classical works. Here, too, his attitude was ambivalent. There exists a long letter about one of them,[26] but after reading it, I frankly don't quite know what he is driving at. I have a suspicion that my father may not have known either. From a different exchange during that time it seems clear that in one case at least the editorial path went anything but smoothly. It concerns the Brahms Violin Sonatas; in the somewhat malicious opinion of a few colleagues this edition gives the impression of the two having worked almost independently of, if not against, one another. My father's letters on that occasion[27] may give a clue for the reasons.

This subject was apparently tinged for Schnabel with some emotion. In yet another letter[28] he describes how he became so annoyed about the way in which his publisher viewed some additional work he had done that he 'threw it at his feet waiving [his] fee'. He reproached himself immediately afterwards for this 'outburst which I recognise with hindsight as the height of madness and folly, but to which I am sometimes prone without being able to stop myself'. Here we have a further facet of his character which now and then became unexpectedly apparent.

Take his remark in a letter[29] about the programme for a forthcoming Italian concert tour. It appears that my father had suggested resuscitating the Korngold Violin Sonata, originally dedicated to them and which they had performed a number of times many years ago. Letters from Korngold seem to make it clear that he and Schnabel were on terms of friendship. This did not prevent Schnabel from writing: 'Under no circumstances do I want to play the Korngold

---

German, is his verse about a world-famous colleague – very likely written not as criticism but to show off his uncanny facility in this genre:

> Als ob's auf kalter Wiese ging,
> So spielt der Walter Gieseking.

[26] See pp. 351–52.

[27] See pp. 349–51.

[28] Dated 22 July 1920.

[29] Dated 13 February 1928.

Sonata; altogether no work whose value is based solely on the composer's youthful age and whose novelty can be likened to that of a freshly minted penny'.

Apparently such outbursts were triggered off by something, someone, anyone, touching a sensitive nerve. It would not be surprising if contemporary music fell into this category. For while Schnabel reigned supreme as an interpreter, his position as a creator of new music was controversial indeed; and though he professed indifference, the lack of recognition of his music must have affected him deeply. Composing was for him of the utmost importance, and we cannot begin to understand him without taking into consideration this aspect of his activities.

XVI

SCHNABEL THE COMPOSER

> 'Creative thinking may mean
> simply the realisation that
> there's no particular virtue in
> doing things the way they've
> always been done.'
> RUDOLF FLESCH

As a pianist Artur Schnabel concentrated practically exclusively on the traditional classical repertoire. But he was also
a (for his time) ultra-modern composer – a further indication
perhaps of the dualism which was one of his most striking
characteristics. It was in this latter capacity that he enjoyed
next to no recognition during his lifetime.

The Berlin music critic Rudolf Kastner expressed it wittily
but maliciously after the first private performance of
Schnabel's Sonata for solo violin[1] in a German pun alluding to
the Second Act of *Die Meistersinger*: 'Dem Schnabel der da
sang, dem ist der Vogel hold gewachsen'.[2]

One can make fun in a more good-natured way. The pianist
Ignaz Friedmann describes in a letter[3] how he had begun to
read the second volume of *The Art of Violin Playing* (which in

---

[1] My father's correspondence, incidentally, contains several letters of
apology from invitees to that performance who most unfortunately had a
prior engagement.

[2] The English translation reads: 'The bird who sang today has got a throat
that rightly waxes'. The German original says 'beak' instead of 'throat'.
Kastner reversed the words 'bird' and 'beak'; and all we still have to know is
that 'Schnabel' is the literal German translation of 'beak', and that in
German slang a 'Vogel' is equivalent to 'bats in the belfry'.

[3] Dated 1 December 1928.

its appendix contains an analysis of one of the Sonata's movements) with fascinated interest until the early hours of the morning, but – 'At around 4 a.m. I came to Artur S's solo sonata and there, I freely confess, I fell asleep. I still don't quite know the reason – but I believe it must have been the late hour'.[4]

However negligible the influence of the composer Schnabel may have been on the contemporary music scene in general, it had a very marked effect on my parent's married life: studying the solo sonata caused my father acute insomnia, whereas my mother was a sound sleeper. The outcome was separate bedrooms. I have no grounds for supposing that there was any different reason from the official one. This result of a composition is to my knowledge unique in musical history.

During the past decade Schnabel's works appear to have gained increased recognition, and I gather that this trend is continuing. I myself am in no way qualified to give a valid opinion; at best, it would be a very subjective one: because of the trouble the solo sonata had caused in our domestic life, Schnabel's compositions were not regarded particularly highly in our family, and I grew up with the distinct impression that they were indigestible. But many years later I was watching the BBC TV show *Face the Music*, in which panellists had to identify compositions played to them. The particular programme included a few bars from a modern piece which instantly appealed to me. One of the experts, Sir Clifford Curzon, who had been a pupil of Schnabel, recognised it without difficulty as one of his late teacher's compositions. I am convinced that, had I known the composer's identity beforehand, my reaction would automatically have been negative – further proof for the view that in order to arrive at an unbiased opinion about whom or what we are listening to,

---

[4] Pianists in general seem to have a better sense of humour than violinists. Friedmann was no exception. In a letter describing a grand piano placed at his disposal for practising he writes: 'My piano appears to date back to the time of Stradivarius – but not the quality'. His sense of humour, incidentally, was not shared by his wife. According to my mother, she usually remarked accusingly after he had finished an anecdote: 'But Ignaz, you know that is not true!'

we ought to know the name of neither performer nor composer, as the case may be.

Many of Schnabel's letters to my father clearly illuminate his thoughts and motivations. They contain a number of significant clues to the understanding of his artistic intentions.

He valued my father's opinion considerably although he realised that their ideas were decidedly at variance:[5]

> I have [. . .] composed a major work for mezzo soprano and piano. It longs with anxious impatience to be submitted to your judgement and hopes for mercy.[6]

> My Quintet is now taking [. . .] vigorous steps forwards. Yesterday I finished the Adagio, whose sketch alone covers 41 pages. I believe it has come off as successfully as the first part. It will have only 3 movements. The last one, on which I am about to start, is intended as a relaxing epilogue which – unburdened, and not taxing the listener – is meant to saunter along cheerful, peaceful-happy by-paths. I shall take it with me on our next trip hoping to show it to you. Your warm appreciation of the 1st movement has given me great satisfaction and pleasure.[7]

> Thank you, too for your offer – very gladly accepted – to perform my Quintet. Therese has made a copy for you which is

---

[5] To quote briefly once more Carl Flesch's *Memoirs*: 'The erstwhile young Viennese salon composer leapt across the intervening stages of Brahms and Reger, Franck and Debussy to join the company of Stravinsky, Hindemith and Schoenberg – a development which seemed to lack organic continuity and inner necessity' (p. 251).

[6] Letter dated 27 July 1914.

[7] Letter dated 16 July 1915. There can be no doubt that my father did not place any real value on Schnabel's compositions. Was his 'warm appreciation' mainly the result of friendship and tact? There is a parallel situation with Julius Röntgen whose compositions my father freely criticised, as he says in the English edition of his *Memoirs*, thereby causing Röntgen some heartache – without, however, damaging their close friendship. I was intrigued to read at the start and again at the close of a letter to Röntgen (21 September 1910) some very flattering sentiments not on all fours with the generally negative opinion expressed in the *Memoirs*. Sandwiched between the two are critical remarks:

> I know that you don't object to minor critical observations [. . .]. The Allegro energico is very sprightly, except that for me the Coda jars a

a veritable masterpiece – no doubt bearing in mind the high standards you apply in these matters.[8]

I am entirely confident that you will be able to master the technically problematical passages in my work with far less trouble than you assumed in the first shock of encountering them; I have endeavoured to make everything playable and I am convinced that a lot of it will lose its sting quite soon, once you start giving it your close attention.[9]

My heartfelt thanks for your so detailed, thorough and affectionate letter. I have dealt with your specific queries in the enclosure; would you please examine and appraise the changes I have made based on your remarks, suggestions and advice and give me your opinion whether the changes have brought about the improvements you had in mind? Some passages I left untouched in spite of your pertinent critique, because I just don't see how I can add or subtract a single note without adversely affecting expression, intention and neatness as I see them. Conversely in other places where you did not raise any queries at all, I have made small amendments in order to express my original intentions still more clearly; I hope I have achieved this.

I am very sorry to hear that you are regarding the 5th piece with such disfavour; I myself happen to like it best – in fact I consider it the most valuable together with the third; I can't believe that I am so blind to the qualities (or lack of them) of my

---

little. The 2 solo bars of the violin seem superfluous and without organic necessity [. . .]. Possibly one could delete the variation marked 'Listesso tempo 9/8 measure'; to me it seems a little monotonous. [. . .] I would also draw your attention to the final modulation. It does not entirely fit into the strict harmonics of the work.

Having given free reinto my critical faculties, I must again express my particular admiration [. . .].

In brief, a well-worn method of sugaring the pill. Röntgen seems to have seen it as such. But if my father's letters to Schnabel were in a similar vein, might he have read more praise into them than had been intended? A comparison would have been very illuminating, but regrettably no letters seem to have been preserved.

[8] Letter dated 8 July 1917.

[9] Letter dated 7 August 1919. This does not entirely tally with my father's assessment of the solo sonata: 'Conceived in touching ignorance of the nature of violin technique, the work seemed at first to pose insoluble technical problems' (*Memoirs*, p. 486).

creations to regard as the best those that have come off worst. However, I am not without hope that you may still change your mind, remembering your frank admission that initially you found them all ghastly, but that on closer examination, which you carried out with such admirable patience, you did detect certain attractions which made you glad – or at least not sorry – to have made their acquaintance.[10]

I shall be back home during the second half of March and definitely count on seeing you. I would like to show you the piano suite (which you don't know yet) as well as the first and hopefully also the second movement of a new string quartet. I am anxious to have your opinion. Your news that you may be performing my sonata in Königsberg makes me very glad.[11]

What – apart from possibly reading too much into interspersed praising remarks – I find remarkable in these letters is Schnabel's diffidence coupled with humour and the acceptance of a divergent opinion when coming from a friend of whose competence and goodwill he was absolutely certain; and at the same time also his unflinching determination to continue on his chosen path.

His more general observations and reflections present a similar picture and, in addition, contain some caustic criticism of the public's attitude – all in the unmistakable Schnabel idiom.

Therese has made my 'Notturno' [. . .] her own astonishingly quickly and now likes to perform it, which she does frequently and admirably.

The piece must be regarded as difficult and is evoking a variety of views ranging from indifferent rejection via cold lack of comprehension to benevolent interest and unconditional approval. I anticipated, of course, that the work would give little pleasure to those who are saturated, indolent, with preconceived and ready-made notions on art, not wanting to let go of their musical leading strings nor wishing to know anything beyond them. I prefer untrained and unprejudiced people to those who are happy with their superficial culture. But far be it from me to wish to force anybody to love my works. Nor am I

---

[10] Letter dated 23 August 1919.

[11] Letter dated 24 February 1921.

The beginning of Schnabel's 'Credo',
translated on pp. 283–84

affected by the painful embarrassment of some 'tactful' listeners. As a matter of fact, I don't even want to communicate my secrets.[12]

This last sentence, attractive though it may sound at first reading, does not seem to me to be compatible with the composer's role which is, after all, one of communication. But the remark about the tactful listener's embarrassment reminds me of an answer he gave me about 40 years later. I had been present at the first performance in London of one of his orchestral suites. The piece had meant nothing to me; I simply could not enter into its idiom. I hate lying on these occasions. When, therefore, I saw Schnabel after the concert, I tried to get out of it by saying: 'You know, I shall have to hear this work six times before I can begin to understand it', to which he replied: 'And what makes you think you will begin to understand it after you have heard it six times?' Touché!

I am sure I am right in saying that Schnabel's reply to me was more to the point than some of his programme suggestions. My father had obviously written to him to say

[12] Letter dated 16 July 1915.

that he considered his violin solo sonata too long or, as he expressed it, too ample and detailed. Schnabel:

> I am surprised to learn that you estimate the work's duration at 1 hour. In my view it should take, even at a comfortable pace, no more than 45 minutes.[13] And I have chosen this length very deliberately. I wanted to give violinists the possibility of freeing themselves from the necessity to pad out their programs with 'minuetlet'- and similar arrangements and to loosen their ties with the frequently intruding accompanist (supposing they are prepared in principle to pay serious attention to my work); I wanted to given them at long last the opportunity for perfect programme-building, say – Bach sonata; my suite; Paganini studies. I would find this exemplary.[14]

Freedom from 'minuetlet'-arrangements would be excellent. But his views on programme-building must be called lacking in a certain amount of realism, to put it at its mildest. Moreover, they would hardly have been in the interest of those of his professional colleagues who had chosen to specialise in accompanying. Am I doing him an injustice or had he written that letter tongue-in-cheek? Quite possibly at the time, but if someone had contradicted him, he would no doubt have been ready to defend his utterance to the death.

If not contradicted, he could make fun of his own programme building: 'In other pianists' concerts only the first half is boring; in mine the second half is equally boring'.[15]

Schnabel had a deep love of composing:

> During the coming weeks I intend fully to relax perhaps to compose a little, something which for me is always a pleasure, being an activity which is unforced, without a definite purpose, non-commissioned and secret.[16]

But I believe his most important letter is one which I would like to think of as his Credo as a composer. It contains a few passages that, without reservation, can be called admirable. It

---

[13] In my father's *Memoirs* it says 'almost one hour'. Possibly both were a little subjective in their assessment.

[14] Letter dated 7 August 1919.

[15] From Peter Diamand, in conversation.

[16] Letter dated 28 July 1917.

will help rekindle confidence and enthusiasm in any contemporary composer whose work is as yet awaiting recognition. It is dated 23 August 1919.

I do not harbour any illusions whatever regarding the dissemination and present-day popularity of my works. First and foremost let me say, that – apart from some compositions in my youth – I have so far written no more than *four* pieces of music and this after an interval of eight years (during which I did not compose a single note). Of these, *none* has been published and two have been performed *once*. My development has taken place in complete secrecy and no-one has had the opportunity (normal in the case of other composers) to proceed with me from work to work, to ascend imperceptibly, to condition their ear to the repeated assaults from these tone sequences. In my case, the organic connecting links are not perceptible. But once I have written, say, 20 works that have been heard in public now and again, have been reviled, fought over, defended – then I am confident I shan't have to worry about acquiring a following, after the path has been made a little easier to tread. (Compared with Schoenberg, my works surely are 'Salon Musik'.) I simply *have* to continue in the direction I have chosen. And everyone knows that nothing is as changeable as opinion on what is and what is not difficult or beautiful; the mountain regarded as unconquerable only yesterday is one which most mountaineers manage to climb almost as a matter of course today.

On the other hand, former wide-spread skills have been lost. Works – including some which are impressive-sounding hackneyed common property – regarded as models of pure, noble and clear expression today, were considered coarse, meaningless, dry, artificial, gross excesses of noise yesterday. Of course, I do not claim that anything that is offensive at first hearing must necessarily be good or will be regarded as valuable at some future date (but the reverse is even more true).

And if you say that there will be – in theory – at most 3–4 violinists able and willing to play the work, and that perhaps only experts and connoisseurs with very specialised interests will be capable of enjoying it, then my reply must be that this would be quite sufficient for me and that I neither expect nor desire anything more; for I can see that only the very few are capable of performing and appreciating the most valuable works in their full abundance – even though these be old and traditional.

And who decides the length of a composition? Habit, which always means inertia? The judgement of the least demanding listener in the same way in which the slowest vessel determines the speed of the convoy? Good Heavens, if Stamitz – God rest his soul – (he himself, incidentally, one of the most daring revolutionaries) had known the length of the 8th Bruckner or a Mahler symphony, or the contemporaries of Dittersdorf the size of the Phantastic by Berlioz! There are those who satisfy present-day demands and needs, not by design but because this is where their talent leads them; and there are those who are more creative and able to arouse spiritual needs, to change and refine them, to achieve the gratifying effort of joint endeavour.

How valid can be the impression made by a new composition on a layman, however knowledgeable, considering that you yourself were able to recognise its value and to learn deriving enjoyment from it only after studying it intensively and in depth? No work will be appreciated *before* it has been understood. (This is one of the reasons that you can confidently expect works that neither need nor presuppose understanding to receive the easiest (but at the same time most ephemeral) recognition.) Anything new requires the sacrifice of something old. But this is after all one of the main joys in life, and happy he who is capable of setting himself free at least in the abstract spiritual sphere, and, on occasion, of losing himself. . .

Whether or not we share Schnabel's opinions, I don't think they can be expressed better than he has done in this letter. I have a suspicion that on re-reading it, he thought the same, because he concludes with a sentence which is either 'coquetry' or an understatement untypical of Schnabel:

Please forgive me if I have been guilty of platitudes, but I have been anxious to try and convey to you my fundamental views in these matters.

XVII

FLESCH AND SCHNABEL: THE BREAK

'If we were all given by magic
the power to read each other's
thoughts, I suppose the first
effect would be to dissolve all
friendships.'
BERTRAND RUSSELL

In our family, if we wanted to spread a piece of news in the quickest and least troublesome way, we used to tell it in the strictest confidence to an intimate friend known to be an incorrigible gossip. We could unfailingly rely on everbody in our circle knowing about it within the space of a few hours. But her invariable reply to the request for silence was a dismissive 'Who'd be interested in *that*?' A remark that became one of our household phrases – but it is equally a question one wants to ask oneself again and again when writing a book such as this.

On 30 December 1932 my father severed his personal relations with Artur Schnabel. Separations in the field of music are not infrequent for personal or artistic reasons and can be very traumatic for the people involved. But the general public are usually more interested in the formation of new, rather than the termination of existing, associations; and obviously the parties concerned in this particular situation have little desire for publicity. So is it worthwhile describing the breach in more detail?

An event of this kind can be interesting when it involves important personalities, or if it is simply a good story. During this century the best-known instance was probably the case of

Edward VIII and Mrs Simpson. If it had simply been a
company director called John Smith marrying his secretary
after divorcing his wife and losing his job because the firm
happened to be in her name, nobody outside his immediate
circle would have wanted to know. But the importance of the
Royal Family made the affair at the time a world sensation.

What has this got to do with Artur Schnabel and Carl
Flesch? One of the intriguing characteristics of the letters
exchanged between them is the fact that one feels tempted to
draw a parallel to the development of an 'affair': the initial
unconditional mutual devotion – needless to say, purely
platonic; the gradual cooling-off more sensed than consciously
recognised – by one party, anyway; the careful preparation of
the ground by the partner planning to leave; the avoidance of
an open discussion; his 'injured innocence' – all the elements
are present; only the sex is missing.

The interpretation and evaluation of the correspondence is
entirely my own. At the time of the break I was no longer
living at my parents' home; and anyway my father was not in
the habit of discussing professional decisions in depth except
sometimes with my mother.

It started with Schnabel's decision in 1920 to suspend his
public chamber-music activities. He must have discussed this
step in personal conversation with my father; at any rate there
is no correspondence before a letter dated 24 February 1921:

> My Dear Carl, My heartfelt thanks for your very cordial letter;
> I had not in fact expected from you anything else than the
> benevolent sentiments you have expressed. You are making my
> difficult task of replying so much easier that for this reason
> alone I am particularly grateful for your help and understand-
> ing. With this, in fact I have said it all. No need whatever to
> emphasise that if I should resume my chamber music activities,
> I would wish to do so only with you; equally that I shall miss
> our music-making enormously, something which I have always
> loved and valued (not to mention the most regrettable reduction
> of our meetings, exchanges of views and friendly discussions).
> But since I have as yet no firm idea about my next season's
> plans, I felt that it would be highly irresponsible towards you
> and art itself, for me to enter into commitments which I might
> have to honour later in an unwilling state of mind and therefore
> badly. I fully appreciate that an association with someone who

can offer his services only 'subject to final confirmation' makes a viable concert schedule an impossibility. I similarly appreciate that my successor will not agree to a sharing arrangement between him and myself (say for engagements abroad, since I intend definitely not to appear on German concert platforms).[1] Hence I shall have to console myself with the hope that we shall, whenever possible, make music privately and in secret – something I know I shall very much want to do. I only wish that Becker[2] were to show the same understanding as you do for the path I have chosen – possibly the wrong one, yet mine own – so that no residuum of anger and resentment towards me remains. Relinquishing the pleasure of our joint travels is, I repeat, a sacrifice that wrings my heart – but I have to try and resist even the most beguiling temptations. I am sure I shall frequently be sitting in the audience at your concerts wishing nothing more than to be with you up there sharing in your activities. In the end, the separation will cause Becker and you less anguish than me, for I have *greatly* changed.

In other words, the separation is one for which the partner who is leaving provides well-founded reasons and which leaves no nasty after-taste; on the contrary, he maintains that it is he who makes the sacrifice. This extends to more practical matters, too. Apparently my father had pointed out that Schnabel's withdrawal would cause a financial loss to the other Trio partners. Schnabel replied:

I cannot agree that there is any justification for your assertion that I am causing you a financial loss. It cannot be substantiated in any way and I could even maintain that my decision has enabled you to avoid a loss.[3]

---

[1] This does not go quite as far as the assertion by Cesar Saerchinger in his book *Artur Schnabel* (Cassell, London, 1957, p. 136) that he 'announced he would abstain from playing in public during the following season in order to devote himself exclusively to composition'.

[2] Hugo Becker (1863–1941) had joined the trio in 1914, leaving the Marteau Quartet, until, because of Schnabel's withdrawal and Flesch's annual stint at the Curtis Institute, it became dormant. When it resumed, intermittently, Piatigorsky took his place. 'Artistically, [Becker] had the reputation of being the most outstanding 'cellist of his age, until Casals dethroned him and his competitors' (Flesch, *Memoirs*, p. 296).

[3] Letter dated 24 February 1921.

He then refers to foreign exchange regulations – an argument which, almost seventy years on, is clearly not worth examining.

Schnabel's decision had not been a sudden one. Already a year earlier he had approached the pianist Carl Friedberg with the suggestion that he should replace him temporarily; I don't know whether he had done this with or without his partners' knowledge. Friedberg was not only an excellent pianist – probably the most prominent pupil of Clara Schumann – but also a very modest man:

> My Dear Mr Schnabel, Your request honours and pleases me – I shall be very happy to substitute for you in the Trio for one year – 'substitute' – to replace you is impossible. But I shall do my best to minimise the loss suffered by the public through your absence. And I promise Becker and Flesch to look after the precious property entrusted to me as best I can until your return.[4]

Unfortunately the new trio combination did not last long because the unfavourable season in 1922/23 resulted in a marked deterioration of concert life, particularly in chamber music. Moreover, my father accepted a teaching appointment in the United States which kept him away from Europe for the larger part of the concert seasons 1923–1928. For this reason one cannot say with certainty whether or not the association with Schnabel would have been resumed at the end of one year; but whatever the intentions, it was the first step towards what was to follow later.

On 7 August 1927 my father wrote to Schnabel, offering to include an analysis of one of the movements of his solo violin sonata in the appendix to the second volume of his *Art of Violin Playing* on which he had been working a good deal during his American concert tours (at that time, of course, they always involved long train journeys):

> I intend [following a review of classical works in historical order] to deal [. . .] with the very youngest composers. I am placing you in this category notwithstanding the sardonic smile that no doubt is on your lips whilst you are reading this.

Considering his critical attitude towards this particular work

---

[4] Letter dated 7 February 1920.

Carl Flesch, Hugo Becker and Artur Schnabel

my father's offer seems surprising. I can't help feeling just a little suspicious about the motive: was there a (possibly subconscious) objective – for instance, an attempt to place matters on their previous footing? One might compare it with a valuable gift from one partner to another in the hope of shoring up a slowly disintegrating relationship. I have no doubt that my father's offer must have meant a lot to Schanbel even though I have not found any written acknowledgement.

Indeed, joint chamber-music activities were resumed after my father's return from the United States, although on a smaller scale. A letter from Schnabel in 1928[5] testifies to his renewed interst, possibly re-awakened by the long separation:

Please forgive my long silence [. . .].[6] I was surrounded by

---

[5] Dated 13 February.

[6] What Schnabel writes is an untranslatable 'Sei nicht ungehalten über meinen so lange gehaltenen Schnabel'.

people wasting my time. [. . .] I greatly look forward to our joint concert tours.

Occasional sonata and trio evenings continued – for instance, an appearance in Vienna in 1930, which apparently did not receive much press coverage. A letter from Schnabel[7] can be seen as a significant foretaste of things to come:

> My Dear Carl, I too have heard only very little about our concert though what I did hear came from the most demanding and discriminating circles and was unreservedly laudatory. As for myself, I value enormously the memory of the concert and its preparation. But nowadays it appears that mediocre public offerings are talked about everywhere provided that they are blatantly advertised, whereas unusually valuable performances, recognised as such, attract very little attention unless accompanied by the necessary noise. I am afraid nobody is making such noises for us (for me, at least, no-one ever has, although I would not mind), nor do I think we shall find anybody willing to do so, because our type of concerts do not fall into the most profitable category.
>
> So what about the future of our Trio? I like playing, as you know, but someone like Mr Milovitch, Piatigorsky's owner [*sic!*], probably has no interest in our ensemble and will rush our young friend from pillar to post, hire him out, and possibly degrade him. He will have no time for rehearsals and without these – the most enjoyable part – I myself derive no pleasure from the whole undertaking. I'll have a word with Piaty during the next few days and then assess the position.

I believe that was the beginning of the end, the preparation of the alibi.

Joint concerts became ever rarer, but this did not yet express itself in correspondence. On the contrary: Carl Flesch to Artur and Therese Schnabel on the occasion of their silver wedding:[8]

> Dear Therese, Dear Artur, We all would like to express to you our heartiest wishes on your silver wedding. It is now 22 years that we, dear Artur, have been united in joint work, have

[7] Dated 24 May 1930.

[8] Letter dated 8 June 1930.

Gregor Piatigorsky

learned to value and love each other, have gone through many experiences together, some pleasant, some unpleasant. All this has forged a firm bond between us which – whatever the future may have in store – will always bind us spiritually together.

I assume that this undated letter is Schnabel's reply:

My Dear Carl, I have been very remiss in not having thanked you earlier for your last letter, which pleased me very much indeed, and whose contents and spirit moved me deeply. I, too, am aware of the certainty of our personal and essential solidarity, and am glad of it; it means to me higher endeavour and better mutual recognition: in brief, life itself and in addition stimulus and confirmation. And I regard and value as a particularly happy mark of our relationship the mutual confidence in the cleanliness of our chosen paths, even if at one time or another they do not run in tandem. Genuine friendship can thrive only where there is affection and respect; in their presence we do not have to fear occasional frailties – our relationship remains our safe property.

The unusually high-flown tenor of these communications permits of the interpretation that both parties were anxious to behave as if nothing was amiss. But Schnabel's allusion to 'paths that do not always run in tandem' is hardly coincidental.

My father urged Schnabel to declare definitely whether or not he was still interested in future chamber-music concerts:[9]

> Regarding our trio activities generally, I have to state that Piaty absolutely denies no longer being interested; he says that the lack of interest is on your side. I have to confess to you frankly, my dear Artur, that in this matter you are an enigma to me. At any rate, one thing is certain: you don't seem very eager to continue playing trio with us. Your reasons are, of course, your affair. I have to tell you that Piaty and I are of a different opinion. For us this type of activity is a necessity and we are not all that concerned whether or not it is a little more or less profitable. You ought to get clear in your own mind what you wish to do in this matter in future. You see, I shall be playing in public only for a few more years and I would like to include chamber-music in my activities. When I asked you during a walk in spring 1929 to make a decision in this matter, you replied with a clear 'Yes' and we subsequently fixed the various dates for last season. Now you have said 'No'. So, what is the precise position?
>
> Of course, I don't have to tell you that for me you are a unique personality and that I would truly regret no longer being able to play with you. On the other hand, I do not want to give up trio playing during the next few years. I trust you appreciate my point and I should be grateful if you would let me have your frank opinion in this matter.

Obviously, Schnabel's reply was negative as is shown by a further letter from Flesch:[10]

> I have noted with very great regret that you don't want to continue playing with Piaty and myself. This is the end of a musical activity that has, over many years, been a unique experience for me. I have tried very hard to comprehend your reasons for this step, but in vain. You are looking at the matter from an intellectual instead of, like me, a spiritual point of view. The difference between us appears to be that for me chamber music satisfies an inner need whereas you can perfectly well do without it. In contrast to you I believe that it is just the best type of public that are interested in this kind of music. The

[9] Letter dated 9 September 1930.

[10] Dated 22 September 1930.

present difficult times will not make any difference. However, in all the circumstances I cannot but agree with your decision, because joint music-making should always be based on the inner motivation of all the parties concerned; without it, nothing really satisfactory will emerge.

Again it was Carl Friedberg who took Schnabel's place, and the Trio Friedberg-Flesch-Salmond gave some very successful chamber music cycles.

One of the 'official' reasons that Schnabel gave for his refusal to continue with the Trio can be surmised from my father's reply. I am sure he gave several of a general nature. But I have little doubt that the real one was simply that he no longer wished to collaborate with my father – or else why should he, only two years later, have formed an association with Huberman and Piatigorsky? In other words, while the original motivation for ceasing to perform chamber music in 1921 had been a feasible one – the expressed wish to devote one year exclusively to composing[11] – those put forward in 1930 cannot be regarded in this light.

The situation must have presented Schnabel with a very awkward dilemma. A letter dated 29 April 1932 may be regarded as an attempt to resolve it:

> Our conformity of views and our [. . .] friendship means very much to me. But I believe that, happily, we both are the type of people who can accept that friends may hold – and act on – opinions that are not in accordance with, or even quite opposed to, our own. These differences which provide attraction, stimulus and profit, can enhance the value of a relationship. (Points of agreement and disagreement frequently are 'twins'.) It depends on fundamentals. Ours permit of a relationship that may be called happy and fruitful, based as it is on constant affection, respect, absolute confidence and continual mental flexibility. We need have no fear about the continuity of the first three; may the last-named – the virtue of flexibility – remain with us for a long time to come!

With hindsight, the underlying idea seems unmistakable.

---

[11] Which, according to Cesar Saerchinger's biography (*op. cit.*, p. 325) resulted in two completed works, the Second String Quartet (1921) and the Piano Sonata (1922).

In the same letter Schnabel refuses a Paris sonata recital which apparently had been offered to my father. It is significant that he passed the proposal on to Schnabel – I am sure he would not have done so if he had had any inkling of the real situation. Nor did Schnabel use this particular opportunity to give any indication of his – if my interpretation is correct – true feelings or intentions. Rather the opposite, for he continues:

> I would, of course, have very much liked to play with you, but, as always when I receive an enquiry from Paris, I have to decline.

There follows a list of reasons, concluding with an aside that sums up Schnabel's contradictory nature in one sentence:

> Pity, because this city does attract me very much, although (or because) I have never managed to evoke a real response in Latin countries or even gain a toehold.

For the rest, I can let the correspondence speak for itself. Schabel to Flesch (7 December 1932):

> Dear Carl, You said to Piaty that for the past few years my conduct towards you has not been compatible with real friendship. I don't know what actions or omissions on my part could have given you that impression.
>
> What I do know, however, is that I would find it quite impossible knowingly to behave towards you in a manner that could imperil our relationship or even cast as much as a passing shadow. For our bond is a happy and valuable part of my very existence. And for me the kind and degree of this all-embracing unity affecting as it does soul, sentiment and spirit are unchanged and to my mind unchangeable.
>
> It would pain me very much if there were to be an incipient loosening of the ties between us. This is what I wanted to tell you in a few words before we discuss our discord in detail (if this is your wish).
>
> For today just my sincerest regards and very best wishes. I remain always your old A.S.

Flesch to Schnabel (30 December 1932):

> Dear Artur, Your letter in which you assure me of your immutable friendship has surprised me greatly. Its contents

The Flesch–Friedberg–Salmond trio

become increasingly paradoxical, the more one measures them against the practical steps you have taken in the face of our previous artistic and personal connexion.

Piaty advised me officially the other day on your behalf of your and his project concerning a Brahms cycle with Huberman next spring.

Since you were clearly anxious to avoid a personal meeting, I was forced on my part to ask your emissary to transmit to you my opinion about this step. I gather from your letter that he has duly carried out this mission.

First and foremost, I am anxious to make it clear that it is not the fact of your chamber-music change of front that is bugging me. When in 1921 you detached yourself from the Trio, freedom of action on both sides was the logical consquence.[12] Equally, your choice of partner is entirely your own affair,

---

[12] Flesch obviously and understandably did not recollect Schnabel's assurance that, if he were to return to chamber music, it would be only with the original partner(s).

particularly since my innate antipathy towards Huberman might make me appear prejudiced. Nevertheless, I have to say that during the past few years I became more and more puzzled about your sudden sympathy for him, especially if I remember the untiring derision with which you used to refer to him in former years.[13] One of you must have undergone a considerable change in recent times. [. . .]

How you are going to agree artistically, only the future can show.

However, what I do reproach you with is the fact that from 1929 onwards you declined, for reasons that were never clear, to give any chamber-music performances in Berlin or in Germany generally, but that you took – with impeccable taste in the final year of my concert career – the first opportunity of collaborating with someone else. I don't believe that, your great dialectical gifts notwithstanding, you will succeed in reconciling this with your definition of friendship.

While I am aware of the official version, namely that the initiative was Huberman's, I know you sufficiently well to be in no doubt that your actions are entirely governed by your own wishes and interests. In any case it is not unknown to me that you had been contemplating artistic collaboration with Huberman for some time as well as the fact that you had tried as long as 2 years ago to interest Piaty in this project. In parallel with this artistic estrangement I could well recognise your efforts during the past 2 years to restrict our personal relationship to the conventional minimum.

These are the facts I have to state in the face of your assurance of immutable friendship.

Without making too many words I am anxious that you should fully understand me in this our hour of separation. I am neither 'angry' nor is it my intention for us to become enemies. What I want is nothing but the termination of our personal relationship. I have no talent whatever for simulating something I no longer feel. I can't bring myself to smiling conventionally at someone if I don't feel like it. I have during the past few months frequently been thinking how very awkward it must have been for you even to shake hands with me during our occasional meetings. I consider it cleaner and more dignified to

---

[13] Whilst I believe this to be correct, I should, in fairness, refer to Schnabel's letter dated 16 July 1915 (see pp. 137–38); in it he gives a measured opinion of Huberman which did not show any trace of 'derision'. There is nothing in his subsequent letters about this subject.

bury our friendship finally rather than embalm it by artificial and unnatural means.

Although this is the parting of the ways, I shall artistically remain as near to you as ever, and always enjoy listening to your playing in concerts, radio or on the gramophone. In this way the best of you, your art, will be preserved for me.

Schnabel to Flesch (2 January 1933):

Dear Carl, Your letter has greatly saddened me. You give notice; you terminate our friendship. It is for you to arrange your relationships, but you cannot dispose of mine. You can't give me marching orders. Where I was friend, I am and remain friend. To be a friend is an attribute, a possession, an organ. Whether I am shaken off, banned, repudiated, no longer needed, even forgotten by another party: I was and unconditionally remain friend, as a part of me that cannot be killed off separately. If you don't want to see me again, I won't force myself on you. If you do want to see me – I am here, and you will meet a friend. Your old A.S.

Injured innocence as well as the stereotyped farewell remark stereotypically uttered by the one who is leaving the other: 'I shall always remain your friend'.

But Schnabel did not let matters rest there: he made a personal approach to my mother. Thereupon my father wrote again (25 February 1933):

Dear Artur, it has given me some pleasure to know that you felt the urge to talk to my wife about the recent change in our relationship.

It does seem to me that friendship, if it is deserving of the name, is rooted too deeply in one's life to be torn from the soil when it becomes troublesome.

For me personally the artistic cause of our estrangement has meanwhile lost much of its importance whereas I am as yet not in a position to forget the personal background. At this juncture I don't feel able to resume our previous relationship honestly and without reservation. Because I regarded our friendship as something permanent irrespective of changing circumstances, and its continued existence a matter of course, I have genuinely tried to explain to myself your action towards me through the diversity of your character (as opposed to the unity of your artistic personality) and I have, after something of a mental struggle, come to the conclusion that striking and outstanding individualities such as yours cannot be measured by normal bourgeois standards. In spite of this inner process of clarification I don't feel sufficiently free towards you to meet you with the unprejudiced feelings which alone would be worthy of our previous friendship. I must ask you to leave me a little more time.

In the long run the bonds and memories of the many years of friendship proved too strong after all. Flesch wrote to Georg Schünemann on 4 January 1935:

I have made it up with Schnabel, realising that you have to apply the severest standards to the artist as such, but have to show the greatest forbearance to the human being.

The words sound magnanimous, but they contain a harsh judgement.

In terms of our original comparison with the progress of a love affair, the fact that two people should drift apart is nothing unusual. Similarly, every artist has a right, sometimes even a duty, to terminate a professional association and if the occasion presents itself, to form a new one. Yet the reasons which motivated Schnabel to take this step, and the way in which he carried it out, remain obscure.

One may take it as read that my father had not regressed artistically or technically. This is evident from his undiminished successes on the concert platform when, after having emigrated, he was forced to resume his career as a performer. I think it far more probable that Schnabel, who during the preceding years had acquired considerable 'glamour' (something to which my father's personality was not conducive), had become convinced – I suspect not without help from others – that he required a partner who was his equal in this respect, a consideration more of a commercial than an artistic kind but none which he had to be ashamed of for that reason. Every artist is entitled to use his talent in a way that offers him the best chance of financial reward.

What is so difficult to understand is that his choice fell, of all people, on Huberman. Artistically they really were hardly compatible but – more important – he was fully aware of my father's instinctive almost larger-than-life aversion to him.

Hence his action not only showed a quite remarkable lack of tact, but was exceedingly offensive towards one of his best and oldest friends.

It seems, incidentally, that disillusionment set in quite soon and that Schnabel endeavoured to restrict the collaboration to a minimum. According to Peter Diamand,[14] Huberman had a far more commercial turn of mind than Schnabel, and placed undue value on the outward signs of success. A delicate situation arose at one of their sonata evenings when the audience clamoured for Schubert's 'Ave Maria' as an encore – a solo piece for the violinist and therefore a slap in the face *par excellence* for his sonata partner. Again according to Peter Diamand, Schnabel rose to the occasion by saying to Huberman: 'Go on, play it, I'll be able to follow you' – which, indeed, he did, without the score and in exemplary fashion.

That on the other hand Flesch had not been over-reacting can be shown by his relationship with Casals. In his *Memoirs* he characterises him not only as one of the most important artists of his time, but also as a great reformer. In 1907 he had given several trio evenings with him and Julius Röntgen.

> Soon after he formed a permanent association with Thibaud and Cortot whereas I teamed up with Schnabel and Gérardy and subsequently Becker. Thus, our Dutch Trio evenings were to my regret the only occasion uniting us in joint music making.[15]

Thus there was no ill feeling, although my father undoubtedly would have loved to have Casals as his permanent trio partner, but simply a recognition of the fact that he had preferred a different combination. At no point did Casals indicate a lack of esteem for my father's artistic qualities. On 31 January 1937, i.e., long after the Schnabel episode, he writes about a broadcast of the Beethoven Concerto by my father (which, incidentally, forms part of his

[14] See note 7 on pp. 262–63.

[15] P. 235. This is at least as far as public music-making is concerned. I have a subsequent letter (7 December 1912) in which the pianist Harold Bauer expresses his and Casals' pleasure about a recent private chamber-music session.

*Donald Francis Tovey, Julius Röntgen and Pablo Casals
with Adela and Jelly d'Arányi, at Tovey's Northlands home
in 1911*

historical record set[16]): 'Je vien de vous entendre et il me faut vous dire que votre jeu a été *SU-PER-BE*'.[17]

Schnabel always honestly believed in the validity of his opinions however frequently he changed them. One would therefore have expected him to be ready with an explanation of the reason for his behaviour, at least to his own satisfaction. It is all the more surprising that this does not seem to have been the case; at any rate, if an explanation existed, he did not make any attempt to pass it on to the person principally affected. This seems to have been one of the rare occasions when his attack-and-defence mechanism, usually so well developed, failed him and he had to confine himself to high-sounding protestations of friendship and general platitudes in place of concrete arguments, regardless of whether they gave the true reasons or not.

[16] See note 2 on p. 16.

[17] See opposite.

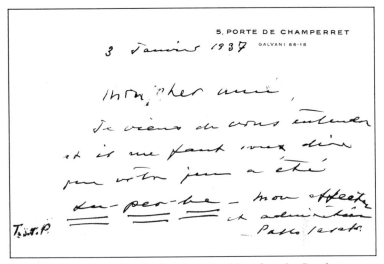

*Casals to Carl Flesch after hearing him play the Beethoven
Concerto*

Obviously no-one wants to tell an old friend to his face that
he no longer regards him as an adequate partner, if this is
indeed his opinion. But it would have been the easiest thing in
the world for a man of Schnabel's dialectic powers to underpin
his decision with arguments of a general musical character.
That he did not do so but – I believe one is entitled to say –
made a mess of it indicates, I think, how uncomfortable he
must have felt. This could also be the most likely reason for
his having 'forgotten' to refer, in *My Life and Music*, to his
friendship and collaboration with my father extending over
several decades. Even so, the whole episode remains an
enigma.

How difficult such a situation must be for both parties can
be seen from the relationship between Julius Röntgen and my
father. In his *Memoirs* he describes how their joint sonata
recitals gradually fizzled out 'as, with advancing age,[18] our
technical discrepancy was becoming increasingly noticeable
whilst at the same time Schnabel aroused in me the need for
technical and artistic perfection which Röntgen was no longer

---

[18] Röntgen was his senior by almost twenty years.

able to satisfy. But we remained life-long friends'.[19] This may
have been due to Röntgen's uncommonly magnanimous character, but I have little doubt that the manner in which my
father handled the situation played its part. It shows what you
can do if you do not want to hurt the feelings of a man of
whom you are extremely fond. The Nederlandse Muziek
Archievan have been kind enough to let me have a copy of a
letter my father wrote in 1915. Apparently Röntgen had
complained to him that some Dutch Schnabel-Flesch recitals
had been announced. I must admit that his reply gives me the
distinct impression of lacking in candour, but it provided an
explanation that was a model of tact and avoided any loss of
face:

> I must confess to you frankly that where sonata recitals in
> Holland are concerned, I find myself in something of a quan-
> dary. When I started my association with Schnabel we
> exchanged the mutual promise to give concerts exclusively with
> one another – with the sole exception of sonata evenings with
> you. Three years ago we received the offer of a concert at
> Arnhem, which I was forced to accept because Schnabel was
> not prepared to lose his fee due to my attitude, however
> commendable. For years he urged me to give joint concerts with
> him in Amsterdam, Rotterdam and The Hague at our own
> expense. I always refused, because I could not bring myself to
> compete in this way with your and my sonata recitals, even
> though these had gradually tended more and more to become a
> thing of the past. [. . .] To compensate Schnabel I had to agree
> to accept Dutch engagements at fixed fees.
> I want to tell you that I myself found this dualism very
> disagreeable, but it was due to circumstances beyond my
> control. It is undeniable that you and I are offered for our joint
> concerts considerably lower fees than those for appearances in
> which I play with Schnabel. It is an inescapable fact of life that
> Dutch concert promoters have always been prone to offering
> their own artists only half the fees they are prepared to pay to
> foreign musicians. I would like nothing better than to play with
> you very often indeed if we could achieve halfway acceptable
> terms. Do believe me, dear friend, that I myself feel the
> situation most keenly [. . .].

[19] P. 215.

It is worth mentioning that my father, like Schnabel fifteen years later, had clearly tried to postpone an open discussion for as long as he possibly could, but once it had become unavoidable, he, unlike Schnabel, made the best of it.

As a matter of fact, the Schnabel-Flesch Duo did play together once more in London, not in public but in a house concert at the private residence of Sir Robert Mayer, the founder of the famous Children's Concerts, who lived to the age of 103. I remember little of the occasion and do not believe that it gave pleasure to either player. The vital spark had been irretrievably lost.

Schnabel spent the War in the United States. My parents managed, after surmounting many dangers, to reach safety in Switzerland. From there they kept up occasional contact. And when my wife and I, early in the War, contemplated evacuating our baby son from London to America, Schnabel unhesitatingly agreed to give the guarantees needed for his entry visa. The plan was subsequently not pursued in view of the U-boat danger. I distinctly remember the precise moment when we dropped the idea: we had been trying to find someone who would take our baby to the USA and received an offer from a man who made a point of the fact that he was a strong swimmer.

The last opportunity I had to hear Schnabel play was after the War at a London concert where he performed the second Brahms Concerto. One felt it to be a farewell. I shall never forget the occasion and do not expect to hear another performance anything like as beautiful and moving. It leaves a lasting memory of everything that was beautiful and great in him.

According to Peter Diamand, Richard Strauss, shortly before his death, expressed the same view in somewhat more robust language. He heard Schnabel play in Zurich in 1946 and since Strauss' attitude during the Hitler period had been open to widespread criticism, Schnabel, on meeting him after the concert, adopted a markedly reserved attitude towards him. Next day Strauss marched into his hotel room, unannounced, with the words: 'I don't care a shit about your opinion of me. But your playing yesterday was so out of this world that, having heard it, one can die in peace'.

XVIII

ATTACKS, MISUNDERSTANDINGS AND MORE INNOCENT MATTERS

'I don't care what is written
about me, so long as it isn't
true.'
KATHARINE HEPBURN

We all of us are on occasions exposed to attacks or unintentional misinterpretations of our motives and actions. How they affect us depends more than one might think on how we react. Frequently, if we disregard them, they die a natural death.[1]

On the other hand, if we take any action we may be

---

[1] I can offer an example from my own experience. Some readers may remember the incident, during the London Olympics in 1948, of a Russian competitor being arrested for shoplifting – she had allegedly stolen a hat. As a result not only the entire Russian team but also the Bolshoi Ballet, which was making a guest appearance, immediately broke off their stay in London. *The Sunday Times* asked me to explain the 'Non-appearance Insurance' aspects of an event of this kind. In the course of the interview the reporter suggested that I mention the names of some of the artists in whose insurances I had been involved. Naturally I declined, since these matters are strictly confidential. The only exception I was prepared to make concerned a musician who had died some years ago and had himself frequently and freely mentioned the fact that he was insured.

When the article appeared I was flabbergasted to note that it had been turned round in quite an ingenious way so as to create the impression of my having disclosed details about practically the whole of my clientele. I feared professional ruin and seriously considered suing the paper or at least forcing it to publish a correction. However, on the advice of an experienced friend I decided to await developments before taking any steps. And lo and behold: nobody ever referred to the article although the incident that had triggered off the interview had been attracting considerable public attention and many people had no doubt read the interview.

achieving the exact opposite of what we had intended, by drawing specific attention to the falsehoods published about us. Some people don't mind; indeed, for them, bad publicity is better than none. But for most others, no matter whether well-known or not, the better course is to ignore such allegations unless they concern fundamental matters which one cannot permit to go uncontradicted.

My father, whose instinct for publicity was altogether not very well developed, usually preferred to let matters rest. This allowed one or two errors to creep into musical history that are worth correcting.

There is the 'Marlene Dietrich Case', for instance. We found it intriguing at the time without attaching any real importance to it. Nowadays, of course, one might think differently, with everybody consulting solicitors on the slightest provocation with a view to assessing the chances of a libel suit. On this basis the Flesch family might have had a chance to move into the millionaire class, but the idea did not occur to anybody at the time and I don't think my father ought to be blamed for the opportunity missed.

Marlene Dietrich originally studied music and intended to become a professional violinist. According to her memoirs she had been a Flesch pupil, a statement which she embellished with a few interesting details: my father had been so severe a teacher and had demanded such unreasonable exercises that she had had to give up the violin due to the physical and psychological damage done to her.

My father was rightly convinced that he would have remembered a pupil with the looks of Marlene Dietrich. He therefore wrote to her several times requesting to let him know when exactly she had been his student; no reply. I, too, wrote once with the same negative result.

The mystery was solved when, many years later, Miss Dietrich entered a Paris restaurant in which my father together with my sister – who has related the story to me – happened to be having lunch as well. This was an opportunity he did not want to miss. He had a waiter take his visiting card to her asking for a brief chat. She invited him to her table where the matter was cleared up.

Miss Dietrich had tried to enter the Berlin Hochschule für

Musik as a student but unfortunately had not passed the entrance exam. Apparently my father had been a member of the committee that turned her down. Understandably perhaps, she felt that, told in this way, the story would spoil her image, and so she decided on a version somewhat more flattering to herself. In either case, one might say that indirectly my father was responsible for her film career, something which many people will no doubt regard as his greatest claim to fame.

I have since noticed that Miss Dietrich must have forgotten the Paris meeting – which admittedly took place more than fifty years ago – for she repeats the original story in her latest memoirs, *My Life*.[2] She also gives a description of my father's teaching methods which is both the most critical and at the same time most concise assessment I have ever read: 'Bach, Bach, Bach, always Bach!' Luckily for him, this rather one-sided method seems to have been missed by other musical experts.

Rather weightier are some allegations made against him regarding his relations with one of his best pupils, the late Josef Wolfsthal. They appear in a biography of the cellist Emanual Feuermann,[3] were repeated by Artur Weschler-Vered in a Heifetz biography,[4] and are going to be referred to in a second book by Weschler-Vered, *Songs Ephemeral* (which contains a chapter on Wolfsthal).[5] In fairness, I ought to add that Mr Weschler-Vered includes in that book a number of corrections I have made available to him. Since, however, he has put the two versions alongside each other without giving his own opinion, leaving it, as it were, to the reader to decide, this cannot be regarded as really putting the facts straight.

If any of the stories were true they would point to serious personality defects of my father. In cases of this kind one wants to ask oneself whether to waste time and space on dealing with these allegations or to treat them with the

[2] Weidenfeld and Nicolson, London, 1989.

[3] S.W. Itzkoff, *Emanuel Feuermann, Virtuoso*, University of Alabama Press, Tuscaloosa, 1979, pp. 115ff.

[4] *Jascha Heifetz*, Rober Hale, London, 1986, pp. 38ff.

[5] *Op. cit.*

disregard they deserve. But since they are contained in biographies that claim to be taken seriously, it would seem appropriate to answer them in a similar context. Moreover – and more importantly – it may be assumed that the situation is not unique and that its description can afford an insight into the direction in which sometimes even the closest teacher/ pupil relationship may develop.

And finally it gives a useful illustration of the risks run by authors – other than novelists – who do not take the trouble to check the reliability of their sources; it can only result in their book losing credibility as a whole. There appear to exist no legal remedies against libel on persons who are no longer alive. I very much doubt that the allegations would have been made if my father had still been living – which would have been all to the good for the books concerned.

Wolfsthal was for many years almost certainly the best Flesch pupil around. The amount of care and trouble expended by his teacher on both his professional training and generally is well documented in a number of letters from Wolfsthal himself, as well as from his family.

Something of my father's regard for him can be found in a letter of 27 November 1916 to a concert promoter;[6] in it he apologises for being unavailable since he will be on tour:

> However, if you are looking for a really good musician – although *not* a draw – to take part, I would like to recommend my pupil Josef Wolfsthal, Berlin, Berchtesgadenerstr. 5, in my opinion altogether the best violinist of the youngest generation (he is only 17). He would accept a fee of DM 100 in order to introduce himself in Br[emen?] and you would be very pleased with him.

In later life, however, Wolfsthal turned out to be a disappointment to my father as a human being. I am not in a position to judge whether or not this adverse opinion was well-founded; my own recollection of Wolfsthal is favourable if somewhat faint. My father has it differently and complains in a diary entry already quoted about pupils' ingratitude – somewhat surprisingly, if one reads the very numerous letters

---

[6] See p. 308.

Carl Flesch recommends Josef Wolfsthal to a concert promoter

of thanks he received, which would almost be sufficient to fill a
(tedious) volume themselves. But the diary is quite specific:[7]

> I have had amazing experiences in this respect – especially with
> my late pupil Wolfsthal who during the last years of his life
> developed a veritable pathological hatred towards me – and that

[7] Entry for 14 October 1931.

after I had done for him everything one human being can possibly be expected to do for another.

The fact that Wolfsthal originally revered my father is shown by a number of his early letters; for instance, in 1916: 'You are the only person who assists me by word and deed'.[8]

That something was not quite as it should be can be sensed from a letter dated 24 October 1930:

My Dear and greatly honoured Professor, Paul von Schlippen-bach[9] has on account of Thibaud's presence in Berlin, coupled with the fact that unlike him I do not regard Thibaud as the greatest living fiddler, somewhat lost his head; so much so in fact that I should not be surprised from what he said, if he sooner or later might make false statements about me [. . .]. I would like to make it clear to you that I have spoken to him about you only once, and that at his instigation. [. . .] I remarked on the differences between your and my bowing.

You would do me a great service as a friend if you could let me know in case anybody were to talk to you in a way capable of affecting our friendly relations. I would be most anxious to take the originator of such talk to task.

This does not sound at all like 'pathological hatred'. And since Wolfsthal died unexpectedly only four months later, there did not remain much time for developing it, either. Indeed, I can find nothing in the documents at my disposal expressing any hatred or, for that matter, pointing to any character defects on Wolfsthal's part.[10] We should therefore not dismiss the possibility that my father misinterpreted Wolfsthal's attitude towards him and generally did him an injustice in judging him in such an unfavourable way. But on the other hand he was not given to making such allegations lightly. Are there possibly additional indications below the surface?

---

[8] See also pp. 82–83.

[9] A painter and mutual acquaintance who liked to be involved in the musical scene; see also p. 91.

[10] The above mentioned biographers deduce a number of them from other factors, but I am not concerned with these since I am dealing only with material directly available to me.

Josef Wolfsthal in 1916

These could be in the first place the allegations themselves that were made against my father and with which I shall deal presently. The point to note here is that neither of the two biographers can possibly have known of them first-hand: Wolfsthal was no longer alive, and to my knowledge there are no written records. The adverse statements must therefore have been made by people near to Wolfsthal who – understandably – may have taken exception to remarks made about him in my father's *Memoirs*. Since we may disregard the possibility that they invented them, most of them must originally have come from Wolfsthal himself. We should not overlook that the relationship between him and Flesch was not dissimilar to that between son and father (Wolfsthal himself had lost his own father comparatively early). It is well-known that such a relationship can decisively deteriorate for reasons which on the face of it cannot be explained.

In addition, on closer reading of Wolfsthal's letter, one begins to have some doubts about the sentiments he expresses. For one thing Wolfsthal may well have talked a little more freely – i.e., in a less complimentary way – than he lets on about the difference between his and my father's bowing. I don't believe, though, that this could have been a point at issue between them, if only because my father specifically remarks in his *Memoirs* that Wolfsthal's 'bowing particularly was near absolute perfection'.[11]

Next the sentence in Wolfsthal's letter: 'I have spoken about you to [Schlippenbach] only once, and that at his instigation'. Now, why should he not speak to a mutual acquaintance about his teacher; or to, put it another way, why should he deny it unless what he said was derogatory?

And this peculiar introduction regarding Thibaud: what could it possibly mean, except perhaps an attempt at prejudicing my father against Schlippenbach as the bringer of unfavourable tidings by pointing out that there was at least one violinist (Thibaud) whom he preferred to his friend Flesch?

In brief, I suspect there is rather more in all this than meets the eye. But I don't want to split hairs. The main question is whether the serious slanders which the biographers have taken on board contain any vestige of truth.

Wolfsthal was Carl Flesch's assistant at the Berlin Hochschule. It is alleged that when Wolfsthal became severely ill, my father transferred his pupils to Max Rostal without more ado – writing him off, as it were, while still alive. It is no doubt true that he did arrange for Rostal to take them over, but – as, indeed, Rostal himself has confirmed[12] – of course, only in order not to leave them unsupervised during Wolfsthal's enforced absence. Nobody was contemplating the possibility of Wolfsthal's sudden death, but only that of the illness and subsequent period of recuperation taking some time. A temporary re-arrangement of the pupils' studies was therefore something any teacher with a sense of responsibility would

---

[11] P. 274.

[12] In conversation.

Carl Flesch with Max Rostal in the 1930s

have done as a matter of course; quite apart from the fact that it would have been out of question for my father to arrange for a permanent transfer without the agreement of the Hochs-chule management, who would clearly not have gone along with a suggestion so utterly reprehensible.

It has further been alleged[13] that Fritz Kreisler had lent Wolfsthal a valuable violin and that at my father's request my mother suggested to Mrs Kreisler that she should ask her husband to press Wolfsthal for its return. The reason? My father was jealous of Wolfsthal's success and hoped to curtail it by depriving him of that instrument! And this is not meant as a joke but as a serious allegation. I don't know anything about the story itself except that it is impossible. I don't even know

---

[13] By Itzkoff in *Emanuel Feuermann, Virtuoso, op. cit.*, pp. 115ff.

whether and for what reason Kreisler had lent Wolfsthal one of his fiddles, but if he did, then presumably it had been at my father's instigation. The most likely explanation for this matter – assuming it happened – is that Kreisler had asked for the violin's return and that Wolfsthal had not complied with this request as promptly as Kreisler would have liked; he may have mentioned this to my mother or my father, perhaps asking him to intervene.

My father himself not infrequently lent some of his violins to pupils, and not exactly unsuccessful ones either – as witness several letters of thanks from, for instance, Henryk Szeryng and Szymon Goldberg. The suggestion that he asked for them to be returned when the pupils became too successful – instead of being proud of the fact – throws a fascinating light on what some musicologists seem to believe makes a teacher tick. Equally novel is the idea that the possession of a first-class fiddle could decisively influence a violinist's career. I had always imagined that success came first, borrowing or buying a first-class instrument later. And, after all, Wolfsthal had been proving for many years that he could achieve outstanding success without borrowing an instrument from Kreisler.

Equally amusing is the story[14] of a quartet evening with Wolfsthal when my father messed up a difficult passage which Wolfsthal sitting at the second desk had to repeat shortly afterwards and did so brilliantly and faultlessly.

My father, considerably irritated (apparently there is, in the biographer's view, an unwritten law to the effect that if the teacher makes a mistake, the pupil has to be sufficiently tactful to repeat it), is said to have commented, piqued: 'Well, it shows that you had a better teacher than I did'.

A pity that neither biographer contacted me before putting this nonsense on paper. I could have told him that I had heard my father, who liked to play quartet with his pupils from time to time, make this remark almost regularly when happening to miss some tricky passage – laughingly, immediately, and in no way 'piqued'. His spontaneous and almost infallible mastery of the violin repertoire was one of the qualities that never ceased to impress his pupils, and he was the last person to have to

[14] *Ibid*. p. 20.

worry about the occasional mishap. The way he said it, it was witty; meant seriously, it would have made no sense at all. Indeed, this saying became so much a matter of course for me that I was occasionally tempted to use it on his behalf, as it were. I remember meeting the cellist Gaspar Cassadó, who was married to a very attractive Japanese lady. I mentioned to her the name of a good-looking Japanese violinist who had studied with my father, asking her whether she happened to know him. 'Know him', she replied dryly, 'I almost married him. But then I decided against it – his violin playing was not good enough for me.' At which I turned to Cassadó with the remark: 'How lucky for you that my father was such a poor teacher – or else you would not have captured your lovely wife'.

But even in his description of my father's relations with Feuermann,[15] the subject of his biography, Itzkoff discloses a remarkable lack of knowledge. He seems to have imagined that the head of the Berlin Hochschule's violin section could decisively influence the selection of a cello teacher. Feuermann had put in for a teaching post at that institution and, shortly before a decision about his application was due to be made, he and my father had a joint engagement to play the Brahms Double Concerto. On that occasion, so writes Itzkoff,[16] Feuermann decided to be particularly careful:

> Flesch, whose technical means were limited [*sic*], needed all sorts of concessions and help from his partner. Feuermann managed to do this so unobtrusively that everything sounded perfectly natural; the ensemble was faultless. Two weeks later Feuermann had his professorship at the Hochschule.

In other words, out of gratitude to Feuermann for helping him with a concerto that was really beyond his technical capacity, my father made sure that he got the Hochschule position.

As it happens, the Double Concerto was one of Flesch's repertoire pieces, one which he played frequently with prominent cellists. I myself was present at several outstanding

[15] P. 101

[16] *Ibid.*

performances with Piatigorsky.[17] And whatever criticisms one might have of Carl Flesch's playing, a 'limited technique' was definitely not one of them. He certainly did not need the forbearance of any duo partner. Feuermann seems to have shared this opinion; at any rate he wrote to him before the concert: 'I hope it will be a pleasure not only for me. Although I have so far never played the Double Concerto by heart, I trust I won't be inferior to you in this respect'.[18] Flattery? Not very likely, for this was not Feuermann's way. Moreover, he knew Flesch's high opinion of him.

One thing we can concede: the concert did actually take place. But practically everything else, I am afraid, is fantasy – even the statement that the ensemble was faultless, for, as it happened, my father reported laughingly on his return from that particular engagement that he had lost concentration for a moment and missed an entry. Feuermann, 'with mischievous sang froid', as he put it, played it for him.

An experienced writer with whom I once discussed the idea for this book disclosed that a biography or similar work was likely to have the best chances of success it if contained as much unfavourable material as possible about as many people as possible – and not necessarily excluding the subject of the book. One might almost be tempted to assume that the author of the Feuermann biography had taken this advice too literally. But I don't think so. The mistakes, however curious, are bound to be bona fide. If he had had any malicious intent, I am sure he would have been able to invent better and more credible ones.

Is it petty to quote at this point a critical (in both senses) opinion about Feuermann? I don't think so – for it is the opinion of Hugo Becker, until his retirement a leading exponent of his art. It is interesting because it demonstrates a

---

[17] A letter (6 October 1932) from his former trio partner Hugo Becker, inviting him for a visit, ends: 'Perhaps we could on that occasion play the Double Concerto, which we annotated together at one time so beautifully (and unnecessarily!)'. Orchestral appearances with Becker must have dated back to around 1910–20; to play the work my father did not have to wait for Feuermann, who was born in 1904.

[18] Letter dated 21 July 1928; see p. 316.

*Emmanuel Feuermann on
playing the Brahms Double
Concerto; see p. 315.*

critical opinion not generally held (and in my view going too far). Becker compares Feuermann with Piatigorsky:[19]

> Piatigorsky's talent lies more in the direction of the emotional, Feurmann's in that of dexterity. Last year I heard the latter play the Schumann Concerto in Munich. Technically excellent, but as unromantic as can be. You simply can't perform Schumann without passion and rapture. I have never heard this – in parts very poetic – work played with less feeling and spirit, and I consider it a matter for regret that so capable a performer has remained so under-developed in these two directions. If he were a pianist or violinist, the public would never forgive him. But who understands anything about cello literature?

While it is true that, as far as I recollect, Feuermann was anything but sentimental, I cannot remember a performance by him that left me dissatisfied.

Difficulties can also arise – in common with so many other professions – in questions of copyright and intellectual

[19] Letter dated 13 July 1933.

property. I myself did not know until some years ago that the name Flesch meant anything to Russian musicians until a friend took me to the Green Room after a concert by a Russian chamber orchestra. The effect created when I was introduced made it clear that Russian violinists are well acquainted with my father's written works. As Soviet Russia at that time had not yet joined the Berne Copyright Convention, this fact had passed me by. But since I had written the last chapter of my father's *Memoirs*,[20] I have had, at least, the satisfaction of having been translated into Russian.

Into this area belong also the so-called 'revised editions' of important violin schools sometimes used by comparative unknowns as a means of gaining publicity. I possess a letter from Andreas Moser's son,[21] asking my father to appear as an expert witness in a law suit against the publishing house Simrock in order to suppress an unauthorised version of the Joachim-Moser violin school. The revision had been carried out by the violinist Ossip Schnirlin who, as far as I remember, was not particularly popular with some of his colleagues. In the case in question he intended, *inter alia*, as Moser wrote, 'to include in the work the reconstruction of a Bach piano concerto changing it into a violin concerto modestly adding "by Bach-Schnirlin"'.

Another – culturally far less important but nevertheless irritating – kind of falsification was applied to a story which originally had come from my father himself. Arriving for a concert in Iowa, USA, he was interviewed four times on the trot. Expressing his surprise at the flattering attention he was receiving in that particular town, the fourth journalist rudely disillusioned him: Iowa boasted only one newspaper but, perhaps surprisingly, also a college for journalists, whose students regarded all visitors as legitimate targets for their practical exercises. My father considered this a sufficiently amusing story to write it up and offer it to the Berlin *Vossische Zeitung* which duly published it. (I am reproducing it as

---

[20] My father's *Memoirs* dealt only with events up to 1928; it fell to me to write a last chapter completing the story up to his death in 1944.

[21] See also p. 160.

Appendix VII,[22] not only because I think it is quite charmingly written but also because it shows the enjoyment he derived
from stories against himself.)

A few months later I read the self-same story in the Berlin
humorist magazine *Ulk* – without naming names but unmistakably about him: it specifically mentioned Iowa. The story
was identical, with just one slight difference: in this particular
version the artist was on a concert tour which was proving
singularly unsuccessful. When he was interviewed so unexpectedly frequently he believed that his luck had turned at
long last, until, to his deep disappointment, he was appraised
of the true facts.

This is again one of those cases which, if it were to happen
today, could cost the paper a great deal of money. But if this
thought had occurred to anyone (which it did not), one would
also have had to take into consideration the possibility of an
action for libel proving professionally damaging: quite likely
the paper might have tried to prove justification, and although
this attempt would undoubtedly have been a failure, the
defence would obviously have collected every scrap of even
remotely critical reviews. As everybody knows, it is easy to
extract for publicity purposes something favourable from even
the worst notice; if one tried hard enough the opposite ought
to be equally possible – a perfect case for letting sleeping dogs
lie and treating such matters with the contempt they deserve.

Sometimes, of course, a case can create more agreeable
publicity – namely when the 'bone of contention' is the artist
himself. A letter to his former pupil Joachim Röntgen from
my father after his arrival in Switzerland during the War:[23]

> A piece of gossip that may amuse you: the management of the
> Geneva Conservatoire are suing the paper *La Suisse* for libel on
> account of little me. The paper had fiercely attacked the Music
> Academy because they had failed to engage me having instead
> allowed Lucerne to get hold of that tasty morsel – myself. In
> consequence acerbic correspondence culminating in a lawsuit,
> with myself as chief witness.

[22] See pp. 368–69.

[23] Dated 6 February 1944.

I don't know the result of this storm in a tea cup – presumably my father's untimely death put a natural end to it.

Times have changed. What would we say today to a letter from the conductor Felix von Kraus, written in 1913 when the pianist Gottfried Galston applied unsuccessfully for the post of Professor at the Munich Music Academy:

> [. . .] Incidentally, I have been told that Galston has been exhibiting, in the music shop Schmied, a photo of himself wearing a 'fantasy costume', something which many people have found very strange. Personally I don't particularly mind whether someone allows himself to be shown in a bath robe, uniform, as Pasha or as Eunuch. Since the question of Mr. Galston's professorship has been resolved in the negative, the matter is without practical importance, but otherwise it would have made it very much more difficult according to the way people are talking about it.

I wonder what people of those days would have said about the dress sense in vogue today.

Respect for older people, on the other hand, had ceased to exist then as now. This is shown, for instance, by a somewhat malicious story about Leopold Auer, who became my father's successor at the Curtis Institute of Music in Philadelphia. He had reached the venerable age of 82 and some Flesch pupils were not ecstatic about the change. However eminent he was, one had to face the possibility that he might be no longer at his best, hence the joke: 'Have you heard the latest Auer sensation?' 'No?' 'The other day, during a lesson, he suddenly woke up.'

Needless to say, this story did not emanate from my father. On the contrary, Auer and he were on the best of terms. Auer wrote on 22 January 1928:

> Your decision to discontinue your successful work in Philadelphia will no doubt be greatly regretted by musicians and music lovers alike, but especially by myself since I have been chosen partly to replace you – a difficult task considering my age and my other obligations. I shall be happy to follow your kind suggestion of attending a lesson in your class [. . .].

Auer was not without a sense of humour. When in 1912 my father sent him a copy of his newly published *Basic Studies*

A letter from Leopold Auer

(*Urstudien* in German), he wrote him a letter of thanks in which he played on the double meaning of 'Ur' which in German can mean 'basic' or 'very old': 'At last something really new in violin technique. Is this why you called it "Ur"-Studien?'

Finally, a remark following the death of Ysaÿe. A variety of violinists claimed to be his rightful 'successor'. Robert Perutz had no such aspirations:

> Piastro[24] reports that Elman is very worried about the enormous responsibility resting on him since Ysaÿe's death. The whole world now looks expectantly up to him. Yes, it must be terrible to carry such a weight on your shoulders!

[24] The brothers Josef (1889–1964) and Michel (1891–1970) Piastro were both Auer students at the St Petersburg Conservatoire; both, too, settled in the United States. It is not clear to which Perutz is referring.

XIX
SKETCHES

> 'The sublime and the ridiculous
> are often so nearly related that
> it is difficult to class them
> separately.'
> THOMAS PAINE

Fritz Kreisler

A good deal has been written about this man – one of the greatest violinists of his time, if not the greatest. But one or two aspects may not have found their full expression in official biographies. In his *Memoirs*, my father, a life-long friend and admirer, dealt at some length with his artistic and personal development. In his youth he was the Bohemian incarnate until his marriage brought about a profound change, and it is intriguing to compare some of my father's remarks in his *Memoirs* with the rather more informal ones in his diary.

Memoirs (of a performance of the *Adagio Religioso* by Thomé):

> It was an unrestrained orgy of sinfully seductive sounds, depravedly fascinating whose sole driving force appeared to be a sensuality intensified to the point of frenzy.

> Kreisler's Bohemian period came to an end in 1902. [. . .] The woman whom he loved and married [. . .] knew how to guide him, to ennoble his characteristic sensuality and to refine the wild and unbridled elements of his temperament. Without endangering the seductive qualities of his playing, Kreisler let his style be determined primarily by musical requirements [. . .]. The quality of his tone was unmistakable, incomparable and un-equalled.[1]

[1] Pp. 118 and 121.

322

Diary:[2]

> To understand Kreisler you have to have heard him as a very
> young man before he was forced by his wife into an ordered way
> of life. At the time he possessed a lasciviousness of expression –
> the violinistic equivalent of original sin – whose fascination was
> second to none. All he had to do was to transfer his mode of
> living into his playing. A few years later he was on his way to
> going under irretrievably when his wife pulled him out of the
> morass by his ears, and ever since she has not lost the habit.
>
> Thus actually, Kreisler as the public knows him now is no
> longer the genuine article. If you observe him today, steady,
> quiet, restrained, always with a somewhat rigid appearance, you
> would not credit that he was once a man lashed by unrestrained
> impulsiveness, oozing salaciousness on the violin, seductive,
> arousing all the so-called 'bad' instincts – in brief, an exceed-
> ingly exciting artist. In the long run there can be little doubt
> that he would have been destroyed by this hypertrophic
> sexuality as a man as well as an artist. Hence it was perhaps a
> good thing that he met his wife when he did, even if ever since
> he has had no longer as comfortable a life as before.

The difference between the two passages is not so much the
portrayal of Kreisler's playing during his youth (about which
the *Memoirs* leave no doubt either) as the description of his
relationship with his wife, though even the diary is still rather
restrained about it. It was an open secret – in fact rather less
than a secret – that Mrs Kreisler was the dominating figure in
that marriage. She kept him under close control – and no
doubt knew the reason why.

My mother was told of an occasion when a mutual
acquaintance was visiting Mrs Kreisler who was ill in bed and
could not attend a public dress rehearsal of the Berlin
Philharmonic Orchestra where her husband was the soloist:
'He comes on at 11.20, so he will be finished at 11.55. Green
Room, congratulations, etc., until 12.30. He doesn't have to
stay on after the interval. Taxi at 12.35, he should be home by
12.55. It is now 13.05 – *why isn't he here yet?*'

Sometimes his wife's remarks led to amusing situations.
The diary again:[3]

[2] Entry probably for 18 March 1931.

[3] Entry for 12 September 1931.

Kreisler, of unmistakably Jewish origin, but baptised early in his
youth [. . .]. His wife would like to convince everybody that
basically he is an 'Aryan'. At a party she once pronounced:
'Actually Fritz has very little Jewish blood in his veins'. At which
Godowsky: 'Oh, I didn't realise Fritz is that anaemic'.

The general devotion to him found expression in public as
well as in private. The American conductor and arranger Sam
Franco wrote to my father from New York in 1920:[4]

> My arrangement of Rimsky-Korsakov's 'Hymn to the Sun' has
> been so successful that at the request of the publishers Carl
> Fischer Inc., Kreisler has made a similar transcription based on
> mine. This means more to me than the fact that Mischa Elman
> has been playing my arrangement for the last 2 seasons and has
> made a record of it which has been sold by the thousands.[. . .]
> Kreisler is one of the few German artists who during the war
> has been consistent and whose noble and manly stance has
> earned him the love and respect of all classes of society. It is for
> this reason that he has become an artist of such unique standing
> with a following second to none.[5]

But there were also other, rather less admiring, expressions
of opinion. I can't judge (but can imagine) how far these were
due to personal animosity by colleagues not as successful. A
letter to my father[6] by Sylvain Noach – who held successive
posts as leader of the Boston, St Louis and Los Angeles
Symphony Orchestras:

> Kreisler has [during the last season] been the absolute sovereign
> among violinists, and since this year he was without real
> competition, he could afford to play even more out of tune than
> usual; it was the widely circulated story of his 'war injury' that
> made up for all his shortcomings. Perhaps you have already

[4] Letter dated 16 July 1920.

[5] Franco is, of course, referring to the First World War, during the first half
of which America remained neutral. Kreisler had served in the Austrian
army at the Russian front, but early on had sustained a foot injury which
made him unfit for further service. He was able to return to the United
States at the end of 1914, but retired temporarily from concert life when
America's entry into the War made him an 'enemy alien'. His first
re-appearance at Carnegie Hall on October 1919 was a personal and artistic
triumph (see Boris Schwarz, *Great Masters of the Violin*, p. 300).

[6] Dated 4 August 1915.

Fritz Kreisler by Emil Orlik

heard the answer given by Elman sen. to the question why his son Mischa had not been appearing in public during the previous winter season: 'Where is Mischa supposed to play? He hasn't got a war injury!'

It has to be remembered that this letter was written in 1915, when the United States was still neutral and by no means entirely anti-German. One cannot blame the American agents who, for publicity purposes, milked Kreisler's war injury for all it was worth (and more) even though Kreisler had been anything but a war hero. Apart from every soldier's normal fears he had the artist's additional worry of permanent damage

RIVER HOUSE
435 EAST 52ND STREET
NEW YORK 22. N. Y.

February 8th 1955.

Dear friend Bertha.

Many thanks for your kind wishes
to my 80th birthday, which brought
back to us both sad memories of happier
times, when my dear friend Karl was
alive, and when the active exercise of
our artistic profession brought us often
together. But, alas, these are bygone
times! Once more, many sincerest
thanks. With best wishes and much
love from us both
always your very cordially
Fritz Kreisler

A letter from Fritz Kreisler to my mother

to his hands. His colleagues' irritation at his 'unfair' publicity is understandable; obviously it did not occur to them that given similar circumstances they would have done precisely the same.

Kreisler sometimes experienced hostility in the press, too; this may well have had political reasons, Robert Perutz wrote to my father (probably in 1920) that

Kreisler has again been vilified in New York. One of the papers has gone so far as to write – 'Kreisler should leave playing the fiddle to younger virtuosos'. His concerts, of course, continue to be sold out.

This review is ridiculous, because apart from anything else it called him – a man in his mid-forties – old and out of date. But it shows that even the greatest of the great are not immune from occasional hostility and a bad press. In Kreisler's case it did not affect his phenomenal worldwide successes. His concerts were filled to overflowing practically wherever he appeared, inside and outside the USA.

In London he gave, during the 1920s and '30s an annual recital at the Albert Hall, again a regular sell-out. At that time this particular venue combined London's largest audience capacity with the worst possible acoustics. The old joke that, in some seats, the echo allowed you to hear two concerts for the price of one was literally correct, as I can confirm from my own experience. This state of affairs was to some extent remedied during the War when, after the destruction of Queen's Hall, the Albert Hall had to be used for concerts more frequently than before. But during the inter-war years the acoustics were simply terrible.

Many people expressed the opinion that it was below the dignity of an artist in Kreisler's position to give concerts there, sold out or not. Confronted with this, Kreisler replied: 'But why should I make a present to the British people of £1,000 a year?'

I can confirm this figure – a very substantial amount at the time – because one of these concerts was the very first public event I insured against cancellation at the start of my insurance-broking career. And at the same time I experienced my first insurance loss of this kind: the concert had to be cancelled due to public mourning following the death of King George V. In this particular case it was possible to find another date a few weeks later. Undoubtedly Kreisler suffered a certain financial loss all the same, but he did not make an insurance claim – whether out of consideration for the young son of his old friend or because he simply forgot, I do not know.

But it does show that his '£1,000 present' remark was meant as a joke and did not give a true picture of his personality. He was, to my knowledge, not avaricious and, being one of the best-paid artists of his time, had no need to be. He was, indeed, well-known for giving his services free for charity relatively often.

I possess a number of his letters to my father, though none sufficiently interesting to warrant quoting here. But I would like to reproduce his last letter to my mother on the occasion of his eightieth birthday.[7] It bears witness of the friendship between the two families and the mutual affection of the two artists for one another.

Willem Mengelberg

Although Mengelberg and my father had been on friendly terms for many years and had collaborated in numerous concerts, the correspondence contains no really interesting letters. But a letter to my father in 1937[8] from a member of his orchestra, a violinist, sounded so improbable to me at first reading that I suspected its contents to be pure invention. On the other hand, I knew its author to be a reliable man who, moreover, knowing of the longstanding friendship between Mengelberg and my father, had no reason to tell him anything that was not in accordance with the facts.

To get a second opinion I showed the letter to a Dutch musicologist who after reading it was by no means as surprised as I had expected him to be. For that matter, it did confirm some of the comments my father had made in his *Memoirs*.[9] He regarded Mengelberg as one of the leading conductors of his time, but with rather more than his fair share of faults and weaknesses. In particular, he was well-known for his tendency to spend an undue proportion of rehearsal time talking instead of making music. If it is true that our bad habits become more marked as we grow older, Mengelberg has to be regarded as a prime example bordering, if the letter is to be believed, at times on the pathological.

> [. . .] What is happening here in the 'Gebouw' can only be regarded as a bad joke.
> Rehearsals are scheduled to start at 9 a.m. Mengelberg

---

[7] See p. 326.

[8] It is dated 26 January.

[9] Pp. 228ff

usually arrives at half past nine. He asks members to tune their instruments, but hardly have we started when he shouts: 'Enough! Silence!' The strings are still entirely out of tune and we are sitting at our desks, frustrated. For the next 20 minutes he makes a speech about a previous concert (and what I am writing you is, on my honour, literally true): 'Well, I always knew that you are tenth-rate, but yesterday? That was 5%, a disgrace! But that, of course, is the result of having guest conductors' (B.W. [Bruno Walter] and V. Beynum [*sic*]). 'They are the ones who play a work through just once or twice without rehearsing it properly ['Durchspieldirigenten'] and who rely on their smiles instead (deafening whistles and booes from the orchestra). What do you know! I am being booed because, for once, I am telling these 20% musicians the truth (calls from orchestra: 'Get off! Too old! You're talking nonsense!')

'What did I have to come, of all places, to Amsterdam for!? [. . .] to work with this gang. [. . .] 10 years ago I would have said – You or I, but today I can no longer do this, the time for it is past. The board no longer listens to me either, this is why audiences are getting smaller and smaller. Soon nobody will be coming here at all.

'The programmes say – "Conductors: – Walter, Mengelberg, van Beynum", Ha ha! As if there were here really more than one conductor . . . . . . What do you Dutchmen understand of works by Tchaikovsky? . . . . .'

At about 10 o'clock, having rehearsed 5–10 bars, he'll say something like 'If that's how you want to play, then please without me. It is enough for me to see the way you are lounging around. [. . .]'. etc.

10.15. He hits the stand with his baton 10–20 times like a madman shouting – 'Where is van Beynum (the second conductor)? You come here! You conduct!' Van Beynum: 'But Mr Mengelberg, why?' He: 'Don't talk. If you have something to say, do it later'. He puts on his coat: 'Good-bye, I'll become conductor in The Hague. They'll receive me with open arms'.

Mr. Stips (member of the Board) appears: 'But Mr. Mengelberg, do calm down, everything will work out alright!'

Mengelberg: 'Break! But in 10 minutes everybody back at his desk!'

About 7–8 minutes later [. . .] he shouts: 'Where are you all, we won't get through in time, get on with it!' (Renewed tuning with exactly the same result as before. Nobody in tune, as he does not give us even one minute's time.)

Now he starts rehearsing for about 15 minutes, stopping the orchestra innumerable times. At 11 o'clock members begin to chat unrestrainedly amongst themselves; he talks louder and louder about crotchets, quavers etc. When after 10–15 minutes he has finished, he says: 'Well, nobody has been listening, but I have done my duty and explained it all'.

It gets to noon, members want to stop. This infuriates him and he alleges that the orchestra have been holding him up all morning (we haven't finished a single page yet). The wind section leave; he asks where they are. Answer: 'It's 12 o'clock'. Mengelberg: 'OK if you don't want to learn, let's finish'. Everybody leaves and he calls loudly after them 'Saubande' (scum).

2 months ago we did a Liszt Gala. Programme: Great Mass, Faust Symphony. He had 7 (!) rehearsals. By the 6th [. . .] he had finished with the 1st movement of the symphony [. . .]. During the last rehearsal we went through its 2nd movement. At noon (after 21 hours' rehearsal) he said: 'I can't do the third movement with you, you are not good enough. We'll play only 2 movements at tonight's concert, that is 23 minutes music, we'll than have an interval of 35 minutes to give the audience time for coffee'. He dismisses the male choir who have been practising the final chorus for weeks on end.

At the concert in the evening [. . .] a written announcement that for technical reasons only 2 movements of the symphony are going to be performed. In fact 22 minutes music, 40 minutes interval, and then the Great Mass (during [. . .] the rehearsals for which he had called the ladies in the choir 'dried-up lemons' [. . .]).

Next day the press reviews. *Telegraaf*: 'One ought to throw out the artistic directors. Mengelberg was very bad, the whole thing a let-down'. *Handelsblad*: 'Inexplicable how anyone can dare to put on a Liszt concert like that. Mengelberg *killed* the Faust Symphony'. *Rotterdamsche Courant*: Mengelberg manages to make his orchestra play badly just by looking at it', etc. etc.

Next morning he causes roars of laughter in the orchestra by saying 'I won't allow myself and my excellent orchestra to be insulted by these snotnoses. [. . .] I know how to make music'.

Gieseking played Liszt. [. . . During the rehearsal] he proposed changes asserting (as he always does in these cases) that they were what Liszt had written himself. Gieseking did not agree. He played magnificently. Mengelberg next morning: 'It wasn't bad, but Liszt can be played better. G[ieseking] is a good pianist but not a good musician.' According to him nobody is really any good.

The letter goes on to detail incidents such as Mengelberg bowing to empty sections of the hall during a concert; getting drunk at a jubilee ceremony for a member of the orchestra; slapping the face of a board member during a disagreement, and so on. It concludes:

> Now you know just a little of what is going on here [. . .] would you have credited it? [. . .] Don't you think the man is a pathological case?

There is nothing in my papers to indicate an answer. What puzzles me is that the management put up with him as long as it did. Eventually Mengelberg had to leave Holland, because of his collaboration with the Nazis during the War. But if half of what the above letter says is true, the Dutch must have been relieved to see him go. Since I am confining myself to using only material in my possession, it is not my task to deal with the 'history' of his case, not even his actions during the German occupation, about which opinions seem to be divided. In particular, I do not know whether my parents were in touch with him during that time, but I do know – and this may be significant – that there was no animosity towards him on my parents' part. This is clearly shown by a letter my mother wrote to Dutch friends in 1943 on the death of Frau Mengelberg, who had obviously been spending the last part of her life in Switzerland:

> I have just returned from Frau Mengelberg's funeral and am still greatly moved by it [she explains that my father could not be present due to a simultaneous concert engagement, and continues] I am glad I was able to pay my last respects to her, so that at least one compatriot was present on foreign soil [my mother's original nationality had been Dutch]. I had sad and at the same time beautiful memories, for we had known each other for many years and had been experiencing identical emotions during many concerts. For her it was a blessing to find rest without having to go through the sufferings of another futile operation.
>
>   I felt very close to him. Although many of his acquaintances attended, one had the feeling of great loneliness. He kept his

composure marvellously well, but it seemed to me that he was still completely benumbed. It must have been very hard for him that none of his Dutch friends were able to be present.

Mengelberg ended as a tragic figure but the impression persists that the tragedy had begun much earlier.

Hermann Scherchen

An illustration of Carl Flesch's interest in modern music, regardless of whether it concerned the violin or not, is his relationship with the conductor Hermann Scherchen,[10] well-known for his promotion of contemporary works. He had clearly taken a liking to the young conductor – who could not be regarded as always 'easy' – and had used his influence with wealthy patrons in obtaining for him the financial support he needed for the realisation of his plans. Scherchen made extensive use of this 'facility' and subsequently (for instance, on 11 January 1938) fully acknowledged the help he had been receiving: '[. . .] through your approach to Franz von Mendelssohn you indirectly started me on my career in 1913 [. . .].'

His first letter to my father, written in that year,[11] has been preserved:

[. . .] The performance of the Chamber Symphony was at the same time my debut as a conductor. Just as I performed this work without any urging from Schoenberg – merely desiring to recreate one of my strongest artistic experiences – I am now feeling the urge to produce his symphonic poem *Pelleas und Melisande* as well as his five orchestral works as yet unperformed.

My parents were not well off; in order to earn a living I was forced to play in orchestras as well as cafes. In practical terms,

[10] 1891–1966. Self-taught as a musician, he played the viola in the Berlin Philharmonic from 1907 to 1910. Scherchen's first conducting post was in Riga in 1914, and he was interned in Russia for the duration of the First World War. He held a variety of posts after the resumption of his career, establishing himself as a leading exponent of contemporary music.

[11] 11 September 1913.

Hermann Scherchen

the purpose of my [next] concert is [. . .] to start myself on my career as a conductor.

The cost of this concert would be about 4,000 Marks[. . .]. The favour I am asking you is to recommend me to people known to you who might be willing to act as patrons. It concerns a balance of 2,000 Marks plus a stipend that would free me from the most pressing financial worries during this coming winter. [. . .]

Mr Schoenberg has nothing to do with the concert except that it is concerned with his works which have filled me with great and profound enthusiasm [. . .].

I hope you will forgive me for troubling you. [. . .] For me this is obviously a question of vital importance.

One may assume as a matter of course that he had in the first place approached Schoenberg himself but that the composer had declined to support him except, as Scherchen writes, by 'not raising any objections to the performance'.

During the ensuing years, those of his letters to my father that have been preserved seem usually to have contained requests for assistance in one way or another; the last one,

dated 11 January 1938, from Vienna, is also interesting for
other reasons:

> My Musica Viva Orchestra is a far greater undertaking than
> would appear at first glance. It has kept free from all the
> inhibiting nationalist, racist and political ties so prevalent
> today. [. . .]
>
> 25% [of its members] are Jews (what that means is best
> demonstrated by the fact that for the past 7 years neither of the
> great Viennese orchestras – Philharmonic and Symphony – has
> engaged a single Jewish player); influential Viennese circles
> immediately attributed a racist and political background to my
> orchestra (the 'formula' read – 'a Jewish left-orientated under-
> taking'). Professor [Joseph] Marx even christened it 'Musica
> Telaviva Orchestra' and [the MP] Herr Rimaldini introduced a
> motion in Parliament requesting that we should be refused a
> labour permit [. . .].
>
> In spite of all this we have so far overcome all obstacles
> through our great and genuine successes; in our third concert
> we had even President Schuschnigg and in Naples the Italian
> Crown Princess in the audience. But fresh difficulties will be
> kept in reserve albeit invisibly, and will no doubt surface the
> moment we experience financial complications. [. . .]
>
> May I emphasise my belief that the great value of our work
> lies in the fact that it is being carried out entirely independently,
> i.e., without being subject to interference from public authori-
> ties or any other influential circles working behind the scenes.
> I believe I am entitled to point to the great moral importance of
> this orchestra and to ask my friends to do everything in their
> power to contribute towards safeguarding its existence. [. . .]
>
> It is for this reason, that, at this turning point, you, esteemed
> master and friend, are one of those I am asking to afford me
> your valuable help in the same way in which you already did it
> once before, at the beginning of my career, namely by using
> your contacts with important patrons of the arts.
>
> The orchestra made its debut on 28 November 1937; its
> second Viennese concert took place on 6 November[12] (start of a
> Mahler cycle with the IXth and the *Kindertotenlieder*); the
> third on 15 December (IIIrd Mahler). In between we toured
> Italy from 2–8 December. On 18 January our official Ravel

---

[12] One of the dates cannot be accurate unless Scherchen intended to add a
qualification to the first.

celebration will take place in Vienna under the patronage of the French ambassador M. Puyaux and on 27 January we shall be performing the VIIth Mahler as well as some of his songs.

Bata (Zlin, in Czechoslovakia) have engaged us for subscription concerts and Italy has invited us for a second tour in April. In June we shall be playing under important American patronage during a three-day music festival in USA. And finally we are ourselves organising monthly subscription concerts [. . .].

It would make me very happy to know that you approve of all this and that you will try and support me through your connections.

Since my father was at that time already an emigrant living in a foreign country and the patrons of his acquaintance were mostly of Jewish origin, I am pretty certain that he was, on this occasion, unable to assist. In any case, political conditions forced the Orchestra to dissolve two months after this letter was written – another small contribution to the history of the influence of the Nazis on the arts.

Max Dessoir

Professor Max Dessoir (1867–1947) was lecturer in philosophy and psychology at the Berlin University; he was also an expert on musical aesthetics and had quite a number of books to his credit. As a hobby he played the violin, for which he showed little talent but all the more enthusiasm. My father owed him a considerable debt of gratitude: it was he who had made the initial suggestion to him of writing his main work *The Art of Violin Playing*. And once the plan had taken shape, he volunteered his constant advice on style and arrangement of material, giving unstintingly of his time.

Personally, I always found him somewhat pompous and unbending, but having since read some of his letters I think I did him an injustice: he had a good sense of humour and genuine modesty. He writes, for example, a thank-you letter for the *Basic Studies*, which my father had presented to him:[13]

---

[13] Dated 19 March 1919.

Max Dessoir

My wife particularly likes the silent exercises (for which I can't blame her). Incidentally I find it quite droll that the publishers have reserved performance rights for these, too.[14]

And some time later:[15]

There now, I had been expecting to take along with me on holiday a large bundle of sheets filled with mysterious signs and characters, and instead you have just been loafing about not doing any work at all. But I must warn you – if on our return on 15 September you cannot produce to me a further part of your book, I shall visit you every day and play to you for a whole hour.

I believe this threat had the desired effect.

[14] A similar idea had apparently occurred to my father on a different occasion, as is shown by his entry in the visitor's book of his friend, the publisher Franz Ries: see opposite.

[15] Letter dated 5 August 1920.

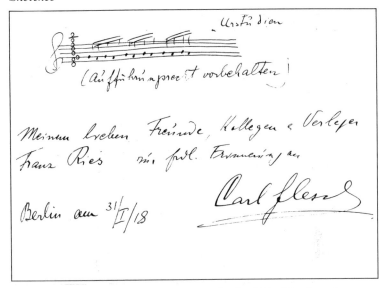

Carl Flesch's entry in the guest-book of his friend and publisher Franz Ries: 'Performance rights reserved'

And in 1928, on publication of the volume of *The Art of Violin Playing*:[16]

> Now the whole great work lies before me, finally completed. [. . .] Let me tell you what a pure and real joy it has been for me to be of some little help.

I myself have a personal reason for appreciating his kindness: his wife happened to be a sister of Professor Heinrich Triepel, lecturer in constitutional law at the Berlin University. When I heard that he was to be on the examining board for the 'orals' of my university law finals, I knew that he would have seen beforehand all the written work done by the candidates appearing before him and his colleagues on that day. Mrs Dessoir was kind enough to ask him unofficially how I had done so far. He replied that I would have to be very unlucky still to fail. The relief afforded to a candidate by information of this kind has to be experienced to be believed!

[16] Letter dated 23 September 1928.

Painters

Whilst living in Berlin, my parents were friendly with a number of painters, three of whom I would like to mention here.

Eugen Spiro was best known through his sketches of musicians, collected as a portfolio under the title *Im Konzert*. There was hardly a well-known musician who escaped his net. In concerts he was a familiar figure, sketching pad on his knees, busily drawing during the performance. Whether the music stimulated him or whether he took it in at all, I don't know. What I do know is that he was able to bring out the essential characteristics of his subjects with a few simple pencil strokes. There exists a sketch of the Schnabel-Flesch duo, for instance, where Schnabel is unmistakably recognisable although the drawing shows only the back of his head.

A large oil portrait of my father which he himself had commissioned has now found its permanent home at the Lucerne Academy of Music, where he taught from 1943 until his death. I always considered it somewhat stiff and formal, whereas a small painting of my mother, done at the same time as a present from the artist, has come off particularly well. Spiro was clearly most successful when allowed to create freely and spontaneously.

Max Oppenheimer ('Mopp') had a quite different, highly individual style. However little one knows about art, there will always be some painters whose work one recognises at first glance. I used to say that for me this applied in the main to van Gogh, El Greco – and Mopp, admittedly, the latter some distance behind, but for me with the inestimable advantage of being the only one of the three I had met personally.

He, too, was deeply interested in music. Almost half the subjects in his book *Menschen finden ihren Maler*[17] are musicians. I consider his drawing of my father[18] particularly good.

Emil Orlik had nothing to do with music if you disregard the fact that his flat happened to be in the same block as ours.

[17] Oprecht Verlag, Zurich, 1938.

[18] See p. 26.

Carl Flesch and Artur Schnabel by Eugen Spiro

He was a 'compulsive' painter, wherever he happened to be. Drawing was as natural to him as writing. He was also well-known for finding it almost impossible to miss any opportunity of attending a public event or meeting a well-known personality. I also gathered – I was too young at the time to appreciate it fully – that his tastes were somewhat indiscriminate where women were concerned.

He embellished for my parents a copy of the programme for

The oil portrait of my mother by Eugen Spiro

a charity concert on board an ocean liner on its way to America. He asked my father to draw two separate lines which he would then use as part of two drawings he was going to make. The result – the heavy lines are my father's – can be seen on p. 346.

Enigmas

Whether all the unexplained, inexplicable things on earth deserve the term 'supernatural' is a question to which I would not want to attempt an answer. But I would like briefly to describe some experiences either of my own or told me first-hand, all touching on the musical sphere – and inexplicable, at least for me.

To begin with, something comparatively minor which, however, gave me much food for thought at the time: in his *Memoirs*[19] my father deals at some length with his

---

[19] P. 164.

A poster of Carl Flesch by Mopp

time in Bucharest (1897–1902) as 'Court Violin Virtuoso'
to the very musical Queen Elisabeth, who was also a
well-known poetess under the pen-name 'Carmen Sylva'.
He gives a detailed description of the Queen's private
concert studio where he made music usually several times a
week.

Carmen Sylva's music room

One day, browsing through the stock of a dealer specialising in musical memorabilia, I came across the photo of an ornately furnished room in which a white-haired lady surrounded by half-a-dozen young girls was listening to someone playing the piano. Without the least hesitation I exclaimed: 'This is the studio in which my father played hundreds of times!' On investigation it turned out that I had been right. The remarkable fact is not the million-to-one chance of my ever finding such a picture, but the immediate and quite certain knowledge that this had been the place which my father had filled with music innumerable times.

More important is an episode which I can only call a 'miracle'. My father had obtained two tickets for a Toscanini concert in London and, as my mother happened to be ill, had offered the second one to my future wife. I took them to the concert hall in my little two-door Morris Minor. On alighting, my fiancée, who had been sitting in front next to me, slammed

Mopp by Orlik

the door with full force without noticing that my father had put his left hand into the door frame in order to pull himself up from the rear seat. He uttered a cry of pain, we opened the door, immediately – and his hand was entirely uninjured, as a subsequent X-ray confirmed.

To this day I can hear the bang of the door closing. Afterwards I tried carefully to re-enact this incident with my hand in the door frame: impossible – it would have been entirely crushed. By all the laws of nature this event should have spelt the sudden and irretrievable end of my father's career, and I have never been able to explain to myself or anybody else what preserved him and us from this seemingly inevitable catastrophe.

A case told me by Peter Diamand, originally private secretary to Artur Schnabel, after the War the originator of the Holland Festival, and subsequently for many years Director of the Edinburgh Festival, concerns no lesser person than Mozart. I have known him (Peter, that is, not Mozart) for many years and his credibility is beyond doubt.

At a gathering following a performance of *Don Giovanni* at the Edinburgh Festival, with Daniel Barenboim conducting, one of the singers claimed to be a medium, and some of those present, including Jacqueline DuPré and Peter Ustinov, decided to test her powers there and then. After a rather boring appearance by one of Ustinov's uncles, Barenboim expressed the wish to speak to Mozart who – by means of the usual knocks – duly made his presence known and declared himself by and large satisfied with the evening's performance. Once of his queries concerned a passage which apparently had been played as a solo by the leader of the cello section; Mozart considered that it should have been played by the whole section, 'unless it could have been someone like –' at which moment a chair travelled in the direction of Jacqueline duPré.

With a view to checking the genuineness of the phenomenon Peter Diamand then asked Mozart which of his operas had been the first to be performed at the Holland Festival. '*Magic Flute*', Mozart replied. 'Wrong', said Peter, '*Figaro*'. Neither was prepared to give way until Mozart seemed to lose patience and volunteered the name of the conductor on that occasion – Josef Krips – at which Diamand suddenly realised that his recollection had been at fault and that *The Magic Flute* had indeed been the first Mozart work to be performed. Incidentally, he is satisfied that the medium had no knowledge of the true facts, probably not even of his previous position in Holland.

A doodle by Emil Orlik

Carl Flesch, Carl Friedberg, their wives, Elli Ney and her daughter drawn by Emil Orlik on a transatlantic voyage

A case that will give pleasure to believers in astrology was told in my presence by the son of a German violinist, personally known to me, who had spent a large part of his career in South America. One day he called on a concert agent. When they came face to face it turned out that they were look-alikes; that they both sported beards; that both had undergone an operation for the removal of a brain tumour which had cost both of them the sight of one eye; that both were professionally concerned with music albeit in different capacities; and – you have guessed it – that both had been born on the same day.[20]

[20] But perhaps this violinist had 'psychic powers' anyway. Many years later I was amused to come across a letter from Szymon Goldberg in which he described him, at the time a boy of 17, and asked my father to hear him. Goldberg's assessment contains the sentence: 'With Paganini he shows a very good trait: he jumps blindly – and hits the target' ('Er springt ins Blinde und trifft').

My last case is that of a British medium, a man well into middle age who had made his name through a series of TV appearances in which he had, with spectacular success, put members of the audience in touch with relatives who had 'passed over'. Since the experiments had been conducted under the strict supervision of a well-known and highly respected psychiatrist at a renowned London hospital I had been considerably impressed and some months later contacted

*Emil Orlik's embellishment of a
concert programme on a transatlantic
voyage, duly signed by the
participants*

*An invitation by Eugen
Spiro*

him in the hope of clearing up a number of matters that had
puzzled me following the death of a relative. (My hope,
incidentally, was not fulfilled.)

During the seance he declared that he was seeing my father
in the company of a few bearded men and that the name of
'Joseph' was being mentioned. This rang a bell with me: my
mother's maiden name had been Josephus-Jitta, and in her
youth beards had, of course, been *de rigueur*. My father had
presumably been in contact with her family. Anybody who has
ever attended a seance will have had experience of the medium
'fishing' by means of vague utterances until one of them fits
sufficiently well for the gullible client – not the medium – to
supply the apparently supporting facts. In this case I was the
typical gullible client, but he wasn't the typical medium. 'No',
he said, 'that's not it.'

A member of my family who was also present jokingly
suggested that the 'Joseph' in question might be Joseph
Joachim. 'Yes, that's it', the medium affirmed, very positively.
I am convinced that the man had never heard Joachim's name,
let alone my father's, so that he cannot have been alerted to the

significance of this combination. Of course, one could never be quite sure, but the idea of my father playing chamber music with Joachim (in heaven, I hope) was sufficiently hilarious to make me dine out on it repeatedly. My listeners were usually somewhat sceptical, some going so far as to suggest that my father might have changed over to the harp.

Many years later I made the acquaintance of one of Joachim's grandsons – the son of his daughter, who had also played the violin. During our meeting I came up, of course, with the Joachim story. But instead of laughing, my companion became pensive: 'This is rather curious. We, too, have been in touch with my late mother through a medium several times. She also told us that she was playing chamber music with my grandfather. She even named some of the participants – including someone called "Carl". Until today we had no idea who that might be.'

I wish I could add that I had encountered yet a third medium who independently confirmed the matter. Unfortunately, so far I cannot. The difficulty is, of course, that such revelation would have to be unasked and spontaneous; any suggestion on my part would largely invalidate the proof. Moreover, I am not in the habit of seeking out mediums and clairvoyants. So I do not expect the question to be resolved. But if it should be true that there is chamber music in the hereafter, I do hope that Joachim will on occasion permit my father to play first violin.

Appendix I

FLESCH AND SCHNABEL
ON EDITING CHAMBER MUSIC

The collaboration between Carl Flesch and Artur Schnabel in the preparation of new editions of chamber music did not always run smoothly. This appears to be particularly noticeable in the joint edition of the Brahms Violin Sonatas (Edition Peters) which clearly shows up the areas of disagreement between the two artists. The letters that follow will serve to illustrate the background to the dispute.

Flesch to Schnabel (26 July 1926):

Dear Artur,
I am sending you by the same mail the corrected violin parts of the three Brahms sonatas. [. . .] I have also perused, albeit cursorily, your corrections of the piano score in order to gain an overall view and at the same time to hunt for additions I might have missed in the violin part. The general impression is favourable. In particular, I consider your identification of the periodic build-up very interesting and instructive. This illustrates to the student the construction of the work in a natural way and makes it necessary for him to give this aspect his full consideration.

Your suggested fingerings are somewhat over-abundant and perhaps you may, on second thoughts, wish to omit some which you consider superfluous. But they are no doubt excellent and to the point. This leaves, as the only difference of opinion between us, the metronome marks on which I have to comment at some length.

I am bound to state that in this respect both you and Peters have not acted in an entirely correct manner. The agreement between us has not been adhered to: when last year I could not consent to inserting metronome marks within a movement and neither of us was prepared to give way, we decided to ask the publishers, Peters, to act as referees. They sided with me and this seemed to be an end to the matter. Now, to my surprise, the piano score contains precisely the same metronome marks as your original manuscript. This means that both you and Peters have acted incorrectly, i.e., contrary to our agreement. Nevertheless, I don't intend to make too much of this and to add yet another to the many games played latterly by you and Peters. Moreover, I am

349

loth to try imposing on you anything that is contrary to your artistic convictions.

The only possible solution is for me to confine in the violin part the metronome marks to the basic measures but for you to place them in the piano part wherever you deem fit. This will clearly show that I do not consider the latter method necessary. If, however, any violinist should happen to incline towards your opinion, he could always turn to the piano score. If we deal with the difficulty in this way, I believe that it will not prove to be an obstacle to publication.

On the other hand, I would like seriously to suggest that you carry out a thorough re-examination of the basic tempi. I have expressed my detailed reservations against them in the corresponding appendices and would just like, in this letter, to add one remark: during the many years of our collaboration on the concert platform I have frequently had an opportunity of noticing that your tempi were subject to changes at different periods. There were times when your inclination was towards speeds that were too slow and others when they were too fast. Now this is something very natural and no doubt happens to every artist as a result of subconscious impulses that almost defy definition. However, the decision on basic tempi is a *joint* matter and therefore has at least to conform closely to my own ideas, too. In the 3rd movement of the D minor Sonata, for instance, the all-too-fast metronome marks are not only a negation of our own artistic usage, but also of every Brahms tradition that in course of time has taken the form almost of holy writ. I do ask you therefore, dear Artur, to meet me in this matter as fully as your artistic conscience permits. If opinions differ, then the decision on basic tempos has to be a compromise [. . .].

Schnabel's reply appears, unfortunately, not to have been preserved, but can be deduced from the next letter from Flesch, dated 8 August 1926:

Many thanks for your letter of 7 August and the positive artistic accommodation you have shown me. To be sure, in the last resort one cannot argue about tempi one wishes to adopt, they are not a question of musicality but of certain subconscious mood changes converted according to need into accelerated or slowed-down movements. When you and I had our first rehearsal of the Brahms G major Sonata, Opus 96, you took the Adagio ♪ = 88. Since I had in mind ♪ = 58, the gap was too wide to be bridged and we deleted the work from our repertoire. In 1920 I substituted at short notice for Rosé in a sonata recital with Bruno Walter. Imagine my surprise when Walter took the movement with ♪ = 56. So, the opinions of two of the most important musicians of their time can diverge by as much as ♪ = 176 against ♪ = 56! I can't imagine any greater difference.

However this may be, we have met half-way. If perhaps you happened to be in a 'fast' period, mine may have been somewhat sluggish and I believe we have found the golden mean.

Meanwhile I had written to Peters to the effect that if need be I might agree to leaving out from the violin part any metronome marks altogether, confining them to the piano score. However, in view of our agreement there is now no reason why I should maintain this proposal and I agree therefore the metronome marks of the initial tempi. I shall be confirming this to Peters.

Turning now to your proposal to delete the metronome marks within the movements, I don't at any price want to impose on you – I respect your artistic intentions and personality even if I can't always go along with the underlying tendencies. I would suggest therefore that you discuss and decide the question of internal metronome marks in the piano score with Peters. I agree beforehand with any decision you arrive at and shall confirm this in my letter to Peters.

These differences of opinion appear to me to be symptomatic of a more deep-seated resistance on Schnabel's part, evident from a letter which he had written almost exactly one year earlier (16 August 1925) when, it seems, the metronome question had been a bone of contention for some time already. But the letter is interesting regardless, because it touches on some intriguing questions concerning editions generally. At the same time I must confess to finding it somewhat obscure and can only hope that my translation represents his thoughts accurately.

Dear Carl,

During a talk one is often interrupted; hence, before I visit you today, allow me quickly to put into writing something that can perhaps not be expressed as easily in a personal conversation.

A new edition of the Brahms sonatas is, from a musical point of view, entirely unnecessary. Proof: the enormous circulation of these works for many decades in the existing (only) edition. Even the most clue-less ignoramuses have been using it without hindrance. Performances of these sonatas range from good to bad to indifferent in all shadings between right and wrong (according to understanding). Talented people develop by themselves and don't need commentaries – indeed, should be spared them. Conversely, lack of talent cannot be remedied by 'editions'.

So, I repeat: musically, a new edition is, in this case as nearly always, completely superfluous; at a pinch it can be justified if – and only if – it shows very *personal* characteristics. But I know: a new edition 'on a realistic (and this means unmusical) basis' is a capitalist trick; it is needed to replace by a new source of profit an existing one that is showing signs of drying up. To achieve this, one makes use of 'names' almost regardless of cost. But at this point it becomes, for me, a matter of concern. I am not a 'name'. He who invokes my name invokes my person; thus I answer, as requested, with my person from whom perfection and infallibility are not expected.

I don't look down on the problem as from a far-distant star where I would have a function but no opinion of my own. My function is to have an opinion, and this is what is required of me (commissions of this kind cannot, in all honesty, have a different purpose). I form, and arrive at, my opinion – freely and not confined by narrow rules – with all the understanding and conscientiousness at my disposal; with humility and obsessive dedication; and with a combination, as far as achievable, of knowledge and inner motivation. For me, this process is always a source of happiness; the result gives me satisfaction no matter whether or not it is objectively of value; it represents my maximum effort at that point in time. My opinion at that stage is a matter of course and (hopefully) never my absolutely final one. When I have done, and enjoyed the process, it matters not if for once, perhaps this time, the 'world' is not made aware of the fruits of my labour. My interest in the fortunes of my work in the 'market' is very slight. I have done my duty vis-à-vis my person; and that is sufficient.

As far as I am concerned, part of my work can be deleted or the sonatas published as untouched as they had been before; it is just that my name is added on the title page, which protects the publisher and provides me with a certain amount of money – which was my reason for undertaking the work in the first place, But!!! Work of this kind places you under an obligation.

Incidentally, I will gladly accept, with thanks in advance, any suggestion that will carry my person forward.

I would like to retain as a memento one copy of the completed product, however it has turned out. Apart from this, I repeat, the 'primordial condition' can be cheerfully restored. On possible trimmings we can consult with each other.

Where does arbitrariness begin, where does respect for the holiest end? Who determines the boundaries? Perhaps, after all, arbitrariness again?

A metronome at the beginning is as sinful as it is in the middle, and every bow stroke requiring a change in breathing, every sound-determining fingering, is an intrusive offence.

Perhaps our Mozart Edition is bad; it is not entirely impersonal and not without courage.

I reject the imputation that I should acknowledge as the final stage in my development that at which I had arrived in Malmö some time ago. It baffles me why my alleged preference for faster tempi should be less justified than yours for slower ones.

Au revoir at 10 o'clock.

Don't take it so much to heart!

Your A.S.

A letter which, like almost anything coming from Schnabel, it is a pleasure to read. For me, it leaves only one small nagging doubt: is he for or against 'editions'?

Appendix II

THE SCHUMANN VIOLIN CONCERTO

At the Düsseldorf Whitsuntide Festival in 1853 Robert Schumann heard the 22-year-old Joachim give a performance of Brahms' Violin Concerto. It inspired him to take to the medium himself, and his own concerto was composed within a fortnight, by 3 October 1853. But after Schumann's death in 1856, Joachim, supported by Brahms and Clara Schumann, came to the conclusion that the work should not be published, and the Concerto languished in the Prussian State Library in Berlin, until in the 1930s Joachim's great-niece, the violinist Jelly d'Arányi, decided that it should see the light of day. Two letters to my father refer to it.

Letter from Georg Schünemann:[1]

> I have just signed the contract [. . .] concerning the Schumann Violin Concerto. I shall be publishing it next year but would ask you not to mention this to anybody as yet, because I have still to complete the score and produce a version with piano accompaniment.
> It has 3 movements, is in D minor, was written in 1853, and requires considerable virtuosity as it is technically demanding. Kulenkampff is expected to give its first performance this spring or summer. Joachim did not want it published at the time, in fact, Schumann's heirs had vetoed it, but I have now succeeded in getting it released! I am certain it will interest you, I shall write you as soon as I have completed the necessary work.

Letter from Georg Kulenkampff:[2]

> The Schumann Concerto has had a great deal of nonsense talked about it. I have adapted the violin part, as has Hindemith. Both pretty similar – I am playing bits of each. In my opinion the original score is, in its unadapted state, impossible! How happy Schumann himself would have been with changes for which he had vainly asked Joachim several

[1] Dated 23 November 1937.

[2] Dated 15 March 1938.

353

times; Moreover one forgets all too easily – and this applies particularly to Schumann's stubborn elderly relatives – that Schumann himself thought *very highly* of his violin concerto (and this was before his illness) and was in fact very fond of the work, even though undoubtedly written (in the space of a fortnight!) in an exaggeratedly explosive style.

Isn't it a remarkably paradoxical sign of the times that this season's most important compositions number amongst them the revival of an old Schumann concerto whose performance had originally been prohibited!

Appendix III

CORRESPONDENCE
WITH CONTEMPORARY COMPOSERS

Erich Wolfgang Korngold to Carl Flesch about his Sonata for piano and violin (15 October 1913; the name of the month is barely legible):

Dear Mr. Flesch,

Many thanks for your two kind letters.

Please take the 'g' in the 14th bar of the final movement flageolet as you suggest, I myself have in fact always hummed this note in falsetto . . .

It is sufficient if the tempo of the violin is taken a little more moderately ($\quad = 88$–92) with an accel. only from the D major onwards where the scherzo appears in the enlarged violin theme, down to the 1st movement's ancillary theme where the theme in quavers leads the violin to the metronome mark $\quad = 100$.

As regards the quavers to be repeated, please note: the accel. starts in the 11th bar *before* Tempo I ($\quad = 100$ is maintained up to that bar). $4\frac{1}{2}$ bars on but before Tempo I there begins a big ritardando, so that the accel. cannot be particularly substantial. If it is too difficult to repeat the quavers with a speed of $\quad = $ [illegible] then please play *simple* eighths, But in that case please let me know so that I can re-arrange the printing accordingly.

After the first 4 entries of the violin the violin part reads (I believe it is different in your copy).[1]

In reply to your first letter I would just like to say that although in the Adagio you do have to undertake the ascent to the high E without a lead, you are in that risky passage *yourself leading*!

Ernst von Dohnányi about his Violin Concerto (4 January 1921):

[. . .] I have no special requests, I assume you will have noticed in Wiesbaden that the violin comes through well provided the orchestra does the accompaniment delicately and I think this something one may hope for with Nikisch. The harp is obbligato and not easy; in

[1] See facsimile on p. 358.

355

*Ernst von Dohnányi asks for advice. The notation at the
end of the letter is probably my father's.*

particular, the final passage does not come out if the harpist does not
play every note. Perhaps you could draw attention to this during the
rehearsal.

On the other hand he also asks for advice (7 December 1926):

Dear Friend,

Many thanks for perusal and advice which I shall naturally take to
heart. I was aware of the fact that fourth double-stops are not easy to

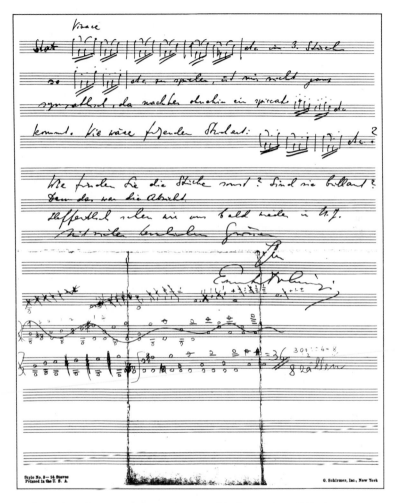

play; that they pose almost insuperable intonation difficulties was, however, news to me. I had been under the impression that this applied only to fifths which I take care to avoid for precisely that reason. However, in the particular passage in question the parallel fourths are an integral part of the *intellectual* content (the work was originally a piano piece) for which reason I don't want to give them up. On the other hand I would not like to resign myself to never hearing them played in tune. I think that the following compromise solution should present no difficulties for playing in tune.[2]

[2] See facsimile above.

The letter from Erich Wolfgang
Korngold quoted on p. 355

You will note that I have put an x where I replaced (albeit reluctantly!)
the fourths with octaves. Is this OK? What do you think of the pieces
altogether? Are they brilliant (for this was the intention)? [. . .]

Josef Suk, on the impending performance of the *Fantasia* with
Nikisch (19 May 1911):

One more request. Please tell Nikisch that all cymbal beats should be omitted except the one in *pp* just before the end. I must, incidentally apologise – *today* I would have orchestrated or composed some passages differently from how I did them – after all! – 10 years ago.[3]

Without wishing to be presumptuous in any way, I myself am just wondering whether Suk, instead of apologising, might not simply have made the changes he had in mind if he no longer found some of what he had done satisfactory? There are, after all, sufficient precedents. It is interesting to speculate why he did not do so and generally to compare the differing attitudes of composers to this problem.

[3] See also pp. 152–53.

Appendix IV

CORRESPONDENCE ON THE CLASSICS

Discussions about interpretation are, of course, not confined to modern works, and even established artists, if sufficiently modest, are glad to seek the advice from colleagues with specialised knowledge.

My father had obviously enquired of Karel Hoffmann, a member of the Bohemian String Quartet, about Dvořák's 'Dumky' Trio, Op. 90; Hoffmann replied:[1]

> I myself play the last movement of the Dumky Trio
> Lento maestoso MM ♪ = 70
> and the C minor lento (♪ = ♩) ♪ = 54.

An answer to an enquiry by Carl Flesch, presumably regarding ties in the third movement of the Beethoven Violin Concerto came from Eusebius Mandyczewski,[2] the archivist of the Gesellschaft der Musikfreunde in Vienna, on 2 May 1915:

Dear Sir,

Unfortunately, the hand-written manuscript of the Beethoven Concerto is not in our possession, but in that of the Royal Library. Since I was glad to find a reason for having another look at it myself, I visited the Library and was able to see the precise beginning of the last movement.[3]

---

[1] Letter written in 1916; I have been unable to locate the original.
[2] Eusebius Mandyczewski (1857–1926) was an eminent Austrian muscicologist. He studied composition in Vienna with Robert Fuchs and Gustav Nottebohm. In 1880 he became both archivist to the Gesellschaft der Musikfreunde and the choirmaster of the Singakademie and from 1896 taught history of music and composition at the Vienna Conservatorium. He was also noted for his work as editor, not least of the complete edition of the music of Brahms, whose close friend he had been.
[3] See facsimile opposite.

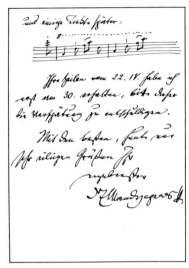

*The Gesellschaft der Musikfreunde reports on the Beethoven
Violin Concerto*

Carl Flesch to Ricardo Odnoposoff (23 April 1933):

As regards the Mozart D major Concerto, a cadenza is not only unnecessary, but in fact disruptive since it can destroy the mood.

If you don't play a cadenza, then you have to omit the few bars before the fermata. I myself usually play the subsequent ending one octave lower on the G string and then the second time as originally written.[4]

---

[4] The Mozart Concerto is K218, not K211, which is also in D major; he is obviously referring to the second movement.

Appendix V

CARL FLESCH ON THE BACH SOLO SONATAS AND PARTITAS

A lecture given at the Victoria Hall, Geneva, on 10 June 1944;
it was probably punctuated by illustrations.
Translated from the French by Rachel Neaman.

The six sonatas for solo violin mark one of the key points in the work of this great composer. They are perhaps the most perfect expression of Bach's genius; although the instrument limits their execution, they are the reflection of an immense musical world. Through their richness of expression, through their variety and especially their richness of inspiration, they remain for us one of the great mysteries of music, before which our admiration knows no bounds. Besides, are they not among those works of which one can never tire? The problem we have is to know how Bach conceived of these huge works at a time when the technical possibilities of the violin were very limited and were in any case a long way from permitting the execution of so complicated a work. This is, furthermore, one of the reasons that they were never played at that time and temporarily fell into oblivion. This state of oblivion lasted until the middle of the nineteenth century. As far as we know, Lipinsky was the first to be capable of performing them. Viotti, Spohr and several other violinists also attempted to without, however, finding in this work sure enough ground on which to apply a technique that was still inadequate.

Finally came Joachim, who discovered the inestimable value of these masterpiece and revealed them to the public. It is to him that we owe the first public performance of the three sonatas and three partitas in their entirety.

Since then the works have come so far that it would take too long to describe. These sonatas are now part of the repertoire of every violinist who has reached a sufficient level of technical ability. Unfortunately, the tendency over the last decades has been to treat these marvellous sonatas as pieces of virtuosity and bravura, stripped of expression, causing them to be played on the whole too fast, at the expense of their expressive character.

The six pieces for solo violin collectively known as 'sonatas' are divided into two parts which differ essentially in their format and conception:

1   The three sonatas
 i   in G minor
 ii in A minor
 iii in C major

2   The three partitas
 i   in B minor
 ii in D minor
 iii in E major

The sonatas follow classic sonata form – *adagio*, fugue, slow movement, finale – while the partitas are in the form of a suite of dances which calls to mind the classic French dance suite – *allemande*, *gigue*, *courante*, *gavotte*, *menuet*, and so forth.

The rather light-hearted character of the partitas distinguishes them essentially from the sonatas, but what is of interest is that they reveal to us a quite different Bach, one who is not afraid of evoking the popular and peasant character of a set of dances of the time.

Sonata No. 1 in G minor begins with an *adagio* whose richness of expression is quite unbelievable. This movement should be interpreted very slowly in order to preserve the grave character of the demisemiquavers and hemidemisemiquavers. The fugue that follows is *allegro*. Then follows a rather slow *siciliano* and a finale that is presto (but not too fast!).

Sonata No. 2 in A minor consists of four movements, *grave*, fugue, *andante* and *allegro*.

Sonata No. 3 in C major, one of the greatest of Bach's masterpieces, begins with a very simple *adagio* whose slow, very slow tempo must be *absolutely constant*! The fugue is one of the most difficult parts to execute and here the problem of chords comes into question (see below, methods of interpreting).

Partita No. 1 in B minor (*allemande, double, courante, double, sarabande, double, tempo di bourrée, double*) is very difficult to interpret because of the complexity which comes from having parts which intersperse with the movements. A rather slow piece alternates with a *double* in a special form.

In Partita No. 2 in D minor (*allemande, courante, sarabande, gigue, chaconne*) one has the very clear impression that the composer saved himself for the *chaconne* which represents the most important piece in the six sonatas in terms of its length, its range and its expression.

Partita No. 3 in E major (*prelude*, *lourré*, *gavotte*, *menuet I* and *II*, *bourrée*, *gigue*) begins with a prelude in a pleasant form, full of originality, characterised by repeated passing notes (which replace the pedal, discussed below).

The issue of interpretation remains the greatest problem to resolve, since Bach did not give (as composers usually do) any information concerning phrasing and fingering. Only some dynamics – those fortes and pianos, on the whole few and far between – come to us from the composer. Although this problem has preoccupied the majority of the eminent violinists of our time, none of them has managed to impose his own ideas totally. The problem is further complicated by the issue of chords with three or four voices. In the time of J. S. Bach, because of a special bow (which could be tightened at will according to the requirements of the moment), these chords could be executed simultaneously, for the bow played all four strings at once. In spite of the obvious advantages of this bow, its weakness of expression in the single-voiced melodies led gradually to its abandonment.

Certain other violinists searched for still other solutions, such as the Norwegian violinist Ole Bull who constructed a very low bridge on which the strings were more or less at the same level (Fig. 2).

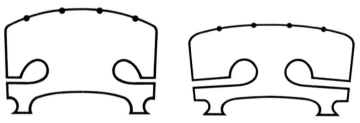

Fig. 1: normal bridge   Fig. 2: special bridge

In spite of the advantages of this bridge, obvious in the execution of three- and four-voiced chords, they were not sufficient in the execution of a monophone melody and led to its abandonment.

Today, the problem has been resolved by broken chords. The chord must be played in such a way that the note of the melody line is brought to the fore (that is to say, it must be held last) which at times leads to chords spread in reverse from the top or, as normal, from the bottom (fugue in C major). Other problems face us; among them that of notes of passage which replace the organ pedal (Partita No. 3 in E major) and that of notes repeated several times as if Bach wanted to hammer them into our heads (*chaconne* in D major). As for the question of pure execution, it is difficult to resolve with respect to the different bowings (sautillé-staccato, spiccato, and so forth) which did not exist in Bach's time. One must, before all else, strive to understand what the composer wanted to express and, if the methods of expression are there to facilitate and improve the expressive character of the performance, why not use them?

In the eighteenth century some bowings were still considered 'indecent', to quote Leopold Mozart speaking of certain bowings required by the very execution itself.

The question of style is difficult to resolve, style being of course the expression of an age destined to change. What is certain is that J. S. Bach probably never heard his work performed as he conceived of it (because of its technical difficulties) and this argument will perhaps ease the task of those who seek the expression wanted by the composer himself.

Appendix VI

CARL FLESCH
ON LALO'S *SYMPHONIE ESPAGNOLE*

The former Hubay and Flesch pupil Mrs Mili Lups has been good
enough to permit me to quote from a letter in which Carl Flesch gave
her some advice on an article about Lalo's best-known work. The
original is with a Dutch music archive and bears the marginal note
'Very important for all violinists'.

Edouard Lalo, originally a violinist and violist in Paris [. . .], soon
became known as an excellent composer for his instrument. [. . .] But
the only work that has become really popular is his Symphonie
Espagnole. He had originally composed it for Sarasate who took it into
his repertoire. It is a work that uses Spanish rhythms very effectively.
Curiously enough, though, Lalo has also been influenced by Hungarian
rhythms. In the fourth movement you frequently encounter the typical
Hungarian appoggiatura-like brief note on the strong beat:

which strictly speaking has nothing to do with Spanish music. Musicians of the older generation have told me that at the time it was
composed the Symphonie Espagnole was regarded as very modern.
This very passionate piece was, as a matter of fact, not all that suitable
for Sarasate's smooth style of playing, and it achieved its rightful place
only later, through Ysaÿe. No wonder that, as a Hungarian, Hubay felt
particularly attracted to this piece, discovering in it a kinship with the
Hungarian way of feeling.

And now, my dear Mili, you'll have to hark back to your own
recollections about Hubay's interpretation. For instance, about the
verve of the first, the elegance of the second movement. Was the third
movement performed or was it omitted? The passion of the fourth
movement. The last movement's rhythm carrying all before it with the
ingratiating middle part on which one can best demonstrate the Spanish

366

Habanera rhythm. Do you remember any details, for instance, how he taught the difficult ending of the last movement? And whether he insisted on the triplets in the last movement's middle part being played in the same tempo, thus

and not

Appendix VII

ESCAPE IN IOWA

Carl Flesch contributed this article to the *Vossische Zeitung* of
8 May 1926; see pp. 317–18.

My concert tour through the United States took me this year to Iowa
City. Although it has a total population of only about 20,000, it
boasts a university with no fewer than 8,000 students. A college of
this kind will teach practically any discipline the human mind is able
to absorb, from medicine and law via journalism to the artistic
professions such as music, acting, etc.

After a journey of 36 hours I arrived early in the morning and
proceded to my hotel. There two young men were already waiting
for me, introduced themselves as reporters of the 'Daily Iowan' and
showed considerable interest in matters that were none of their – or
anybody's – business. Having answered their searching questions as
best I could, I took my seat in the dining room in order to recharge
my batteries with one of those famous American breakfasts.

However, I was not allowed to indulge in this agreeable occupation for long: two ladies from the 'Iowan Telegraph' asked me to see
them on an urgent matter. Fearing that any hesitation in complying
with their request might irretrievably damage my popularity with
the Iowan public, I denied myself my usual habit – as pleasurable as
it is unsightly – of crushing my grapefruit with a spoon in order to
extract from it the last drop of juice. The two girls, one blonde, one
brunette, asked me the make of my violin, Stradivarius' dates of
birth and death and his marital status, if any. Having stilled their
thirst for knowledge with a few freely invented facts and figures, I
started unpacking my overalls – my tails – trying to rid them of some
of the creases they had acquired during the long journey.

Whilst occupying myself with this chore, two emissaries from the
'Iowan Express' called with the request to fill them in about my
family life and any favourable or unfavourable views I might have
about jazz. This persistent interest shown me by the Iowa media
sharpened my sense of artistic duty and responsibility and caused me
a certain amount of disquiet – something that is best remedied by

close contact with one's chosen instrument. I decided therefore on a brief rehearsal with my accompanist. At the same time I could not help admiring the important position occupied by American journalism seeing that even a small town like Iowa was able to support so many different newspapers.

On leaving the hotel my way was barred by two young ladies who entreated me not to withhold from the readers of the 'Iowa Despatch' my views on the differences between American and European concert life.

'This is the fourth interview since my arrival', I remarked with considerable pride. 'I don't suppose there are more than four papers in Iowa?' 'What do you mean?' one of the young ladies replied, 'Iowa has only one.'

'But damn it all, who are the people who have been asking me about everything under the sun since my arrival?!' 'Well', the younger of the two replied with quiet satisfaction, 'we are students of the faculty of journalists, and whenever a famous man visits Iowa, the whole class interviews him as an exercise.' 'And how many students are in your faculty?' I asked with as much outward unconcern as I could muster. '236', was the answer.

It became clear to me that only immediate flight could save me from further attentions by the rising journalistic generation, I ascertained the whereabouts of the nearest Turkish Bath and emerged from its protective steam only shortly before the appointed hour of the concert.

Appendix VIII

LETTER FROM THE BATTLE FRONT

This letter was sent to his mother by a young German cavalry officer at the Russian front; it is dated 24 July 1915 (see p. 189).

Dear Mum,

You are always complaining about hearing so little from me, although during the past few weeks I have written to you several times.

Allow me to say that you and all of you at home seem to be having an entirely wrong idea about the war and its dangers. Armin at the Loretto Heights ['Loretto Höhe] is of course at enormous risk because he is in one of the most fought-over sections of the Western Front and under constant artillery bombardment. I read about it recently; the way it looks, if you and Uncle and Aunt were to see it, it would make your hair stand on end. The dead still lying where they fell during the assault, hundreds of them, pell-mell, with hands convulsively clenched, bodies bloated, skins pitch black from putrefaction. The stench of such a battlefield makes my horse snort with fright and horror and refuse to go on. This is how an animal feels, and you are arguing which is the greatest danger spot.

The German troops lack the elaborately constructed dug-outs and judiciously laid-out trenches of the Russians, who are able to retreat into positions prepared many months in advance and looking more like fortresses with their camouflages and a great many other refinements. Yet eventually everything does get taken by assault, albeit mostly at the cost of very heavy casualties. The attacker is always at a disadvantage; long marches during the day, trying repeatedly to storm those positions, with their machine guns behind every firing slit. And then, fighting until nightfall, attacking again and again until the Russians retreat or – at present more likely – the German infantry retreat into foxholes hastily dug under enemy fire.

On top of this it rains – no, the heavens opened for 48 hours, mercilessly, onto our infantrymen who on days like these, without any chance of getting food or drink, have to try and squeeze, fully equipped, into the mire, their rain-filled foxholes, without proper cover; and who, within a few hours, will inevitably have to start

370

fighting all over again when the regular Russian night attacks start, which are conducted with dreadful tenacity.

At 1 or 2 o'clock at night the field kitchens, having driven through rain, fire and storm, arrive and station themselves in some ravine behind the lines, where they have some little cover; and then they come along, our boys, one squadron after another, one man from each unit laden with mess tins: 'Quick, hurry up, they are doing all they can to spot us, we want to get back before they see us, it is getting light already'. And that's the first food our people get to see since early morning.

For two nights I was detailed to the staff of an infantry regiment, standing by, horse fully saddled; in our immediate vicinity a machine gun hammering away, rifle bullets whistling and swishing through the tree branches, Russian grenades exploding from time to time with an ear-splitting crash. I myself was comparatively safe in a narrow gorge, but our infantry – ! One man was just coming back, shot only through the hand, yet crying – 'It's absolutely impossible, the swine are under cover, and we, we have to get at them through wide open spaces, it's hopeless' – and on he went, still crying.

The engagement continues until well after daybreak, the Russians advance, our infantry has to retreat farther and farther – great agitation at the command post, the commander observes the scene through his telescope – 'what's that?!' 'Your Excellency, the infantry are retreating, the field artillery have stopped firing.' The command post is situated on a hill affording a panoramic view, we stand behind trees for cover but are able to observe the whole battlefield with its undulating hills and cornfields. Just then, a report comes in from the division lying next to us: 'The Guards are advancing again, the Russian attack has been halted through a supreme effort by our troops and artillery'. His excellency looks up from the telescope: 'Major von Willich, a dispatch rider!' The cavalry division is positioned under cover on a hill slope. Acting Sergeant Babbel, a native of East Prussia, is commanded into his Excellency's presence: 'You ride down there and transmit my order to the infantry: the present line is to be held at all events!' 'Yes, sir.' He mounts his horse and gallops directly in the direction of the firing.

Arriving at the artillery emplacement, the gun crews are lying underneath their guns, carabines in hand, in the air continuous whizzing, on the ground the dust thrown up by striking bullets – as if someone at the sea shore had taken a handful of little stones and scattered them in the sand in one go – that's how the machine guns are spraying their bullets. A jolt – a bullet has gone through his uniform, breast-high, but only his uniform. A hundred metres ahead are our riflemen, he has to go up to them through open terrain, the

Russians have seen him, a horseman coming at them through the
thick of the engagement. More firing, more noise, now he has
reached the infantry lines – spots an officer – shouts: 'You are to hold
on whatever happens, the 16th Fusiliers are on their way!' The
officer just nods and passes the message on. The miracle happens,
the line holds; and the yet greater miracle – the dispatch rider,
leading his foaming trembling horse, reports back to his excellency,
unharmed.

And you ask and argue how dangerous it is? Just visualise it: on
horseback in an engagement, everybody else lying low, hidden,
using every clod of earth, every mound for cover, not 100 metres
away from the enemy lines. It is hardly credible that anyone might
get out of this without being hit. Buschak, my batman, riding
behind me, received a stomach wound just as we were emerging
from a wood to go on patrol.

Another time we, six troopers, had to stop behind a shed, within
earshot of the enemy, we couldn't get away at first as the shed was
entirely free-standing and visible to the enemy. Our field artillery,
thank God, pinned the Russians down in their lines, but still we
could go neither forward nor back. The German infantry appears on
the scene, fierce fighting ensues, a battery commander, although
under cover, gets hit in the head, we have to retreat, we rush along
the line of fire towards a gorge, at first we are unscathed except for a
damaged lance, we have almost made it when one of us falls with a
bullet grazing the back of his head!

The risk is greatest when you least expect it. You in Berlin have
simply no conception of the cost of this advance, of our forces'
achievements and of their losses. The regiments in our Division are
on batallion strength, two Russian squadrons equal one of our
regiments! And then last night, due to failure of communication
with one of our infantry patrols, a Russian batallion, guardsmen,
gigantic fellows all of them, infiltrate into our lines, make a surprise
attack on the batallion from the rear, drive it, already disarmed,
before them, the whole front wakes up, the artillery has to be silent,
a terrific hand-to-hand combat ensues, our pioneer corps who
happen to be in the front line constructing wire entanglements, join
in and wildly hit out with their axes, no-one shoots, the fight is
decided in dead silence with bayonets and rifle butts, the break-
through fails, none of the Russians gets back – our 16th Fusiliers fire
into the retreating crowd, two machine gunners alone account for
about 400 Russians and stop shooting only when their vision is
completely blocked by the wall of corpses piled up before them.

All this is fact, is the reality here, although in Berlin one has
become *apathetic*, and by and large doesn't seem to know anything

of all that, apparently visualising our 11th Army as taking a walk into Russia. So now you may tell Aunt Claire that the war can in fact be quite dangerous from time to time.

Briefly, some different matters. My Iron Cross hasn't arrived yet, instead of the six asked for they sent only three, but I am on the list, and at the next opportunity, in a few weeks' time, I expect it to be my turn. Please go to Frau von Willich – I hope you have seen her already once before – and ask her for the Officers' Association's invoice – including that for the second order. Additionally 10 marks are due for the compass she enclosed in the last parcel. I hope the other items ordered have been sent off, the rubber bowl is very good and we both would ask you to go and buy the items we have requested, exactly as described and as soon as possible.

So bye-bye, love to everybody including Tucke, and please write how Lena is doing.

Sincerest regards from your grateful son

Leo.

INDEX

Another Toccata Press book
for violinists and violin enthusiasts

Max Rostal

BEETHOVEN

The Sonatas for Piano and Violin

Thoughts on their Interpretation

**With a Preface by
The Amadeus Quartet**

**With a Pianist's Postscript
by Günter Ludwig**

**and a History of Performance Practice
by Paul Rolland**

In this book Max Rostal, one of the world's most renowned teachers of the violin, distills sixty years of experience to provide a guide to these perennial favourites, both for the performing musician and for the general reader. This is the first full-length study of these works in English since the beginning of this century.

'What Rostal has produced here is a highly detailed, intelligent and immensely thorough guide through all ten sonatas'
Robert Dearling, *Classical Music*

219pp, illustrated, 207 music examples, bibliography, index

0 907689 05 1; £12.95 (cased)
0 907689 06 X; £6.95 (paperback)